GOLD DUST ON HIS SHIRT

Visiting a neighbour, Hudson Bay Mountain, c.1923.
From the left: Edwin (in front), Arthur, Verner, Ingeborg
Nelson with baby Irene, and Mrs. Donald Simpson.
(*Author's collection*)

GOLD DUST
ON HIS
SHIRT

THE TRUE STORY OF AN
IMMIGRANT MINING FAMILY

IRENE HOWARD

Irene Howard

BETWEEN THE LINES

Toronto

Gold dust on his shirt: the true story of a pioneer mining family

First published in 2008 by
Between the Lines
720 Bathurst Street, Suite #404
Toronto, Ontario   M5S 2R4
Canada
1-800-718-7201
www.btlbooks.com

LIBRARY AND ARCHIVES CANADA CATALOGUING IN PUBLICATION

Howard, Irene
  Gold dust on his shirt : the true story of a pioneer mining family / Irene Howard.

Includes index.
ISBN 978-1-897071-45-8

  1. Howard, Irene. 2. Nelson family. 3. Frontier and pioneer life–British Columbia.
4. British Columbia–Social conditions–20th century. 5. Miners–British Columbia–
Biography. 6. Mines and mineral resources–British Columbia–History–20th century.
7. British Columbia–Biography. I. Title.

FC4172.1.A1H69 2008   971.1′030922   C2008-904450-9

Cover and text design by David Vereschagin, Quadrat Communications
Illustrations by Louise Howard
Printed in Canada

Between the Lines gratefully acknowledges assistance for its publishing activities from
the Canada Council for the Arts, the Ontario Arts Council, the Government of Ontario
through the Ontario Book Publishers Tax Credit program and through the Ontario
Book Initiative, and the Government of Canada through the Book Publishing Industry
Development Program.

To Greta, Brita, and Edith
and in loving memory of Lois and Marie

English like a stone in their mouths,
they translated their lives
into the rhetoric of this country . . .

—Leona Gom, "Immigrants"

I think that those who made so many things
ought to be owners of everything.
That those who make bread ought to eat.

That those in the mine should have light. . . .

Someone is hearing me without knowing it,
but those I sing of, those who know,
go on being born and will overflow the world.

—Pablo Neruda, "The People"

CONTENTS

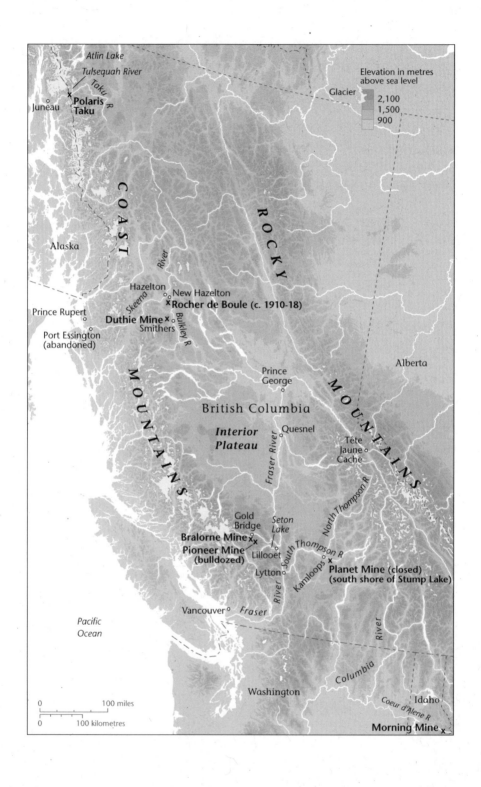

Atlin Lake

Tulsequah River

Taku R

Juneau

**Polaris
Taku**

COAST

Alaska

ROCKY

Glacier

Elevation in metres
above sea level

2,100
1,500
900

Prince Rupert

Port Essington
(abandoned)

River

Skeena

Hazelton
New Hazelton
Rocher de Boule (c. 1910-18)

Duthie Mine
Smithers

Bulkley R

Prince
George

Alberta

MOUNTAINS

British Columbia

*Interior
Plateau*

Fraser River

Quesnel

Tête
Jaune
Cache

North Thompson R

MOUNTAINS

Gold
Bridge

*Seton
Lake*

Bralorne Mine
Pioneer Mine
(bulldozed)

Lillooet

South Thompson R

Kamloops

Planet Mine (closed)
(south shore of Stump Lake)

Lytton

River

Fraser

Vancouver

*Pacific
Ocean*

Columbia

River

Washington

Idaho

Coeur d'Alene R

0   100 miles

0   100 kilometres

Morning Mine x

ACKNOWLEDGEMENTS

Writing this book has been a long journey and I have received much help along the way. It began as a single story about Pioneer Gold Mine that appeared, most appropriately, in "the only magazine published out of an abandoned mine shaft." I would like to remind Charlie Angus and Brit Griffin that in the years in which they were publishing *HighGrader Magazine* (and even after moving on to more conventional quarters), they encouraged me to continue writing my mining camp stories about ordinary workers. They put a value on these miners and their families, made them legitimate as story material, and I thank them for that.

There was so much I did not know. There were few personal documents, for miners don't often write diaries about stoping a rock face, nor do their wives have time or energy to write letters to families back home: washing the Stanfields long johns is hard work. Fortunately for writers, there are librarians and archivists, and I consulted a great many of them in Norway and Sweden, the United States, and Canada. These people were always able to search out answers to my questions, no matter how difficult, and to move my research along a mile or two. Their institutions are acknowledged in the appropriate places in the Notes, and I thank them here in general – though I would rather have delivered a speech, pinned a medal on each one for being always there, patient, reliable, scholarly. I want especially to thank archivist George Brandak of the University of British Columbia Special Collections for his help with many research problems over the years. I send *tusen takk* to the archivists at the National Library of Norway, and the University Library of Trondheim's Gunnerusbiblioteket. I send *många tack* to archivist Gunilla Jingborg and senior archivist Thord Byland at Härnosand Regional Archives in Ångermanland,

Sweden. I want them all to know that with their help I have added a little more to the story of Scandinavian immigrants in Canada.

On the subject of hard-rock mining I was fortunate to have the advice of several geologists. Lewis Green read sections of the manuscript and made detailed comments and suggestions, clarifying many arcane matters about shafts and timbers, flotation tanks, gold that was "free," and gold that was not. He also made available the research notes from his own book, *The Great Years: Gold Mining in the Bridge River*, and shared with me his wide knowledge of the social history of that area. Wayne Merton took me through the new mill at Bralorne when operations there were being revived; he explained the operation of crushers and ball mills. Glen Woodsworth answered my questions about dynamite, and Robert Boyd explained that some gold bricks were more gold than others. I am most grateful to all of my geologists for tutoring me and providing firm "bedrock" for my own reading and study. They have been most kind and patient with a sometimes slow-learning pupil, and I hope they will excuse any oversimplifications and errors.

Interviews, correspondence, and telephone conversations with a great many people in Canada and Scandinavia provided other detailed information. Ingegerd Troedsson offered research suggestions and kindly mailed printed material about Resele, my father's birthplace, which allowed me an intimate glimpse of that area of northern Sweden, especially its folk culture and history. Norman and Olga Gronskei took me on a tour of the abandoned site of Pioneer Mine, re-creating for me scenes from my childhood and adding their own memories. Other old-timers from mining camps invited me to their homes, offered cups of coffee, and told me their stories. Their friendly responses always warmed and encouraged me.

My relatives in Norway, so far away from Vancouver, must sometimes wonder at being involved by accident of birth in the writing of this story of an early Canadian mining family. I want to assure them that they have provided essential historical and geographical background for my mother's part of the story. I salute them here and send them all *tusen takk* for their help. When I visited them they offered hospitality, and it made me Norwegian all over again just to hear them speak with that lilting sound. They swept me up into their National Day celebrations, and I was happy to celebrate May 17 three times in one day, though I wished that I too could have worn the appropriate folk costume. Since then, back in Canada, I've had telephone conversations with them and a rich e-mail correspondence. In response to my requests for specific information they sent long letters and photocopies, corrected my Norwegian spelling, read parts of the manuscript, and even did primary research.

I want as well to offer *många tack* to my translators: to Märta and Hans Lundquister for helping me with difficult Swedish words and sentences and for bringing out their little archives of memorabilia for me to study; to Greta and Ed Nelson for their genealogical research that provided the starting point for my own researches into family history. Greta also translated some Swedish background material for me.

Throughout my career in local history, I've had the good advice and support of some of the most distinguished historians in this province. Jean Barman, Fellow of the Royal Society of Canada and a prolific and talented writer of local history and my mentor of many years, read and commented on individual stories, as did Roderick Barman. They both cleared away the fog when it settled thick and gloomy, and walked a little way with me into the sun again. Robert McDonald remained solidly in the background, not without a little wry humour, but always validating my hopeful venture. Frank Leonard read chapters of the manuscript and made useful suggestions that smoothed out a few rough spots. Keith Ralston was my astute adviser in labour history. I salute also Gordon Elliott, my strict but kindly mentor of respected memory who for so many years nurtured the writing of local history in British Columbia.

Friends, colleagues, and family have been generous with timely and practical help. Poet and literary critic Jean Mallinson read many drafts and versions. She is a sympathetic listener who stayed with me and my paragraphs and sentences, and always put me back on track when I was overcome with uncertainty and lost my way. Elizabeth Walker and Elspeth Gardner read chapters of the later versions and offered sensible suggestions; Molly Ralston responded to appeals for tea and fruitcake; Laverne Darychuk researched family artifacts and sent photographs; Elizabeth Hunter, Charlotte Roth, Jean Wilson, and Barbara Beach also honoured the claims of friendship with many courtesies, large and small, as did Anne Carson Yandle of fondest memory.

Coping with the crazy speed of changing computer technology and the mysterious workings of JPEG and anti-virus, modem and motherboard, was often too much for me. There were days when I just wanted to go back to pencil and paper and reincarnate as Virginia Woolf going shopping for a few pounds of lead type for her own press. Fortunately I had my computer gurus:

Steve Howard, Katherine Howard, Wendy Hutcheon, Sandra Nelson, and Fred Nelson. I offer my heartfelt thanks to them for answering my calls for help and being my kind and patient teachers. I also thank Manzurul Faruque, who served me at the copy shop; he was competent and kindly aware that the CD disc he was taking from me was of inestimable value.

To my good, kind family – Jack, Steve, Louise, Katherine, and Nicholas – I offer special thanks for . . . well, being a family and sustaining me with their love and support. The errands, the garden, the shopping trips, the birthday dinners, the offerings of lentil soup, the solicitous e-mails and phone calls: the Muse of History looked after me in many homely ways. They also helped with the actual book production: Katherine was my editorial assistant; Louise drew the illustrations that appear on the chapter-opening pages.

At the end of my journey I was welcomed by Between the Lines. It was a pleasure to work with this publishing group, and I was happy eventually to have them take the manuscript away from me and set about putting it between covers. I wish to acknowledge with thanks the professional services of their staff, and especially those of editor Robert Clarke for his sensitive and astute reading of my manuscript.

I would like to have illuminated in gold the names of all the people who have helped me. Instead I can only say that I hope they will find this book worthy of their efforts on my behalf – this story of the life and times of one miner's family, a story that is now being sent out into the world to find its readers.

PROLOGUE

This book began over dinner in an apartment high-rise in Vancouver's West End, where my brother Arthur was living out his days, alone. Marie, his wife of many years, had died some years earlier, and they'd had no children. As usual I have brought the Swedish meatballs; he has peeled and cooked the potatoes. He is telling me, once more, a story about a big win at poker that time in camp at Polaris Taku, and that reminds him of the winter the water froze there and they would have gone ahead and evacuated everybody if he hadn't figured out how to get the water running again.

But this time, I really am listening. I'm beginning to understand that he's asking for something. He was here, he had a life – well, not as a mining engineer, he missed out on that alright, but he did things just the same. He was the one who made things happen on the job. Pioneer Mine, the Yukon, Deas Island Tunnel, the logging camps on Vancouver Island ... I begin to see him in his many lives: my brother, the gambler, off to his poker club of an evening, but not before Marie checks him over, straightening his tie; my brother, the surface foreman in charge of the Deas Island Tunnel work crew, dredging the Fraser River, wrestling with it, holding it back; my brother, the highball logger with chainsaw dropping a giant Douglas fir. So I write down the poker story and the one about Polaris Taku and they're published in a magazine. Now thousands of people know his name. Arthur Nelson was there, and he isn't just fading away.

In our large extended family, Uncle Art was our storyteller. He had a capacious memory with a fund of stories that he delighted in telling. They were about our family's beginnings in Prince Rupert and about the mining camps we lived in after that. He told these stories over and over again, reaffirming the Nelson family's place in the world. One of his favourites was about a winter in 1926 when we were living at the Duthie mine for the second time, not even in a log cabin but in a tent halfway up the mountain and handy to the mine workings, office, and cookhouse. The school, in an abandoned log cabin, was a good distance farther down on the lower slope. Standing outside our tent, you couldn't see the school. It was down the trail somewhere among the trees, and I had been walking that trail with my brothers and then by myself since I started school that September, even though I wasn't four until November. It had been snowing all winter, and the trail from our tent to the schoolhouse had become a narrow passageway between two high walls of snow.

One afternoon my mother said to Arthur, "Where's Irene? Didn't she come home with you?" They went outside and looked down the trail, my mother anxious. Then Art saw a little dark object bobbing along. "There she is. That's her." And so it was. He couldn't actually see me, but he could see the hat on my head, the dark blue beret, bobbing along, and then this little person coming into view, walking home from school all by herself up the steep hill between two high walls of snow.

The whole family listens to this story about me, little Irene – how sturdy! how brave! They murmur approvingly. Am I embarrassed by this attention? I am not. For I've come to understand the importance of stories in our lives, how they support and sustain us, as this one has, over the years, supported me. I had this in mind when I began to write the stories in this book about my immigrant parents and the workers and their families in the mining camps where we had lived. Al Purdy had written about Roblin Lake, Margaret Laurence about her hometown, Neepawa, which she called Manawaka, and Alice

Munro about the fictional Jubilee in Ontario. Now I too was writing about hometowns, beginning with Art's stories and those of my other brothers, and they were real places, so little known they might well have been fictional. I was finding other storytellers too, former schoolmates and my brothers' friends from Pioneer Mine, who remembered with such nostalgia and pride the company town that was their hometown, and, oh, the hockey games and the ski carnival, and the dress-up afternoon teas with silver service! Other storytellers I found in archival documents and print, and it was for me to discover their voices.

Sometimes I heard my own amused, ironic voice intruding with that put-down question, "Who do you think you are anyway?" But then the snapshot of our family standing outside our log cabin at the Duthie would flash before me – my mother, her black hair severely cropped, holding me, an infant, in her arms, my father, upright, unsmiling, and their three young sons – and I'd think, "That's who I think I am. This cabin, this family is history, and I am part of it."

So I knew what I had to do. I had to summon all my writerly bravado and write miners like my father and women like my mother down in history. I had to commemorate their labour, their monumental labour. I had to find the words to tell their historic and significant griefs and joys, their strength, endurance, and courage. I had to tell their heroic lives. This was my difficult task.

Fortunately, I knew that I was the little girl who had climbed the trail all the way home and by herself between two high walls of snow. My brother had told me, had told everybody, often, so I knew that's who I was, and that's how I knew I could do it.

First cut at Prince Rupert, 10 May 1908. The railway labourer
has to be able to run a loaded wheelbarrow "blindfolded on
a one-plank runway." *The Empire*, 29 Aug. 1908, p.6.
(*Courtesy Prince Rupert City and Regional Archives*)

ONE

COYOTE HOLES AND BLACK POWDER

DRILLING AND BLASTING FOR THE GRAND TRUNK PACIFIC

In 1905 a thirty-year-old Swede stepped off a ship at one of the eastern seaports of Canada. From there he headed west on the Canadian Pacific Railway to Kenora, Ontario, where the first thing he did was pre-empt a piece of land, for he was of peasant origins, a farmhand, *en dräng*, someone who had worked for the landowner. Here in Canada he himself was going to be a landowner. He would have his own fields and fences, a barn full of hay, his own cow, maybe two cows, even a horse. The streets were not paved with gold, but the possibilities were rich with promise. This was Canada.

"Proving up" a farm was more difficult than he anticipated, or maybe the blackflies and mosquitoes in Northern Ontario discouraged him. In any case he soon joined other immigrants working their way west on the construction of the Grand Trunk Pacific Railway, with its eastern terminus at Winnipeg. In September 1908 he fetched up on Kaien Island on the coast of British Columbia, the site chosen as the railway's western terminus, a place soon to be named Prince Rupert.

His name was Nils Alfred Nilsson, and he was my father. He came from the province of Ångermanland in northern Sweden. He couldn't speak English, but that didn't matter because he was tall and broad-shouldered and could handle a pick and shovel.

During my childhood my father was a miner who went to work every day with his black lunch bucket, hard hat, and carbide lamp, with a little round box of Copenhagen Snuff* in the breast pocket of his shirt. He used to tell stories, beginning "When I was On Construction." Those words are firmly fixed in my memory, along with a handful of other "railway words" that I heard over and over again. Although those words did not form a connected narrative for me, they did reaffirm my sense that my father, the miner, was as strong and solid as the rocks he drilled, for he had worked "On Construction" and at the time that was enough. Those words are not enough now, when I want to tell the story of his years in Canada. But I can write that story just the same, and the start of it all will be about nothing less than the founding of a city and the building of a railway. It will be about immigrant labourers and it will be about Construction – of the city of Prince Rupert, of the Grand Trunk Pacific (GTP) Railway. It will be about how my parents made their separate ways to Canada and found a life together in British Columbia. It will be about a mother, and her growing family, and how she managed to move her household from one mining camp to another. It will be about school days and gold mines. But this story is mostly about anonymous workers, men and women. It is about Nils Alfred Nilsson and Ingeborg Aarvik.

The Prince Rupert townsite had to be blasted out of the rock on Kaien Island. The side of a mountain had to be removed to make a place for the town and for the railway under construction that was the reason for the town. The community there would owe its existence to a boardroom decision that the western terminus was to be on this island at the mouth of the Skeena River and would follow the north bank of the river, not the south bank where the already existing cannery town of Port Essington was located.

Kaien Island was a chunk of the Coast Range that had broken off in eons past, an island-mountain, its cliffs rising steeply from the sea. The heavily timbered mountain slopes disappeared downward into swamp and marsh

---

* A chewing tobacco that the miners called "snoose," from the Norwegian, Swedish, Danish "snus" (snuff).

and bog. This forty-nine square kilometres of rocky raincoast wilderness was not a prepossessing location for a town, but the Grand Trunk Pacific Railway, under the direction of president and general manager Charles Melville Hays, was ready literally to move mountains to realize a vision of a northern seaport terminus for this transcontinental railway. In 1906 the engineers and survey parties had set up camp on the northwestern coast of the island, and the first axemen were hired to start clearing the land. The general contractor in charge of construction in British Columbia was Foley Brothers, Welch and Stewart.

The blasting on Kaien Island began in 1908 and continued for the next five years: the Grand Trunk Pacific was re-creating the geography of Kaien Island, for a mountain cliff rising from the sea had to be brought down to make a level area for railway yards. Thousands of immigrant labourers were employed to drill holes in the walls of rock on the western waterfront of Kaien Island. My father, that Swedish immigrant by the name of Nils Alfred Nilsson, called them coyote holes, and the newspapers of the day referred to them in the same way, without saying how they came to be so called. In the basement of our house on Seventh Avenue in Prince Rupert was a bundle of steel rods – our father's drilling steels, some eight feet or more in length. Pounding a steel rod into solid rock with a sledgehammer: that was drilling. One man held the steel, turning it as a second man pounded it with the hammer. The holes were then loaded with black powder and exploded with an electrical charge. This might seem to be an extravagantly labour-intensive technology to apply to a mountain wall, but even ten loaded drill holes in a bluff could bring down 9,000 yards of solid rock.

By the time my father arrived in 1908, Prince Rupert was already a town of some three hundred people, with all the amenities of town life. *The Evening Empire*, a weekly newspaper established the year before, printed a list of the citizens as a progress report. The town had four hotels, three lodging houses, a bakery, two restaurants with bakeries, and four cigar, fruit, and newspaper shops. It had two meat markets, a hardware store with building supplies and stoves, an electric supply shop, a drugstore, and a dairy. It had two real estate agents. There was an architect, a dentist and a physician, a dealer in coal, and a Chinese laundry. The Canadian Bank of Commerce had an outpost in this rough little town. Because steam shovels could not always usefully replace men in overalls, Bacon and Holland provided wheelbarrow transfer.

But there were no saloons. Or so claimed the editor of the *Evening Empire*, though of course there must have been bootlegged liquor and plenty of it. "There are no loafing places except the G.T.P. wharf," he wrote. The wharf was indeed a meeting place for the townspeople, who were creating a city at the same time as the town's streets and the waterfront yard for the railway were still being blasted out. Blasting for construction of the railway bed began in the spring of 1908, and the first passenger train left Prince Rupert heading east for one hundred miles in June 1911. By that time the young city had a population of 4,184.

The steam-powered Burleigh rock drill had been invented and was used on the GTP construction along with drill and hammer to create not just coyote holes, but coyote tunnels as well, perhaps twenty feet high in a rock bluff. Were these the tunnels that reminded the workers of a coyote's den? They also drilled crosscuts or drifts out from a main tunnel, creating a maze of tunnels. In one blast, 66,250 pounds of black powder and one and a half tons of dynamite brought down 40,000 cubic yards of rock. Crowds of people stood down on the wharf to watch this huge upheaval. This was only one of many such explosions that kept the inhabitants of the new city in a precarious state of alert.

"Explosion Creates Havoc in Hotel, Stores and Homes," *The Evening Empire* headlined in a typical report. "No One Killed – Clock Blown off Mantel, Strikes Ten While Lying on Floor – Some Marvellous Escapes." From day to day rocks flew through the air, crashing onto unlucky rooftops: "A huge rock weighing over six hundred pounds was flung high into the air and crashed down on the roof of Mr. Warks's house just above the parlor. . . . Mrs. Wark was in the kitchen at the time." On another day, a rock in its meteoric course tore through the roof of a tent-house and "struck a chair in which Mrs. McLure had been sitting a minute before." In yet another blasting accident, a worker was hurled three hundred feet into the harbour at Seal Cove. Pedestrians could be nicked in the arm by a piece of flying glass or splattered with muskeg. Boxes of dynamite were sometimes left carelessly on a street corner – where who knows what might have happened to them?

Several short toots in succession of the donkey engine were intended to give due warning of a blast. Other regulations on blasting were also in place, and the mayor instructed police to enforce them. But the exploding rock was erratic, and destruction, injury, and death by dynamite inevitably accompanied the settlement of this community in which the very earth was in a state of imminent upheaval, its inhabitants looking to flee for cover at any time. Not many cities have a founding story like this – not even Rome, its destiny decided by a random flight of birds and not by anything as grand and omnipotent as a railway corporation.

Rome had only seven hills. Prince Rupert was being built on any number of hills. Its streets, like the railway yard, would have to be blasted out of cliffs and bluffs and ridges, and they would have to find their way across marshes and swamps and inconvenient creeks and gullies. The Grand Trunk Pacific had decreed that Prince Rupert was to be a model city, and the company architect's design for curved streets, following the precepts of the City Beautiful Movement, accommodated this difficult terrain. After drilling for the Grand Trunk Pacific, Alfred joined the gangs of anonymous labourers hired by contractors to drill cuts through Kaien Island bluffs to create the city's streets and carry out the plan for the City Beautiful. More coyote holes, more dynamite and blasting, more rocks flying through the air. For the citizens of Prince Rupert, dynamite was a daily hazard. These were dangerous times.

But the labourers at the work site were even more at risk. Through his years of drilling and blasting Alfred escaped serious injury; he survived. But many an immigrant worker did not, and to the cost of building the railway line and railway yard and the streets of Prince Rupert must be added the cost in workers' injuries, and in their very lives. The newspapers reported the names of those men whenever they could. One premature explosion killed a Swede, Bowman by name, foreman on a job to make a cut through a bluff on the foreshore. His four helpers, Austrians and Finns, died in the same blast. They were all "sober, industrious workers," the newspaper said. "It was the worst tragedy in the annals of the city and it was felt keenly."

Only a week later came more tragedy: an Austrian labourer, Rade Mastilo, was killed during grading work on First Avenue when a huge rock became loose while he was drilling. "Mastilo tried to leap clear but failed, and caught by the huge mass, was ground to pulp beneath it. Death must have been instantaneous, though Mastilo's head escaped injury. The drill he had been using was bent and [twisted] like wire in the rock as it fell." These are random events culled from newspaper reports of·that time. They become for the reader nearly one hundred years later a serial narrative of injury and death among the immigrant labourers who built the city of Prince Rupert.

During these years immigrant workers were being organized by the newly formed Industrial Workers of the World, which had spread into British Columbia from the United States. In 1909 Local 126 was formed in Prince Rupert, and the Wobblies, as they were called, soon had their own hall on Third Avenue. The local had some impetus from the Western Federation of Miners, which was active in the Kootenay mining area in eastern British Columbia and had not at that time withdrawn its support of the IWW. The Prince Rupert organizer of the WFM, Patrick Daly, in his report to *The Industrial Worker*, called himself "an old WFM man" and said he had applied to the Seattle IWW to send an organizer to Prince Rupert.

The IWW was an industrial union; that is, it aimed to organize all the workers in an industry under a single banner. This was as opposed to organizing them in separate organizations according to craft or trade so that tailors, printers, carpenters, foundry workers, and miners, for instance, were each in their own union. The IWW was radical and revolutionary and proudly anarchist. Its declared mission was nothing less than the abolition of the wage system and the destruction of capitalism. It was theoretic and philosophical, deriving from the syndicalist movement in Europe. The pages of *The Industrial Worker* were eloquent with impassioned discourse, variously citing Nietzsche, the Bible, Jack London, and on occasion the poet Shelley in support of the worker who "lies torn and trampled where/ Honor sits smiling at the sale of truth." Letters and reports from workers in logging, mining, and construction camps employed a different language: capitalists are "cockroaches," employment agents are "sharks," detectives are "Pinks" (for the Pinkerton agency), workers are "slaves." The main concerns for these workers were wages and working conditions.

In 1911 workers on streets and sewers in Prince Rupert were being paid thirty-seven and a half cents an hour for a ten-hour day, which was up from twenty-five cents in 1909 but still not enough to meet the cost of living, even at a time when a pair of overalls cost only $1.25. They were demanding forty-five cents, and the city council heard the testimony of IWW delegates: with $30 a month to pay for rent and $3.50 for five sacks of coal and a new pair of gumboots at $3.75, a married man with a family could not adequately feed and clothe his family. The aldermen acknowledged the need for a raise in pay. However, they had to deal with the contractors too, and one of them was Alderman Vernor Smith, a superintendent with Foley Brothers, Welch and

Stewart. Smith took a no-nonsense approach to the problem. According to one report – which left the readers free to fill in the blanks – Smith simply told the contractors, "Starve the ——— out." In the end council decided to refuse the increase, claiming possible legal difficulties with the contractors.

On March 1, after two years of fruitless protest and petition, Local 126 went on strike, four-hundred strong against the private contractors, who responded by applying to employment agencies in Vancouver for more immigrants and, at least according to the union, to a detective agency for a few spies. When the Union Steamship Company's *Camosun* arrived on March 4 with unwitting strikebreakers on board, the Wobblies were at the dock to meet them, carrying red banners proclaiming in different languages, "Strike on. Don't be a Scab. Be a MAN." Some thirty men, including the spies, walked off the ship to join the Wobblies. Then followed a month of scuffles, fisticuffs, taunts, and insults in confrontations between strikers and strikebreakers until, inevitably, all-out war erupted in the Battle of Kelly's Cut.

But perhaps not "inevitably." The undercover men were, after all, at work inside the union. They could very well have urged a confrontation at the First Avenue "cut" between Sixth and Ninth streets, where subcontractors McInnes and Kelly had employed a new crew of strikebreakers. City police had erected a barrier around the site, and some officers were stationed down in the cut to protect those at work there. On the morning of April 6, the strikers marched behind a red banner to the various street construction sites in the town, calling on workers to drop their tools and join the march, which many did. They were led by a Norwegian IWW organizer from Seattle, A.O. Morse, probably the man sent to Prince Rupert after Patrick Daly's request for help. But when this army of some one thousand strikers arrived at Kelly's Cut, the new workers refused to walk out. They had only just started work that morning. In his *Memories of the Skeena*, Walter Wicks writes:

> I watched the marching men swarm over the Cut from the back or higher ground when a rock came hurtling over their heads from behind, towards the 'scabs,' supposedly thrown by an undercover man to start the disruption. That started the ball rolling, for soon the air was full of rocks and the Law retaliated with firearms. The police fired over the strikers' heads and reports that they also fired directly into them were denied. However, I personally saw one striker with a bullet hole in his stomach, lying on the

sidewalk writhing in agony, mumbling a prayer in a foreign language to his God. He died later.

That man's name was Milan Nickdevic.

It is not certain who threw the rock or who fired the first shot. Historian Frank Leonard, in *A Thousand Blunders: The Grand Trunk Pacific Railway and Northern British Columbia*, concluded that a peaceful procession was fired on. He further reported that the federal minister of labour, William Lyon Mackenzie King, was briefed by a telegram from the city engineer, which said that "paid agitators ... who themselves got off with their whole skins ... pushed Bohunks, ignorant of our language into the fight." Leonard noted, however, that the message was sent before the violence occurred. In any event, for a company to hire labour spies and to foment violence is nothing wonderful in the labour history of British Columbia.

The violence could have been worse. Even before the strike, a secret meeting of aldermen – the mayor absent at the time – at the instigation of Alderman Smith, sent a note to the provincial capital, Victoria, to request that the cruiser HMCS *Rainbow* be dispatched to the scene to put down an anticipated uprising. Fortunately, the request was not granted, and the navy's heavy guns were never trained on the Prince Rupert workers.

The Grand Trunk Pacific also played a part in this drama. The company did not want to see an increase in wages for street workers because it was paying a lower wage for railroad construction work and did not want to compete with street contractors for workers, who were then in short supply. The company therefore used its influence on city council to help break the strike.

That Prince Rupert was in an uproar, that the Battle of Kelly's Cut was bloody and brutal, there is no doubt. Citizens as special constables armed with rifles and revolvers paraded the streets and joined in the fray. Subcontractor McInnes gave his revolver to a special constable and with his bare hands fought "with rocks and fists." *The Prince Rupert Optimist* further reported:

"Shoot if necessary," was the order and to shoot was necessary.... Sergeant Phillipson was cruelly mauled before he drew gun at all.... Hardly a word of good, clean English was heard from the ranks of the strikers. Their cries were unintelligible, but they gave ground suddenly under the persuasive eloquence of the six-shooters.... Foot by foot the mob, still spitting stones and curses, was forced back.

And now I almost wish that I were writing fiction, because of the fifty strikers arrested, thirty-three had Slavic names and the name of my father, Nils Alfred Nilsson, was not on the list. The Norwegian IWW strike leader, Morse, was arrested, but no recognizably Scandinavian names were listed. I could write a more exciting story by sending Nils Alfred Nilsson to jail along with all those hot-headed, unruly Slavs. Or better still, I could dispose of the Slavs and replace them with grim, steely-blue-eyed Swedes. Such a fiction would have the ring of truth, for after a general strike in Sweden in 1909 thousands of Swedish workers had immigrated to the United States. Just south of the Canadian border, in Portland, Oregon, a Scandinavian Propaganda Club had been formed under the wing of the IWW, with plans for reading rooms and employment offices and committees to visit the sick and disabled. The new immigrants were also to be instructed in the importance of demanding an eight-hour day.

But I am committed to writing from the historical record, sparse as it is for the anonymous railway construction worker and Prince Rupert street worker. And this Swede, my father, the immigrant labourer drilling rock on Kaien Island and in Skeena River canyons, was anonymous to me as well, for when I was younger I no more than anyone else was willing to listen and learn about his early life. What I do know is that he was strong, hard-working, and almost fiercely contemptible of shirkers. Although he was hot-tempered at times – and I saw him fly off the handle more than once – he was not one to hurl rocks and bottles at policemen, guardians of the state. For he was, above all, a prudent man. He had received his naturalization papers in 1910 and now had all the rights and privileges of a Canadian citizen. In 1911 he may indeed have laid down his drills and quit work, if his actions in later life are any indication. There was a time I know of in later years when he did speak up and confront the boss, and to the great acclaim of fellow workers. But I doubt if he would have jeopardized his newly won citizenship by challenging law and order in reckless hand to hand combat in 1911.

I do know that he kept on working. After drilling and blasting for the GTP railway yards and sidings in Prince Rupert and drilling for the streets of the new city, Alfred drilled and blasted on the rock cuts and in the tunnels up the line. Swedes were highly regarded as railway construction workers: James J. Hill, the U.S. railway magnate who influenced the Canadian government to choose the difficult southern route through Kicking Horse Pass for the Canadian Pacific Railway, famously declared, "Give me Swedes and snoose and I'll build a railway to Hell." On the Grand Trunk Pacific, Swedes were similarly sought to do rock work: in a list of work orders one contractor specifically asked for "15 Italians and Swedes to report at Mile 90," which would be in the general area of Kitselas Canyon on the Skeena. Another news item for 1909 listed seven Swedes in a group of workers on construction near Prince Rupert as "experienced rock men." As for my father, he was certainly aware of his own worth. I remember how he used to stand back and survey with satisfaction some piece of his own handiwork. Each time he would proudly declare, "*Ja*," then in English, "It takes a Swede every time." And he would take a chew of "snoose."

Construction on the railroad out of Prince Rupert had started in the spring of 1908, and by 1910 the eastward-bound "end-of-steel" had moved to more than one hundred miles up the Skeena, to the tunnels at Kitselas. The line eastward through British Columbia followed the Skeena north through the ranges of the Coast Mountains to Hazelton, south through the valleys of the Bulkley River, then east again through the Central Plateau and the gorges and canyons of the Fraser River to enter the Rocky Mountains through Yellowhead Pass at Tête Jaune Cache, with Mount Robson, 3,954 metres, towering above it. The construction of a railway through this formidable bulwark of North America's Cordillera was an enterprise of heroic proportions. A London *Times* correspondent visiting Prince Rupert recalled, "On the way to Port Essington, up the Skeena River, one had the impression of being in a naval battle, so frequent were the shots along the banks where the new transcontinental trail was being driven through iron-hard rock."

The railbed had to be won blow by blow by men attacking the rock with steam drills, sometimes even with hand drill and hammer, and tamping dynamite charges into the holes. In his book about the construction of the GTP, British journalist and historian F.A. Talbot provided a first-hand account of this dangerous and arduous work. He visited a construction site near Kitselas Canyon and saw workers hanging from ropes anchored at the top of a bluff and somehow contriving to make footholds in the rock with hammer and drill. Where a cliff dropped sheer to the water, "the men plying the drills were slung on crazy footholds, secured to the rock face by planks and logs held in position by a length of chain and iron dogs* driven into the wall. In these cramped quarters careful movement was essential to avoid sudden acquaintance with the raging waters below, for the precarious scaffolding was but two feet or so in width." One false move and a man could fall to his death.

The dynamite was unpredictable. When a whole cliffside was peppered with holes and charged with dynamite, after the explosion there was no way of counting the number of charges that had gone off and the number that had not. Sometimes the workers went back to the rock pile before all the "shots" had gone off. *The Evening Empire*, May 15, 1909, reported two men killed at Henderson's Camp twenty-five miles up the line from Prince Rupert by a premature explosion: Alexander Watt from Tennessee, and a Montenegrin, name unknown. "The latter, like many a fellow railway grader, is buried in a nameless grave." *The Prince Rupert Optimist*, February 6, 1911, reported that three Italians were killed while working in No. 1 tunnel at Kitselas and eight more workers were injured. They had struck loose dynamite with a pick. "The damage was counted in flesh and blood." The men were buried near the scene of disaster. One week later five more men were blown up in a tunnel near Kitselas when a large box of powder left to thaw at the mouth of the tunnel somehow became heated and ignited: Burgess, Kvornstrom, Ogrezobic, Otisovic, Kova.

In November 1911, the westward-bound end-of-steel crossed the Rockies from Alberta into British Columbia and construction began on that part of the line moving northwest along the Fraser River between Tête Jaune Cache and Fort George (now Prince George). Here the river turns south, but the rail line continued northwest. Tête Jaune Cache, on the Fraser River, was head of navigation for the sternwheelers and the tugs with scows that carried equipment and supplies down the river to the construction sites along the line. Navigating the Grand Canyon, the perilous gateway to Fort George, was a dangerous adventure, especially in the notorious Giscombe Rapids, where scows attempting passage through seven miles of turbulent, foaming white water were frequently wrecked. In June 1913 the *Fort George Herald* counted twenty men drowned "since the beginning of the season," which presumably meant since the breakup of ice on the river in April or early May.

---

* A mechanical device, made of iron, for gripping.

Not only did the workers risk being blown up or drowned, but they could also be killed in a grading accident on the line. The *Fort George Herald*, June 17, 1913, reported: "At 160, a poor devil of a Galician was brought in from Camp 162, just cut in two with a dump car, the fifth dump car accident in ten days." Slavic immigrants were all lumped together as "Galician," which sounded more respectful than the usual "bohunk." Anonymous as these men were in life as workers, when they died they had to be accounted for, recorded, traced to the country of origin. Forms had to be filled in and signed. Vital statistics gave each dead man an identity, as Talbot illustrated with studied and condescending euphemism: "One station-man confessed to me, after a solitary, unfortunate experience that befell him in this connection wherein one or two foreigners were launched into eternity, that he had never realized the activities of consuls before, or the number of relatives these strangers from Europe possessed." The Swedes too, even though sought after as construction workers and future settlers, suffered the usual insulting slurs of the dominant Anglo-Saxon culture: they were "squareheads," "dumb Swedes," and "drunken Swedes." They were prized for their brute strength, a reputation that was perhaps the legacy of men like Big Jack, described by Pierre Berton in *The Last Spike* as "a Herculean Swede who was said to be able to hoist a thirty-foot rail weighing 560 pounds and heave it onto a flat car without assistance."

The two lines of steel that moved westward from the Rockies and eastward from Prince Rupert eventually met at Fort Fraser, just west of Prince George, on April 7, 1914. As the track-laying machines moved forward, laying down wooden ties on the roadbed and on top of them the rails, the grading gangs moved on ahead to prepare the next section of railbed. To accommodate the workers, railroad camps sprang up along the line – the sites identified by the name of the subcontractor, or more usually as Mile 29, Mile 160, or whatever the number of miles from Prince Rupert or Yellowhead Pass. As each section of the roadbed was graded and ballasted with gravel, the men packed their belongings and their blankets and moved on ahead of the track-machine to the next construction camp. They were called "blanket stiffs," or "bundle stiffs."

The contractors didn't supply blankets, but their migrant workers had to be housed and as cheaply as possible. This was accomplished by stacking the men in tiers, an exemplary arrangement for the contractors, but not for the workers. According to a first-hand account in *The Industrial Worker*, July

1912: "Bunkhouses have double-deckers. One small window in each bull pen. Each pen contains from 50 to 60 men. Very few of the pens have floors. I find that most of the stables have floors in – horses cost money, slaves are cheap." The bunkhouses were filthy and stank of dirty socks and underwear and unwashed bodies. Some camps along the line had bathhouses, but taking a bath was an event. The straw mattresses were crawling with bed bugs and fleas, and the men were infested with lice. Sanitation was primitive. At one camp near Hazelton, reported a journalist-cum worker, "a single ditch started close to the kitchen door and went *uphill* to the river. Into this was thrown all the refuse from the kitchen, and the stench arising therefrom in the hot weather was vile in the extreme." Cases of typhoid and diptheria were reported. The *Fort George Herald* mentioned in 1913 that the hospital at Mile 160 was full and the camp inspectors were issuing warnings about using water from the Fraser even for washing because the river was polluted with slops and refuse. The men complained about the food: beans and bacon and ham. They were hungry for fresh meat. "And for the love of Mike, send us a potato," they cried, "or we'll all have scurvy." A Fair Wage Officer from the Department of Labour in Ottawa duly inspected the camps and found conditions "excellent" and the complaints much exaggerated. But the men often quit, fed up with such working conditions. They packed their blankets and walked out of camp and down the line. The result was a shortage of labour.

On the Grand Trunk Pacific, wages were as little as $2.50 for a ten-hour day, and out of this the men paid $1.00 a month for medical care, which was administered by a "horse doctor" at Sealey Lake near New Hazelton in a shed with six bunks. Led by the IWW, the men demanded a nine-hour day, a wage of $3.25 a day for muckers and $3.50 for drillers, and better working conditions, including enforcement of sanitary regulations. On July 20, 1912, Morse sent a telegram to *The Industrial Worker*: "Strike on the Grand Trunk Pacific Construction [along the Skeena and Bulkley Rivers] called today. The men could stand the putrid conditions no longer." The GTP refused the construction workers' demands and brought in scabs to replace them.

Some 2,000 Grand Trunk Pacific Railway workers went out on strike. The strikers could not remain in camp during the strike because they had no ready way of obtaining food in the wilderness along the line. By this time rail transportation was available for part of the distance to Prince Rupert, but many of the strikers could not afford the rail fare because there was nowhere to cash their time cheques. They left the construction sites along the Skeena and the Bulkley and hiked along the uncompleted roadbed to Port Essington or to Prince Rupert, where they pitched their tents and enjoyed the amenities of town life: the hotels and restaurants and shops, the companionship of women, and a social life that was more than the poker and blackjack of the camps, a social life in which they might even mingle with ordinary families. The trek to town was particularly difficult in winter, when the deep snow stopped the work trains from going through. In *Memories of the Skeena*, Walter Wicks said that many workers used to stop at his brother Paul's cabin: "With backs humped and knees buckling, some completely collapsed after having walked forty to eighty miles in the heavy snows that closed all railroad transportation."

One winter the two Wicks brothers worked at repairing the telegraph line. "The snows lay deep, no work trains could come through, and the snow ploughs were working out of Prince Rupert on rails not yet ballasted with gravel," Walter recorded. One day, somewhere near Point Edward, the two of them found a railroad worker "holed up" in a hollow stump. "He's dead," Paul said. But he was not. They rubbed his body until he finally regained consciousness. Then they pulled him down the track to the section crew's camp.

> Four days later he passed us near Paul's cabin, and we refused to accept a valuable watch and chain from the grateful man who indicated he had nothing else in his pockets but that railroad time check. Who was he? What was his name? Where did he come from? Did he have a family? Nobody asked him any questions; he was just another railroad stiff.

From Frank Leonard I learned that the Grand Trunk Pacific recognized three kinds of rock that could be used to establish excavation rates for contractors: solid rock that had to be blasted, loose pick-and-shovel rock, and anything else – a category that included gumbo, a rock-hard clay that changes to a soft, sticky mass when it rains, making it impossible to lay a firm roadbed. Often a whole bank of earth on the steep terrain would collapse in a huge mudslide. Moreover, in winter the high clay banks along some stretches of the Grand Trunk Pacific route, notably just west of Tête Jaune Cache, were like solid rock, but in spring, with warmer weather, the clay thawed and the outer surface softened into a thick mud that oozed down over the tracks.

"Gumbo!" It was one of my father's railway words, enriching our family language. It conferred on him the idea of a creditable past, the details of which, unfortunately, I did not bother to learn from him. But that past allows me now to study archival photographs of construction workers on the GTP and say, "He's there." I look for a tall, broad-shouldered man with a large, straight nose, a high forehead, and a handlebar moustache. For sure, he'll be wearing a felt hat with a brim and he'll have piercing blue eyes. But the photographs are faded; the faces of the men are not distinct; I can't identify my father's nose, certainly not his blue eyes; and in any case a good many of the men have handlebar moustaches and are wearing felt hats with a brim. There were other railway words too that rescued him from anonymity, words that acknowledged the heroic labour of those years before I was born, before he was my father: "On Construction," "coyote holes," "Tête Jaune Cache."

Especially Tête Jaune Cache. Today this end-of-steel camp no longer exists, but five miles further east of where it once was there is a tiny village of the same name, at the junction of the Fraser and Robson rivers in the Rockies. It is at the intersection where the Yellowhead Highway branches north along the Fraser towards Prince George or south along the Thompson to Kamloops. The Tête Jaune Cache of GTP construction days, designated Mile 53, was just down the river from there, and close to a settlement of Shuswaps, whose numbers had been decimated sixty years earlier by a smallpox epidemic. As head of navigation for the sternwheelers that distributed construction materials and supplies from end-of-steel to tote roads down the line, Tête Jaune Cache was more permanent than other camps, with huge warehouses six hundred feet long. It consisted of a row of rough log cabins in a clearing in the forest – bunkhouses, stores, restaurant-cum poolroom and cardroom, often with accommodation for the women camp followers. Sometimes there were even separate cabins for the women. The railway contractors did, however, refuse permission to locate eighteen dancehall girls in the camp, so their promoters settled them five miles distant. And there was plenty of booze, and there were drunken brawls and gunfights and men killed. Special constables were sworn in, and one by the name of Speed was exonerated when he accidentally shot dead a man by the name of Magnuson – probably, as the name suggests, a Swede. The *Fort George Herald* also reported that one James Teaff was acquitted of a charge of murder. He had shot and killed in self-defence a violent gambler who was brutally attacking him. According to one visiting journalist, "an end-of-steel village is a disgrace, but Tête Jaune Cache is indescribable."

By the time I was ready to really listen and learn about my father's life "On Construction," his memories of those years had all been distilled into one special story he liked to tell. One of his workmates used to complain and complain about the bunkhouse and the food, the lice and bedbugs, the fleas and mosquitoes. The sound of his incessant litany became intolerable to a second workmate, who finally exploded: "What did you expect? Hummingbirds?"

My father thought this hugely funny, and it was, but I understand now that those words had become his sardonic mantra. The anger in that remark, the cynicism and mockery, and above all the bitterness and hopelessness must have summed up his own back-breaking, mind-numbing years of drilling coyote holes, restoring roadbeds overcome by gumbo, enduring the ignominies of bunkhouse life in the notorious construction camps of the Grand Trunk Pacific. He told the story over and over again, and in our family, whenever we needed to reconnect with the real world and gain perspective on disappointed or failed expectations, we would recite those words, chanting, "What did you expect? Hummingbirds?"

My father was certainly one of those who left the railroad construction camp during the strike of 1912 and headed for Port Essington. Indeed, he may even have been one of "a dozen or more stalwart Swedes" who three years earlier, in 1909, helped move a piano and other furniture during the fire that destroyed homes and businesses on Dufferin Street just after the New Year. The *Port Essington Loyalist*, January 9, 1909, reported an influx of men from nearby camps at Christmastime. "We have had Swedes, Italians, Slavs and Greeks, and others flocking into town until every bit of accommodation was taken up and the hotels filled to overflowing. All this heterogeneous crowd of men were intent on having a good time, and all had money."

Some six or seven hundred men had arrived, and contrary to expectations, they didn't cause any trouble. The Grand Trunk Pacific Railway labourers were "of a superior class to the average railroader," the paper ruminated. "There was any amount of singing and dancing among the men, but quarreling and fighting was conspicuous by their absence, and our sidewalks were absolutely free from rowdiness or anything in the slightest degree objectionable. A more good-natured crowd of men could not have been found anywhere."

The Prince Rupert *Evening Empire* told a different story. Port Essington was "the most drunken and disorderly place in British Columbia." The town was a hotbed of "professional gambling," blackjack and poker, night and day. Still, I hope, if my father was indeed there, that he would have been judged "of a superior class" by the editor of the *Loyalist*, escaping the stereotype of the "drunken Swede." From my own experience I know that my father certainly enjoyed his beer, and he enjoyed it with his friends: his own homebrew and hot rum too, with a spoonful of sugar, and a silver spoon in the glass when he poured the hot water. There would be hardtack and pickled herring and cheese and someone playing the accordion and everyone singing, in Swedish, "To be in love is real suffering / Those who try it never say no." Then, with a **one**, two, three, **one**, two, three, they would all be dancing the Swedish waltz, kitchen chairs shoved out of the way, as the accordion player strikes up "Life in the Finland Woods."

Those, at least, are my memories of my father in his fifties, and they pretty well fit the idealized description by the *Loyalist* editor of the construction workers on the Grand Trunk Pacific coming into Port Essington for a good time. My father liked to sing. I hear him now, strumming along on his autoharp: "Come Adolfina, come Adolfina, put your arms around my neck / Come Adolfina, come Adolfina, swing with me in the waltz."

It was most likely in Port Essington in 1912 that he met up with a beautiful young widow, recently arrived from Norway to join her uncle and aunt, who were well settled in Port Essington, and her elder brother, a new immigrant like herself. Alfred would have been courting her during the strike. They were married on January 9, 1913. Soon they would have their own, new house. He was no longer an anonymous blanket stiff; he would be Nelson, not Nilsson, and moreover it takes a Swede every time!

In any case, he had never really been anonymous at all, nor had all those other blanket stiffs who drilled and blasted and mucked for the Grand Trunk Pacific. That "poor devil of a Galician" had a grieving family somewhere in Eastern Europe. The man from Montenegro had a mother and father. He might have been married, and left behind a widow with children. Burgess, Kvornstrom, Ogrezobic, Otisovic, Kova, and Alexander Watt of Tennessee – they were all mourned by family, comrades, friends. Those who were not killed on the job, those who were not blown up, drowned, or cut in two, found work elsewhere when they left the GTP. They were miners, loggers, fishermen, carpenters, dredge operators, machinists, electrical workers, plumbers, steelworkers, trappers, telephone linemen, farmers and cowboys, camp cooks and flunkies. They married, built houses, raised families, spoke English, and paid taxes. Later on they would wash their cars in the driveway on Sunday. They suffered unemployment and hard times. They went to war and were killed. They joined unions or not; went out on strike or scabbed, got drunk or stayed sober. They went to church, sang in choirs, played the violin, played poker, built their own community centres and old-age homes. They would be Canadians, and their biggest aspiration was surely for their children, to give them an education, to send them to college or university, to see them take their place in careers and professions where they would never suffer the humiliation and ignominy of being such a one as a wage slave in a railway construction camp.

As for Alfred Nelson and his family, over the coming years they would have to move to wherever work could be found, and they would never be able to live for any length of time in their home in Prince Rupert. There would be cabins, and one winter a tent, and eventually a piece of land with a house and a barn full of hay and a cow called Daisy. But that was only when Alfred was used up and could no longer work "On Construction" or in the mines because of illness. This, too, was Canada.

City of Prince Rupert, early days.
(*Author's collection*)

Resele Gamla Kyrka, the Old Stone Church in Resele,
Sweden, as drawn by O. Ohlsson during a journey
through Ångermanland in 1828. Construction began in
1295, but due to epidemics of disease the church was
not completed until sometime in the following century.
The church was demolished in 1838.
(*Courtesy Länsbiblioteket Västernorrland
Härnösand, Sweden*)

TWO

SARA ERIKA HANSDOTTER

DISCOVERING MY *UPPSTUDSIG* GRANDMOTHER

My father never talked about Sweden or spoke of his mother and father, so it never occurred to me as a child that I had grandparents there. He said only that he was born in the northern province of Ångermanland. Not till years later, and only when I began to read and write about Nordic emigration, did I reflect on the leave-taking of my own father from his native land. For this task I created a Swedish grandmother. I imagined her as a little peasant woman, a widow, standing outside her cottage door, a shawl around her shoulders, head wrapped in a kerchief. She watches her son lift an old brown suitcase onto the cart that will carry him away to Amerika. In my script she is the only one who speaks: "Well, you'll be off then!" No embrace, no tears. She gives him a little package of *tunnbröd* (flatbread) and cheese. "You'll be wanting this," she says. He stuffs it in his pocket, seizes her hand in farewell, and jumps up beside his driver. He turns and waves as the cart clatters off down the road. She stands watching until they're out of sight, then with a sigh goes inside and sits down at her spinning wheel.

This imagined leave-taking was straight out of folk tale, unembarrassed by the archival information that I had yet to discover in Swedish church records. In Sweden's strict nineteenth-century society, dominated by the Lutheran Church, the priest was required to keep a register called *Husförhörslängd* (Household Examination Roll), with a separate page for each farm. The *bonde* (farmer) came first on the page, then members of his family, followed by his farm workers with their families and finally, at the bottom of the page, *pigar* (maidservants). It was there, in the record book for the parish of Resele in the province of Ångermanland, and always near the bottom of the page, that I found the name of my grandmother, Sara Erika Hansdotter, maidservant.

Ångermanland is in the northern part of Sweden, between latitudes 62 and 64, as far north as Great Slave Lake and Whitehorse are in Canada's Yukon Territory, yet without their severe winter climate. The Ångerman River rises beyond Sweden's western border in the mountains of Norway and flows southeasterly to the coast through low mountains, cutting deep valleys with steep sandy river banks – the extraordinary *niporna*, bright with flowers in spring and summer: pink campion, blue monkshood, and especially the anemone or windflower. Ångermanland is a country of pine and spruce forest, and birch and aspen with many lakes and swampy areas. The forest is home to bear and elk, marten and lynx, with blueberry bushes in its undercover. The landscape resembles parts of Northern Ontario – Kapuskasing, Lake Nipigon, Kenora – though with more cultivated farms in the valley bottoms and on the lower slopes of the mountains.

The villages in Resele parish are in these valleys and along the river, and they include Översel, where Sara Erika, the youngest daughter of the crofter Hans Larsson and his wife Lisa Märtha Ersdotter, was born in 1848. The family had twelve children. In those days the farmer sowed his oats and rye by hand, flinging the grain from a basket as he walked. He harvested it by hand with sickle and scythe, for this was pre-industrial Sweden. Transportation was by horse and cart and ferry boat: the railroad did not reach Resele parish until 1887.

Resele parish was largely a farming community, and in Sara's time there was also an unseen farming population of gnomes. Folklorist and scholar Arvid Enqvist interviewed many older people in Resele and neighbouring parishes in 1912 and later published their folk memories. In *Folkminnen från Ångermanland*, he declared that giants, elves, wood and water sprites, and little old men of the flour mill may well have receded into myth and legend, but many local residents still firmly believed in the existence of *vättarna*. They were invisible folk who lived the same kind of everyday farm life as humankind, with their own houses and barns and meadows and their own cattle, which were fat and handsome and usually white. It was thought by some that they were descendants of Adam and his first wife Lucia, who bore children several times a year. God thought that she was too much like an animal; Adam's progeny were increasing too rapidly. He decided to give Adam a new wife called Eve and banished Lucia and her offspring to work as before, but in an invisible world alongside the human world. *Vättarna* are no trouble, unless, perhaps, a cow barn is inadvertently built on one of their paths, in which case the cows don't thrive and the farmer is well advised to move the barn. About five kilometres north of Resele church there is ridge of land called *Vitteråsen* where people often got lost, supposedly because they had wandered off along a path there.

The commercial centre for the parish of Resele is the historic town of Resele, where early settlement can be traced to sometime before the year 1000, when a wooden church is believed to have existed there. So Christianity came early to Resele. Then in 1295 work began on a stone church, constructed around the wooden church. According to tradition, construction of this church was interrupted for seventy years because of the Black Death. Resele is old, and not unacquainted with grief.

In Sweden the Lutheran Church was, until the year 2000, the State Church. In effect, one was born Lutheran and, ideally, was to be guided by the tenets of the evangelical Lutheran religion, which took the Scriptures as sole authority. The usual method of instruction in the Scriptures has been for centuries the study of a catechism, a textbook containing the principles of the Christian religion in the form of question and answer, followed by an oral examination. Martin Luther's Small Catechism of 1529 was first introduced in Sweden in 1595, and by 1686 was being used throughout Sweden. The Catechism is in five parts: The Law, or the Ten Commandments; the Apostles' Creed, the Lord's Prayer, Baptism, and the Sacrament of the Altar, which included instruction on confession and absolution.

The priest visited each village twice a year to offer communion, usually at the house of a leading member of the congregation, duly recording those who received communion. He also recorded vital statistics regarding birth, death, marriage, vaccination, and entry into and departure from the parish, with cross-references to pages for other villages. He tested each person's reading ability and knowledge of the Lutheran Catechism, a task he performed in accordance with church law, for his parishioners, and especially the children, must read God's word with their own eyes. Literacy was the way to the soul's salvation.

In the parish record books for the years I examined, the priests had been saved the labour of writing notes for each parishioner. Instead, they used a system of symbols. The instructions for using the symbols and the key to this elaborate code were given at the beginning of the record book. First came the symbols for the results of the reading tests, which were graded in some detail both for reading aloud and for comprehension.

⌐	Has begun to read	T	Has poor comprehension
⌐⌐	Reads poorly	⊥	Has fair comprehension
⌐⌐	Reads fairly well	⊥⊥	Comprehends quite well
⌐⌐	Reads satisfactorily	⊥⊥	Has good comprehension
⌐⌐	Reads proficiently		

Next came the examination on the Lutheran Catechism. A parishioner had to be able not only to read and understand it, but also to recite it from memory. The priest entered one dot for reading and one for reciting and understanding each of the five sections: ⁙ But then, if the person should at a later examination not be able to recite the Lord's Prayer or the Creed or any other part of the Catechism, the dots would be very small. However, by making good the deficiency, you could earn a compensation of enlarged dots, thus: ⁙

The symbols became quite elaborate, for there were levels of performance and degrees and combinations of remembering and forgetting. For example:

⌐⌐⌐ "Reads satisfactorily from the Book; has good understanding; forgot to learn by heart the fourth and fifth parts of the Catechism."

The priest also assessed mental abilities and attitudes. He did not tolerate laziness: ⌐ .

⌐─┘   "Has good memory and understanding but is lazy."

Finally, he was required to record instances of misconduct and bad behaviour, as reported by reliable sources, and presumably the *bonde* and his
wife, master and mistress, would be so regarded.

∿∿   "Has been disorderly or delinquent. Write the number of the
       commandment which has been broken."
∿∿·   "For drunkenness, make one dot after the wavy line."
·∿∿   "For being quarrelsome make one dot at the beginning of the
       wavy line."

Insubordination, perjury, stealing: for each of these offences the priest
assigned a wavy line with distinctive markings.

But human behaviour is too various to be measured and controlled so
minutely. The system of symbols most likely proved too elaborate and was
eventually abandoned, though in Sara Erika's time it was still in use – in her
case, most eloquently.

From the pages in the parish record books I learned that my grandmother could read quite well by the time she was eight years old and that she
knew some of the Lutheran Catechism. But as a young woman, Sara Erika
had many wavy lines accompanying her name. She was quarrelsome and
known for insubordination (*uppstudsighet*) towards her parents and her employer. Moreover, she had broken the commandments, specifically the sixth.
According to Luther's numbering of the commandments, this was "Thou shalt
not commit adultery." Her name appeared over the years with the notation
"*oäkta*" (illegitimate) introducing the names of her four children. The second
of these was my father, Nils Alfred Nilsson, born on November 24, 1876. Sara
was twenty-eight years old when he was born. Nils Erik Eriksson, his father,
was eighteen. It was a case, it seems, of the maidservant and the landowner's
son: a script right out of a novel or film.

It appears, moreover, that all four of her children had different fathers.
Sara moved from village to village, bringing her reputation with her, all duly
recorded by the parish priest in his record book. He did not approve of her
and judged her severely. Was my grandmother the parish slut? Surely not.
One must not jump to harsh conclusions on the basis of incomplete evidence

or read genealogical data with the eyes of a novelist or filmmaker. So I tell myself, but yet an Ingmar Bergman film comes to mind and I see a young Sara Erika, blonde and buxom, joyously romping in the hay with her farmhand sweetheart, blond and broad-shouldered, in a scene right out of *Smiles of a Summer Night.*

Fantasy aside, I consider the century she lived in, the sheer physical harshness of those times, the life of servitude, the struggle for subsistence. In the parish of Resele, people had experienced famine. In 1867 throughout northern Sweden the climate was unusually cold. Ice and snow were on the ground well into summer; frost remained in the ground and made the earth too wet to plough. When finally seed could be sown, it was too late and none of it sprouted. Not only was there no harvest that year, but there was also no seed for the following year, and the famine continued into 1868. People had no work, they had no money. To eke out their meagre supply of flour they would mix it with moss and straw. When that little bit of flour was used up, they had to go about begging to feed their starving children. In the parish of Resele a committee was formed to provide jobs. Men were set to work cutting wood for burning to make tar, a traditional industry in the area. They received in pay a carefully calculated amount of grain: 3.9 pounds of grain for a day's work, and that would have to feed a large family. Women were set to work spinning flax. For their day's work, they were paid 2.5 pounds of grain for spinning 6.8 pounds of flax or hemp, depending on the quality of the linen they produced.

Sara Erika was nineteen years old in 1867, the year of the famine. The story of the famine is well documented in provincial and municipal records for that time, but what was it like for Sara Erika? She would certainly by that time have left home to become a maidservant, for daughters were sent out early to service and she would have been earning her own living from the time that she was twelve or thirteen years old. When the famine came and disrupted the whole economy, the servants had to live on what their masters could spare them, famine bread perhaps, made with flour eked out with moss and straw? Or she may well have been one of the women in the parish of Resele who was set to spinning flax. It's quite possible that Sara knew hunger.

She surely knew hard work. A maidservant was up early to make the fire in the *kakelugn*, the handsome traditional stove made of decorated tile. She scrubbed and cleaned and polished every day, and she may have been the dairymaid and milked the cows. In the fall, when it was time for *tunnbrödsbakning*, the baking of the hard, thin bread, of *knäckebröd* (hard tack), which could be stored all winter, she built the fire in the bake oven at two o'clock in the morning, so that baking could begin three hours later. In the middle of June, when the cows were moved to the summer pasture where there was a rough cabin, several maids were sent along with this exodus. They were the dairymaids who milked the cows and scoured the milk trays and churned the butter. They cleaned the cabin and provided food for the men who chopped wood and mended fences. The dairymaids made the cheese, and that required some skill, to mix the milk with the proper amount of rennet (made in those days from the stomach of newly slaughtered sucking calf), wrap the soft cheese in a cloth, squeeze out the moisture, and hang the cheese to dry. Twice a year, at harvest time and at Christmas, a new batch of beer had to be brewed, and the maidservant was the one who scoured the water barrels, the brewing tubs, the buckets and casks and wooden ladles and put them to soak in juniper water.

The maidservants did their share of work on the farmstead, but for all that they were not regarded with the respect due them. Women throughout the Western world, not just servant girls and not just in Sweden, were still regarded as lesser human beings, lacking in the ability to think and reason. They were regarded as emotional and easily led astray. They were, after all, descended from Eve. (And yet, I smile when I think of Martin Luther in an earlier century. He did not allow such stern views to invade the happy bedroom he shared with his dear wife Kathe during their long and mutually loving and respectful relationship. He was sometimes embarrassed when she became voluble in company, but he valued her for her shrewd judgement. And she brewed an excellent beer. In one of his letters to her he signed himself "Your Holiness's Willing Servant.")

In the division of labour, women laboured at home. If they had servants to bake and brew and scrub and scour, then those servants were even further down on the economic and social ladder. Even so, whether mistress or servant, all women obeyed the same rules: they must be gentle and submissive, and not talk too much. They were useful and necessary, but they had to know their place, which was to be a helpmeet, provide sexual service, and bring forth and multiply.

Yet there remained the problem of lust, sexual desire, one of the Seven Deadly Sins, a problem only partly solved by sanctifying it in marriage. For sexual desire, even when sanctified, produced too many children and too great a burden on the wife. A Swedish friend of mine remembers that her grandfather was made to sit on *skambänken*, the shame stool, in his church during the service, because he had made his wife pregnant with thirteen children.

The records show that Sara Erika by no means qualified as a proper gentle and submissive woman. She broke all the rules. She was uppity and rude. She had children out of wedlock. However, the priest received his information from the master and mistress, and the records are not likely to show instances of their misbehaviour. At one or another of the farmsteads where she worked, she may have been mistreated by her mistress, even given the occasional slap. It was sometimes convenient to shift the blame for some household misfortune onto a servant. A fanciful story is told in Resele about one unlucky maidservant. Her master and his house guest had spent the evening drinking after a day's hunting. They had then fallen into a drunken sleep until morning, when the guest found that his money was missing. The master blamed his maidservant for stealing the money. It was returned to the guest soon enough, however. For, the story goes, the maidservant, sweeping the floor, suddenly threw the broom outside and was carried away on it like "a bird over the treetops" to the home of the guest, to whom she was made to return the money. She then had to walk home and stand on the shore and shout for the ferryman to bring the boat across for her. This experience so affected her that she became a little odd, no longer right in the head. "Who dunnit? The Butler did it" is surely today's variant on the maidservant's story.

Nor do the records necessarily show that Sara Erika was a giddy, promiscuous woman. She bore her first child at the age of twenty-five, the second at twenty-eight, the third at thirty-three, and the fourth at forty-one. What her sexual life was like in the intervals between childbirths we do not know. She may have been living in true common-law relationships, if illegitimate. Sara Erika knew a mother's suffering: her two last-born died in early childhood – Johannes Malkolm when he was two years old, Pehr August when he was three. Today we would refer to her as a single parent.

I do not claim Sara Erika as an exemplary grandmother. Yet the parish records show that she did at least one good thing. She brought the eighteen-year-old Nils Erik Eriksson into district court at Sollefteå, where he admitted to being the father of her son, Nils Alfred. The inference is clear. She was out-raged by an attack on her person. She did not meekly submit to being raped by the landowner's son. The church records show that the eighteen-year-old she took to court sired four illegitimate children before he married at age twenty-four. He died of tuberculosis at age thirty-one, having married and fathering at least one more child.

Perhaps there is even more to the story. In *The Girl from the Marshcroft*, Swedish writer Selma Lagerlöf tells a similar story of a disgraced maidservant who brings a married man into court to make him admit that he is the father of her child. The maid is not given a name in the first chapter of the novel. She is simply "the plaintiff," and the father is "the defendant." Because she has committed the sin of adultery, no household will now employ her. She has no money to buy food, her child is gravely ill, and the father has refused her plea for help. In court he completely disowns her. When the judge hands him the Bible and is about to administer the oath, she grabs the Good Book to prevent her erstwhile lover from perjuring himself. In her distress for his soul's salva-tion, she says slowly, earnestly and clearly to the judge: "I wish to withdraw the suit. He is the father of the child. I am still fond of him. I don't wish him to swear falsely." The judge is so moved by her moral rectitude that he does as she wishes and orders the case closed. The defendant hangs his head in shame. "'Thank you!' says the judge once more, taking her hand and shaking it as if it belonged to a real man's man."

I doubt if Sara felt any concern for the salvation of the soul of the eighteen-year-old randy youth who had in all likelihood taken advantage of her. Nor on the evidence of the wavy lines with their several sixes against her name in the parish record would she have been regarded by the Sollefteå court judge as the equal of a "real man" in moral rectitude, whatever latitude such real men were allowed in sexual matters. And then also Sara Erika's wavy lines sometimes had crosses above the sixes: $\overset{+}{\underset{\sim}{6}}\ \overset{+}{\underset{\sim}{6}}\ \overset{+}{\underset{\sim}{6}}$, which indicated that she had either "under-gone corporal punishment or Penance, or fallen into dishonour." Evidently in addition to bearing children out of wedlock, whatever the circumstances, she had been guilty of some delinquency that earned her further opprobrium.

Yet was it only because of deeply felt injury to her self-respect that Sara Erika stood before the judge in Sollefteå? Like Lagerlöf's plaintiff, she was a disgraced woman, and like her she had a child to feed. Was it for the sake of her infant son that she took Nils Erik Eriksson to court and made him admit to being his father? She knew about hunger, about famine even. If this were the reason, her action speaks of a certain nobility of soul after all, despite the wavy lines and sixes and crosses. But I am speculating.

The records show that this child, Nils Alfred, the only son who lived to adulthood, followed her from farm to farm until he was fifteen years old. As a farm labourer, he would have walked behind the plough and turned the furrows; planted potatoes and cabbage; mowed the hayfield with sickle and scythe; fed the horses twice a day and rubbed them down and cleaned their stalls; built fences, repaired them. He would have shovelled manure.

Later he became a labourer in the village of Översel, where his mother was living. In the church records there are no wavy lines, or sixes, or crosses against his name, or any other indication of bad behaviour. This is the young man who became my father, and I cannot believe that if his mother was completely unregenerate he would have stayed with her for so many years. When he finally left her in 1897, it was to take his compulsory military service at the age of twenty-one. He became a private in the supply column, and when he finished his military training he did not go back to Översel to live; he went off to work at the Kiruna iron mine in northern Sweden. That was when he said goodbye to his strong-minded mother, who may indeed have given him a packet of *tunnbröd* and cheese to help him on his way. It appears that by the time he left, Sara Erika could look forward to a more stable life and could do without him. In 1898 she married a farm worker, a widower, and, wife at last, may have enjoyed a more settled life.

In 1902, according to Norwegian records, Nils Alfred was in Norway, and in 1904 he received permission to work in the port of Narvik on Norway's west coast. He himself said in later years that he worked on the railway that was being built from Kiruna to Narvik, and that he emigrated from there. That was where he must have bought a little red trunk that accompanied him on his first long voyage and would always be in the family. In 1908 the Resele parish priest moves the name of Nils Alfred Nilsson to the missing persons list in the Household Examination Roll. By that time he had left Sweden and was on his way to Kanada, where just maybe you could live without being watched and written down in a book. He had an English-Swedish dictionary in his pocket and had learned a new English word: "pre-emption." In Canada land is free if you promise to clear it, plough it, and make it ready for sowing; and you must promise to become a citizen.

Sara Erika died in 1919 at the age of seventy-one. Her son was by that time a Canadian citizen raising a Canadian family. He owned a piece of land and had even built a house on it. There are no letters or other documents to say whether or not he had kept in touch with his mother in the twenty years after he said goodbye. But I think I know why he never talked about his parents: he did not want to bring her disgrace with him to Canada. It had followed her far enough. He adopted instead the family of his Norwegian wife, not just her uncle and brothers in Prince Rupert but also those living in Norway, all respectable people. In a letter to his brother-in-law Erik in Norway, he asked, "How is Mother...?" as if he had actually met his mother-in-law. Erik was a school principal and editor of the local newspaper.

I too have followed Sara Erika far enough, and Nils Erik Eriksson as well. I could visit Ångermanland, visit Översel and Yttersel and Myre, consult court records, even discover elderly cousins, but I will not do it. I will not intrude further on my father's past with my twentieth-century sensibilities, my researcher's eagerness to lift every stone, my speculations and imaginings. I will respect his reticence and leave closed a history that in any case can never be fully told.

But now I think of that scene in Shakespeare's *Twelfth Night*, in which Malvolio is asked, "What is the opinion of Pythagoras concerning wild fowl?" Malvolio answers, "That the soul of our grandam might haply inhabit a bird." I do not believe with Pythagoras in the transmigration of souls. But mitochondrial DNA? This is not your ordinary, all-purpose DNA, but the extraordinary DNA that you get only from your mother and her mother and that mother's mother. Sara Erika Hansdotter, our family's Mitochondrial Eve? A grandam who inhabited a bird, and that bird her son, Nils Alfred Nilsson? Sara Erika was destined not to disappear from his life after all, for you cannot emigrate from your genes. His uppity mother was surely with him, my strong-minded, resolute, stubborn father, that immigrant labourer who faced up to many a foreman and boss in his struggle to survive in Kanada, who with shovel and hammer and steel helped to build a city and a railway and proudly declared, "It takes a Swede every time."

At the House on English Hill, 209 W. 7th Ave., Prince Rupert, 1915.
In the middle is Alfred Nelson, with son Arthur; to the right, Ingeborg,
with Verner; the woman at the back may be cousin Anna Orwig.
(*Author's collection*)

THREE

TO AMERIKA AND THE HOUSE ON ENGLISH HILL

"Your mother, she had the Amerika fever." It had been seventy-five years since Tante Kristine had seen her sister leave Norway for Kanada, and she was meeting me, her niece visiting from British Columbia, for the first time. She spoke urgently, in English, wanting to tell me right away as though she needed to give an accounting, the reason why Ingeborg had emigrated. And here I was at last, Ingeborg's daughter, a stranger come all the way from Kanada to find her, but not a stranger either, *for jeg kunne snakke litt norsk*, I could speak a little Norwegian, and understand too.

She drew me away from the crowd of welcoming relatives into her apartment hallway so that she could tell me, her words punctuated by the soft clink of coffee cups in the living room, that it was because of the Amerika fever that Ingeborg had left her family and immigrated to Kanada. Tante Kristine spoke no blame. She was nearly eighty years old and could remember how in Norway the fever to emigrate was a contagion. In Orkanger, where Tante Kristine lived, in Viggja and nearby Børsa – in all the little villages and farms on Orkangerfjord, on Trondhjemsfjord, and in the rest of Trøndelag – the Amerika fever spread, as in the rest of Norway from Oslo to Hammerfest and Tromsø. Throughout all of Scandinavia during the nineteenth and early twentieth centuries crofters and farmhands left the land, and fishermen their boats, answering the call of railway companies inviting settlers to come and take up free land. Amerika beckoned, not least young maidservants seeking an escape from servitude in a new country where you could become the wife of a farmer instead of his servant. Those who stayed behind blamed the Amerika fever, as did my Aunt Kristine, still feeling bereft at the loss of her older sister.

Uncle Thorstein and Aunt Berit and their children had left for Amerika, but that was in 1888, before Kristine was born, so they were people in a story, a continuing story told in letters from Amerika, which included Kanada, farther north and colder. The letters told about Port Essington, where they were now living, on the west coast of British Columbia. In 1910, when Kristine was fifteen, her elder brother Bernt packed his carpenters' tools and said goodbye, he was off to Amerika too, to this place called British Columbia, but he was twenty-six years old, not just part of the story from the Amerika letters, but part of her life.

A year later, in 1911, her sister Ingeborg left her as well. Ingeborg packed her trunk and left Viggja, the little village on Orkdalsfjord where she was born; left her family and the house on the fjord to join her Uncle Thorstein and Aunt Berit in Port Essington. Ingeborg had caught the Amerika fever, just like everybody else, and when I came to visit my Tante Kristine in Norway, she spoke as though it were a physical illness, a terrible affliction that had disrupted the family. The memory of that illness had stayed with her all her life.

I began to understand then what it truly meant to emigrate, to leave one's own country and start again. I had learned early the founding stories of Canada: of the Native Indians, the Explorers, the Fur Trade; of Wolfe and Montcalm on the Plains of Abraham; of Chief Maquinna and Captain Cook at Nootka. And the Immigrant Story, which for me was especially vivid because as a child I knew it belonged to my own family. The mountains of British Columbia enclosed us, and enclosing, embracing them was the Old Country of my parents, divided into two parts, because my mother was from Norway, my father from Sweden. *Norge, Sverige* – they were the Old Country, where my parents had lived at one time but had left to come to Canada.

They were immigrants, and I knew that Canada was a country of immigrants. But not until I stood on the shore behind my grandfather's boat shop and wondered at the Canada Geese swimming about as though they belonged there, as much Norwegian as Canadian; not until I had slept in the house where my mother was born, and met Tante Kristine, who spoke to me so movingly about Ingeborg and the Amerika fever, did I begin to understand the meaning of "emigrate." For then I knew there had to be a leave-taking.

Ingeborg may have taken passage on the *Orkla*, the new steam launch built in 1908 for freight and passenger service on Trondhjem Fjord. Or she may have sailed up the fjord with her father, he at the helm of his handy boat. With a good wind, they'd be in Trondhjem in one and a half hours. Either way her family were with her, offering little last-minute cautions and advice for her health and safety, waiting to say the last goodbye. Then the moment comes, they each in turn hold her close, and as she turns and walks away, they wave from the shore and call their farewells: "*Ha det bra! Ha det bra!*" She turns once more and calls "*Farvel, farvel.*" That is how it must have been. That is how it is to emigrate.

When Ingeborg said goodbye to Norway, she left behind more than her family. She took leave also of centuries of Norse history and tradition. The history of Viggja, the village where she was born, resonates with names and events in the shared collective memory of Norway, and they are commemorated on a cairn that stands not far from the front door of her childhood home. An older brother, Anders, was a member of the local young people's club, which erected the cairn in 1896 and under the heading of "Viggja Ancestors" inscribed these names on it: "Lodin, c. 1015; Rut, d. 1030; Lodin Viggjaskallen; Sigurd Ullstreng." They all figure in the *Kongesagaer*, the Norse *Sagas of the Kings* by the Icelandic skald and historian Snorre Sturlasson, and all are connected with what was then known as Vigg (later Viggen, and now Viggja). Fervent nationalists, these young people chose to erect the cairn on the seventeenth of May, a day commemorating the anniversary of the new Norwegian Constitution, adopted in 1814 at the time of the union with Sweden.

It appears to me that they also elevated in importance the feudal lord, Sigurd Ullstreng: "*STALARE SLAGET PÅ VIGGJA* 1095" (King's Marshal The Battle of Viggja 1095) reads his inscription, and "*GRUNDET NIDARHOLMS KLOSTER 1105*" (founded Nidarholms Kloster 1105). There were bloody battles at Vigg, and archaeological discoveries from that area in 1888 are witness to them: an iron battleaxe and a one-edged sword, both from Viking times in the tenth century. It was in a later century at Vigg in 1095 that Sigurd Ullstreng, a loyal chieftain and king's marshal, fought a losing battle against the rebel Tore, who refused to surrender to the rule of King Magnus Barefoot. Snorre tells of the battle, but he does not call it the Battle of Viggja. He treats it as one of many such struggles during the Christianization of Norway, struggles that were not as important for its history as some others, such as the famous Battle of Stikelstad in 1030, where King Olav, later Saint Olav, met his death.

Sigurd Ullstreng was a Christian, and he it was who established the monastery later called Nidarholm and left to it his lands at Vigg. It was one of the earliest monasteries in Norway and belonged to the Benedictine Order. But his ancestors in earlier Viking times had worshipped the pagan gods and even in his own time in the Trøndelag area there was still some resistance to changing from the old forms of pagan worship to Christian rites.

One of my young relatives in Norway told me that she wrote a school essay about Sigurd Ullstreng, and my own account of him comes not just from Snorre, but also from a recent monograph about him and his lands at Vigg, *Vigga in the High Middle Ages* by Ann-Carin Bøyesen. It is a study guide for teachers with the express purpose of encouraging the study of local history in schools, thereby strengthening the student's sense of personal identity. If indeed knowledge of one's roots does accomplish this, surely Ingeborg Aarvik grew up with a strong sense of self: she knew about Sigurd Ullstreng and Lodin and Rut and Lodin Viggjaskallen – they were right there on the cairn in front of her house. Anders and his friends had evidently read about Vigg in Snorre's sagas and been thus inspired to lay claim to their Viggja ancestors and to the Battle of Viggja. Anders was seventeen years old; Ingeborg was eight, and she was most likely there with all the Aarvik family on the seventeenth of May 1896 when her big brother and his friends erected the cairn to honour their ancestors.

But those ancestors were not all feudal chieftains harrying throughout the land with battleaxe and sword. Among the artifacts discovered at Viggen in 1888 were hearth stones and a griddle, testifying to the everyday home life of the early inhabitants of the village. The griddle was of the kind used today for baking *lefse*, a thin pancake of rolled dough common to many cultures. In Norway it is served buttered, sometimes sprinkled with sugar and cinnamon, and rolled or folded. My niece Ingeborg in Norway bakes *lefse*, and so too did my mother Ingeborg, and her mother Ingeborg-Anna, as did the many Inge-borgs going back through the centuries to Sigurd Ullstreng's time and before; that is, if that griddle found in a coal seam in a hill in Viggja was indeed used for baking *lefse*.

My Ingeborg's mother was Ingeborg-Anna Andersdatter Viggen, daughter of the fisherman Anders whose family, having lived on Viggen farmsteads for over a century, had taken the surname "Viggen." Almost certainly they lived on some part of Sigurd Ullstreng's land, one of the oldest properties at Vigg. The researches of local historians indicate that the house on the fjord where my mother was born and the cairn nearby are also on Sigurd Ullstreng's land.

Ingeborg-Anna Andersdatter Viggen married Elling Erikssen Aarvik from Tysvær, farther south on the coast near Haugesund. Elling Aarvik was a boat-builder, and his grandfather, Thorstein Johannessen, was a sailor who lived in a cottage on the Aarvig farm. They had Danish forebears, a fact that ac-counts for the name ending in 'g', which became 'k' in Norway. An eighteenth-century Aarvig is said to have come originally to Norway to repair the organ in a church in Stavanger on the west coast. The family moved farther north when Elling's father, Erik Andreas Thorsteinssen Aarvig, at nineteen, was sent to the northern part of Norway to teach fishermen about a new, lighter boat developed on the south coast on the Lista peninsula. In 1869 (some sources say 1872), he settled in Viggen and established his own boatyard on Orkdals-fjord. Aarvigs from Denmark became Aarviks in Viggja in the Trøndelag part of Norway. Aarvik and Viggen: those are the names I inherited from my moth-er's family.

I inherited the names and also the knowledge that I had Norwegian grandparents in a place called Viggen. But of the history of Norway I learned nothing from my mother, who by the time I was born was thoroughly Can-adian, though still singing, in her native language, "Can you forget Old Norway?" and still baking *lefse*. Lodin, Rut, Lodin Viggjaskallen, Sigurd Ull-streng: she left them all behind when she immigrated to Canada. And Magnus Berrføt, Harald Hårfagre, Olav Haraldsson, Olav Trygvasson; their women, Astrid, Gunnhild, and Sigrid; Ingegerd and Ingebjørg. The names reverber-ate, they echo through the centuries, heard to this day in the names of the general population of Norway.

Yet she brought something with her of Norway and Norway's history, cer-tainly her own name, the sound and lilt of "Ingeborg," a name with a history.

There were many Ingebjørgs in Snorre's *Kongesagaer*, and one of the most renowned was Ingebjørg Trygvesdatter, who gave staunch support to Olav Haraldsson, the Norwegian king destined to become Saint Olav. For by her cool intervention the king of Sweden finally agreed to relinquish sovereignty of Norway and give him back his kingdom. It would be no small thing to bear the name of this woman.

My mother's nephew Egil Aarvik was born in the Aarvik house at Viggja on Trondheim Fjord and spent part of his childhood there. He recalls with some pride that Vigg is well known as the place where Norwegian novelist (and 1928 Nobel Laureate in Literature) Sigrid Undset chose to have Kristin Lavransdatter, "seasick and exhausted," step ashore on her way to Huseby, where she would be mistress of the manor.

Egil Aarvik became a journalist and was for many years a member of the Norwegian parliament, and also chairman of the Norwegian Nobel Committee, remembered for his annual address at the ceremony for awarding the Peace Prize. In his autobiography, *Smil i alvor: Fragmenter av et liv*, he recalls how Grandfather Elling could build a boat without the aid of spirit level or square, from its first design laid out on the floor to the rigging of the sails. The keel was struck, the ribs fashioned, the deck built in the boathouse on the beach. But much work was done in the little *stue* or living room, which also served as dining room and extra bedroom. Egil Aarvik recalls further that here the tarred oakum was prepared for caulking the seams, and that somehow space was found to place a bench diagonally across the floor, where Elling and his helpers could sit and sew the sails. He had a flowing beard down to his chest, but otherwise was "compact, square-built and nimble as a cat when he climbed the shrouds to fix the sails to the topmost rigging."

My cousin Egil recounted also that Grandmother Ingeborg-Anna was a partner in the building of boats. In the tiny "peanut-sized" kitchen she cooked meals for up to ten people at a sitting (her son Julius and his wife Louise lived upstairs, where Egil was born), and sometimes as well for thrifty customers who came to the house to contribute their own labour to a boat. According to Egil, she kept these men in line. A worker called Samson never tied his shoe laces, and this exasperated her. One day when Samson was walking along the scaffolding in the boathouse he tripped on his shoe laces and fell three metres, landing on his head. "Grandmother felt no pity for him," Egil said. "She wiped the blood from his head. 'You could have tied your shoe laces,' she said."

Ingeborg-Anna had nine children in the course of nineteen years, and only one of them died as a child. My mother, Ingeborg-Oline, born in 1888, was the sixth. She grew up to be a beautiful young woman, but not with the usual flaxen hair of most Scandinavians, for she was from Trøndelag, and Trønders are typically dark-haired. Her hair was so dark that it was almost black. It was long, down to her waist, and she wore it in the fashion of the day, coiled and piled around her head.

At that time Viggen was a little village with the dwellings of fishermen and labourers strung out along the shore. It had a general store with a post office, and a dairy and school. The steamship from Trondhjem arrived several times a week and docked at the quay. By 1910 the young people's club had built themselves a clubhouse. Some older people opined that in their day they didn't have a clubhouse, but they had held dances, had a little whiskey and a good time just the same without spending any money. Undaunted by this grudging response, at Christmas the young people held a successful fundraising bazaar that brought together young and old in the new clubhouse. In a crowd of 180 people, nobody was "noticeably drunk," but everyone was in a holiday mood just the same. "This is what a holiday celebration should be like," declared the leader of the club in his report to the local newspaper. Now that there was a meeting place for young people, he admonished, there was no reason for them to get drunk at Christmas and cause a disturbance. In his next report he announced plans for another ambitious project, a community bathhouse. These young people in Viggja were evidently a spirited group with a lively sense of social responsibility.

What Ingeborg's social life was like I do not know, but the youth club had been in existence for most of her young life, with her brother Anders taking a leading role. Moreover, in 1908 her eldest brother Erik was the editor of the local newspaper, *Søndre Trondhjems Amtstidende* (later *Sør-Trøndelag*). He was also a school teacher and school principal, and in the course of his long life in the town of Orkanger, where he later lived, became one of its leading educators. He was a man of intellect with a keen, wide-ranging mind – the walls of his study were lined with books, floor to ceiling – and he was proudly Norwegian. He, like his brother Anders, had been strongly influenced by the movement for national liberation that led to the separation of Norway from Sweden in 1905, when Norway became an independent country.

Erik maintained this ardent national sentiment throughout his life and acted on it, even to the extent of putting himself in danger. During the Nazi occupation of Norway he continued to publish his newspaper, finding ways of opposing the regime with brief and subtly worded news items. Eventually he was summoned to appear before the local Nazi official, who in the course of his interrogation went so far as to accuse him, indeed, of a "lack of national sentiment." At this Erik Aarvik could no longer remain silent. He became the school teacher, patiently explaining to a rather dense pupil what national sentiment really was. At this display of insubordination, was he seized and turned over to the Gestapo? No, the Nazi boss was so affected by this kindly lesson that he "suddenly clutched his head with both his hands and wailed in naked desperation, 'But what shall I do?'"

Ingeborg Aarvik grew up, then, in an articulate family that contributed to the cultural life of the community. The Aarviks liked to talk; they had spirit, they had ideas.

On the meadows and hills above and beyond the shore were the farmsteads, among them those of the more prosperous farmers. Ingeborg was a maidservant in one of those households. Women were still destined for marriage, not for education and a career, and the daughter of a boat-builder must earn her keep.

On December 19, 1907, when she was nineteen, Ingeborg married the village tailor, Kristian Andreassen Viggen, a fisherman's son, whose family also lived on a small Viggja farmstead. It would appear that theirs was not a village wedding, for they were married in Trondhjem's beautiful, historic *Vår Frue Kirke* (Church of Our Lady), restored one hundred years earlier but dating back to the year 1207. They made their home just east of Viggja along Orkdalsfjord at Nøstmælen, near the village of Børsa. Kristian had tuberculosis, in those days also called consumption, but they married anyway, for Ingeborg was pregnant. Their daughter Inga was born six weeks later, on January 27, 1908. A bride giving birth so soon after the wedding was not unusual in those days. What would have caused some distress and head-shaking in the family was the knowledge that the husband and father had tuberculosis, for Kristian would almost certainly be showing symptoms of the disease when they married. The events surrounding that marriage, which would be cut short by illness and death, suggest a difficult time for Ingeborg, but unfortunately that time never became a part of our family memory.

My mother's story, however, is not altogether lost, for I have found at least part of it in the historical record. A social stigma was attached to the disease: it was considered a poor people's sickness. The very word (*tæring*) (tuberculosis) was taboo. When a family member was smitten, one spoke rather of chronic bronchitis, catarrh, or a nervous condition. Sometimes those stricken with the disease would ignore their symptoms and continue with their everyday life rather than admit their true condition. Kristian may very well have hidden his illness as long as possible, for who would want to have a garment made by a tailor who had tuberculosis?

Norway had a very high incidence of that illness at the beginning of the twentieth century. With Ireland, it had one of the highest rates in Europe. It was only fifteen years after Robert Koch had identified the TB bacillus as the cause of the disease and told the world that it was infectious. The bacillus thrives in unsanitary conditions among the malnourished and indigent in the slums of industrialized cities and then spreads rapidly in the larger community. But it is also spread by unsanitary practices among the general population. Spitting, for example, was almost universally quite respectable in the first decades of the twentieth century, not just at home but also in public places, even in church during the sermon, and the dust from dried spittle on floors and walls and sidewalks polluted the air. Women could spread the disease simply by walking along a floor or sidewalk where the long trains of their dresses became contaminated with TB bacilli, which can live for several months in dry air. According to one researcher, in Sweden TB was noticeably prevalent among tailors because they often made over garments of people who had died of the disease, garments still contaminated with live bacilli.

In 1900 Norway passed a tuberculosis law requiring everyone who had the disease to register with the authorities and introducing measures to combat its spread. The Norwegian Medical Association, founded in 1886, and the Norwegian Women's Sanitary Organization, founded in 1896, were at the forefront of a campaign to educate people about the disease, and they were joined in 1910 by the National Association Against Tuberculosis. Thus began the decades during which a whole country was educated in personal cleanliness, sanitary housekeeping, and hygienic preparation and storing of food.

Judging from the editorial content of *Søndre Trondhjems Amtstidende*, Erik Aarvik was much concerned with the way in which tuberculosis was sweeping the country. "Tuberculosis Ravages" was his headline for one news item: government statistics showed that deaths from tuberculosis had increased from 16.6 per cent of total deaths in 1905 to 17.2 per cent in 1906. South Trondhjem was hardest hit, at 3.2 deaths per thousand, the highest death rate in all of Norway next only to Finnmark to the north.

Erik Aarvik was a man with a social conscience and a compassionate Christian sense of duty. According to his granddaughter, Ingrid Aukrust, during this time, before the founding of the Labour Party, he was a left-wing radical, *en venstremann*, but never actually became a socialist or a member of the Labour Party. "He was first of all a great humanitarian, always with an eye on the less fortunate members of society."

He was eloquent and passionate when he wrote about those people. In an article about the downturn in the economy that shut down factories and left many unemployed, he spoke of "the disastrous struggle between money interests that demand big dividends and the workers' mouths that ask for food" and declared that he stood with the workers, on the side of the thousand homes, the many mouths: "... *de tusind hjems, de mange mundes side*." And with that one phrase he invoked Norway's national anthem, Bjørnstjerne Bjørnson's "*Ja, vi elsker dette landet*" (Yes, we love this land), which embraces, in the words of the poet, "*de tusen hjem*," all of Norway's homes.

Among the less fortunate members of Norwegian society was that large population afflicted with TB. In his newspaper Erik Aarvik followed closely the activities of the local health societies: their public events, with speakers explaining how to avoid infection from TB and how to treat the sick, their money-raising bazaars in aid of building hospitals, the work of their nurses in the community. He cited figures: the hospital in Evjen opened in 1909 and in 1910 had fifty-five patients, 55.9 per cent of them with TB (eleven men and seventeen women). By March 1911 six of them had died. In an editorial addressing the health question, he urged the building of sanatoriums and nursing homes in every community, this with his private knowledge that the dread disease had struck down his brother-in-law, Ingeborg's husband.

The sanitary organizations had been active in Norway from the beginning of the century, certainly during Ingeborg's childhood and young womanhood. Signs were posted forbidding spitting in public places. One of Egil Aarvik's memories of Viggja is of the enamelled sign posted in the young people's hall and in the auditorium that was part of the dairy: "Don't spit on the floor!" He also mentioned that the Sanitary Organization held meetings at which "the local doctor distilled his message into two words: 'soap and water. Use soap and water,' he said, almost belligerently, as he leaned over the benches where his listeners were seated." This memory, so vividly recalling the passion and the energy expended in the fight against TB, is from the 1920s, but it also recalls 1909 and 1910 and the passion and energy of that fight in those years as reflected in Erik Aarvik's newspaper.

From the beginning of the century, sanatoriums, both public and private, were established for those who could afford to pay. Throughout the country tuberculosis nursing homes were also established. These were free, as were hospitals on the coast, where patients had the benefit of bracing sea air, but the number of applicants for both far outstripped the number of beds. There were scarcely any hospitals available for poor people with TB. Many of them simply remained at home to be looked after by their families, with help and instruction from a visiting nurse. It would have been difficult to isolate the patient to prevent the spread of the disease.

There were no wonder drugs in those days, no streptomycin, isoniazid, or pyrazinamide. It would be nearly half a century before the miracle of antibiotics was discovered and these new drugs came to be tested on TB patients. The usual treatment was a prolonged stay in a sanatorium, where patients were given ample meals with plenty of milk and cream and sat outside wrapped in blankets on a wide verandah to breathe the fresh mountain air or the salt sea air. This was called "the cure." A more radical treatment was "lung collapse," which stopped the lung from functioning and thus allowed it complete rest.

The milk and cream Kristian and Ingeborg might have managed, but not the prolonged stay in a sanatorium. Lisbetsæter in the nearby village of Børsa looked after TB patients, but it is unlikely that a village tailor could afford to be a patient there. The names of all TB patients who received treatment in Norwegian sanatoriums or hospitals are recorded in the tuberculosis registers in the Trondhjem State Archives. A search of the registers for 1908–09 did not find the name of Kristian Andreassen Viggen. I can only assume that he remained at home during his illness. Moreover, the parish records where his death is recorded show that he died at home and that he was visited by a doctor in the last stage of his illness.

How long did he continue working as a tailor, cutting material for an overcoat, operating the sewing machine, stitching buttonholes? For eventually the persistent cough and the fever and loss of appetite would defeat him.

When he could no longer earn a living, how did they manage? Did Ingeborg work as a maidservant and look after Inga and nurse Kristian as well?

The Norwegian Women's Sanitary Association sent nurses into the homes of TB patients. They moved in and lived with the family, isolated and cared for the patient, cooked meals, and helped with the children. One such visiting nurse, recalling her experience in the early 1920s, said that she always stayed with the patient throughout the illness, and when the patient died, it was often she who saw to the body and laid it in the coffin. As she said, "When the patient coughed up blood, that was always the worst experience. To see the look in the patient's eyes, the fear. I will never forget it." It is possible that such a live-in nurse looked after Kristian.

To watch a loved one die from consumption was not at all unusual, and several Scandinavian artists were moved to express their own private grief on canvas, among them Norway's Edvard Munch. He painted his sister Sophie sitting up in bed, her thin face illuminated in an aura of light and turned towards her mother, in black, kneeling, head heavy and bowed in grief. The painting is a powerful evocation of pity and sorrow for the young life ended by this disease. In Viggja in 1909, when Kristian was dying, there were many families with children, mothers, and fathers suffering from this disease that invaded the lungs to take away the very breath of life. No artist painted Ingeborg kneeling at the bed of Kristian, but their suffering and grief are commemorated just the same and can be found in the parish record book. On the page where Kristian's death is entered, his name is just one among many entries, but in the column where the priest wrote the cause of death one word leaps off the page: *tæring*. Over and over again, that word. Sometimes the priest just used ditto marks.

Kristian died on 20 November 1909. He was twenty-seven years old. There can be no doubt that the tragic illness and death of her young husband influenced Ingeborg's decision to emigrate. True, she had the Amerika fever, but she also wanted to leave behind illness and death brought about by this other contagion, and in Amerika, the new land that promised so much, there was surely no *tæring*. She was a widow. She had to earn a living for herself and Inga. The Amerika letters from Uncle Thorstein and Aunt Berit made the west coast of British Columbia seem like a place where even a young widow might prosper. Other Aarvik women younger than she had emigrated on their own: Thorstein's twenty-year-old sister, her aunt Josefine Emilie, in 1888, and then his daughters, her cousins Josefine and Albertine, even younger, still in their teens.

Whether in desperation over her economic future or in calm determination to take control of her life, Ingeborg decided to emigrate too and take advantage of the opportunities that Canada offered. Her brother Bernt would be there in Port Essington to help her. He had gone the year before and would be able to help her find work. But she had to make a hard decision. She had a child: Inga was three and a half years old. She would leave Inga behind in Viggja with the grandparents, just until she was settled in Kanada, until she had found work and could support herself; then she would send for her. Inga would accompany the next Aarvik family member immigrating to Canada.

The plan was reasonable enough. Uncle Thorstein had left Aunt Berit and his four daughters behind when he emigrated in 1888, and then sent for them, in stages, in the following four years. This was how it was done. Johannes, Ingeborg's eighteen-year-old brother, was thinking of emigrating, and Inga could accompany him. But what did Ingeborg's mother and father think about her plan? Leave Inga behind? Did they protest, "No, that won't do!" Or maybe, dubiously, "Well, perhaps. But poor little Inga!"

And my Tante Kristine, seventy-five years later: "She had the Amerika fever." Was she at that moment remembering her sister Ingeborg, stubborn, headstrong, and their mother and father, Elling and Ingeborg-Anna, arguing, pleading with her? Tante Kristine could have told me about that, for she was sixteen years old at the time and would have remembered. But those brief minutes decades later in her hallway were an emotional time for both of us, this meeting between Ingeborg's daughter and her Tante Kristine, and scarcely an appropriate time to ask probing questions, not with a crowd of relatives in the living room waiting to talk to their new-found relative from Kanada. When I was able to ask them later, they had no memories at all of Ingeborg, certainly not of any family quarrel with the parents hotly opposing their wilful daughter. So perhaps the parents sadly accepted her decison and waved goodbye.

Did Inga wave goodbye? I will never know, and Inga would remain a shadowy figure belonging to the Old Country of my childhood, except for this: when I was a young mother, I had to wave goodbye to my two-year-old son when I stepped out of our house, not to enter that door again for a year. Like

Kristian, I had tuberculosis. In my time, however, the new antibiotics were available, so with the help of streptomycin and isoniazid and the regimen of "the cure" in a sanatorium, I recovered completely. But the memory of that goodbye is engraved on my heart, suffused with a mother's sorrow and despair and guilt. So too it must have been with my mother Ingeborg when she had to wave goodbye to her child, her Inga.

Other things about Ingeborg's leave-taking I know from documents. According to the emigrant lists, the widow Ingeborg-Oline Ellingsdatter Viggen left for Trondhjem from Børsa (she was living nearby at Nøstmælen) under a contract with the Allan Steamship Line dated July 12, 1911, and she sailed from Trondhjem on the steamship *Aaro*. The document recorded that her destination was Port Essington and she was going to join her brother. These archival emigrant lists are from the Trondhjem Police Office, for all emigrants had to provide this kind of information to the authorities before departure.

Oddly, exactly a week before her scheduled departure Erik published a departing (anonymous) emigrant's story in his newspaper, providing a wry glimpse of how emigrants were likely to experience the visit to the local authorities: "In the afternoon all the emigrants met at the police office to give an account of themselves, and if you didn't have a clear conscience, you were in for trouble." Given the timing, it seems likely that this uncredited story represented a brother's farewell to a sister. It recognized her brave act and implied, even conferred on it, a certain legitimacy. It seems that this good, compassionate man, far from turning his back on his sister, might very well have declared his support in this anonymous yet public way.

In any case we do know that Ingeborg was allowed to leave, and I can imagine her standing on the deck of the steamship sailing out of Trondhjem, saying a last farewell to her country, to her family, to Kristian in his grave, and to Inga. In due course she would have been crossing the North Sea and there, like the traveller in the newspaper story, would have experienced "the poignant moment ... when we would say farewell to our motherland and see the last glimpse of Norwegian mountains disappear beyond the horizon."

Ingeborg's sister Kristine did not emigrate. She remained in Norway, married her brother Erik's publisher, Rasmus Kongsvik, and lived in Orkanger all her life. But Ingeborg was an adventurous young woman who was willing to leave the safe environs of home and family. She had her own plan, and it was simply to join her brother Bernt and Uncle Thorstein and Aunt Berit in

Port Essington on the west coast of British Columbia and make a new life for herself and Inga there.

Thorstein Mathias Aarvik had come to the northwest coast of British Columbia in 1891 with his wife Berit and their four daughters. He had first immigrated to Sioux City, Iowa, where others of his Viggja family had already settled in the farmlands of the Missouri River. But Thorstein could not live so far from the sea. He was a boat-builder and had been one from his youth. By his own account, in 1866, at the age of seventeen, when the Norwegian government appointed his father to travel to northern Norway to teach the fishermen how to build a new kind of fishing boat, Thorstein had been included in the appointment. This was the Lista boat, sprit-rigged and easier to handle under sail than square-rigged vessels. "In the year 1883, I was selected by the Norwegian Government to represent the Norwegian interests at the Fisheries Exhibition held in London, England."

Clearly, the Missouri River in Iowa was not the place for him, and he soon made his way with his family to the Pacific Ocean, where at Chemainus on the east coast of Vancouver Island he began building boats again. He built two sealing vessels; the second one, the *Fawn*, was sent up the coast to Alaska on an anthropological expedition commissioned by the Smithsonian Institute. In 1894 he pre-empted land on the Ecstall River, a few miles from where it empties into the mouth of the Skeena at the village of Port Essington. Here on the river beside a waterfall he built a waterwheel and boats of every kind: rowboats, tugboats, halibut boats. He called his place *Strandheim*, which means a home on the seashore.

At the mouth of the Skeena River, the mountains rise sheer from the river banks, cloud and mist hover over them, and the slopes are timbered with cedar and hemlock, spruce and pine. At the turn of the twentieth century this land was harsh wilderness to the European arrivals but home to the Tsimshian people, abundantly providing for their needs: deer and moose in the forests; cranberries, blueberries, and raspberries; beaver in the ponds; clams on the beaches; and in the river mouth, oolichan, that tiny fish so rich in oil. The rivers, too, had plenty of salmon – and it was salmon that encouraged white settlement on these banks of the Skeena estuary. The first salmon cannery was built on the north bank in 1876, and by 1890 on the south bank three canneries were strung out along the tidal flats of Port Essington. They were the mainstay of that town.

Port Essington was a port of call for steamships coming up the coast. Here freight and passengers were transferred to flat-bottomed, steam-powered paddlewheelers for the journey up the Skeena to Hazelton and beyond. The Tsimshian people had long used this rocky point on the south shore of the river as a camping place; they called it Spokeshute. The town was established by a former Church of England missionary and Hudson Bay fur trader, Robert Cunningham, who in 1871 pre-empted several sections of land. Setting aside a part of the pre-emption for the Tsimshians (he had married a Native woman), Cunningham built a salmon cannery, general store, sawmill, and hotel. He operated sternwheelers on the Skeena in competition with Hudson's Bay Company vessels and, like them, issued his own coinage for use in trading. Spokeshute became Cunningham's Port Essington, and for the first decade of the century the town grew and developed. The main street was a plank walk built on posts above the rock and muskeg. This was Dufferin Street, where the hotels were located – the Caledonia, the Essington, the Queens – and also Ragstad the Jeweller, the Royal Bank, Mr. Shades Shoe Shop, Shelton and Hicks' Bakery, and a Japanese photographic studio. George Frizzell had a warehouse and abattoir down at the wharf, where he installed lighting for the ships arriving at night. Mrs. Frizzel advertised in the *Port Essington Loyalist* as "Importer and Dealer in Millinery and Dry Goods." The town had a hospital and a residence for the doctor (in 1909, she was Dr. Belle Wilson), a dentist, drugstore, and two churches – Methodist, serving mostly the Tsimshian people, and Anglican, serving non-Native people. Port Essington, no longer a trading post, had the amenities of European settlement. If there were sometimes drunken street brawls, the *Loyalist* claimed, nevertheless, that its citizens were orderly and law-abiding.

In winter Port Essington was a small community of a few hundred people, isolated by heavy snowfalls and ice floes in the river. In the spring, when the salmon swam homeward upstream from the ocean, the cannery workers – Chinese, Japanese, Tsimshian, European – arrived to process the catch. Then for a few months Port Essington became a sizeable town of several thousand.

The salmon season was almost over and the cannery workers were beginning to leave when Ingeborg arrived in 1911 near the end of July, but the town was still lively with workers of various nationalities. Uncle Thorstein and Aunt Berit, her brother Bernt, and cousin Mary, married to a young Norwegian, Martin Letnes, were there to meet her when she stepped off the steamship from Vancouver. Thorstein and Berit lived several miles up the Ecstall River, but the Letnes family was well established right in Port Essington, for Martin Letnes was caretaker, and later foreman, of the Cunningham cannery. Moreover, the Aarviks belonged to the Anglican Church in the town. For lack of a Lutheran congregation they had changed their religious denomination, and their youngest daughter, Anna, was confirmed there in 1913. They had also changed the spelling of their name: "Orwig" was easier to spell and pronounce than "Aarvik." Ingeborg was joining her Norwegian relatives, English-speaking now, and comfortably settled in Canada. Of Port Essington she could say, "This is my home away from home."

Ingeborg found a job as a cook in the hospital. She did not stay long in Port Essington because only a year and a half later she married Nils Alfred Nilsson, that immigrant from northern Sweden who was already a Canadian citizen. Just what Thorstein and Berit thought of Ingeborg marrying this Swede is open to question, for it was only seven years since Norway had won its independence from Sweden and the Norwegians had never forgotten 1814, when they went to war against their powerful neighbour. Even today those events resonate for Norwegians and surface in good-humoured jokes about Swedes. Still, no dark hints of opprobrium have trickled down through the decades from my mother's side of the family to suggest that this rough, convivial railway worker was viewed with disfavour. Thorstein and Berit had left Norway twenty years earlier and were more likely concerned with what was happening in Canada than with Norwegian nationalist feelings. Then, too, Alfred was Lutheran, as they were, or had been in Norway, so there was no question of religious difference, although Berit was a devout Christian, which could not be said of my father. They may even have invited Scandinavian railway workers, Danes and Swedes as well as Norwegians, to Strandheim, and it's possible that Ingeborg met Alfred there, or at a church social, a dance, a picnic; or they met on Dufferin Street when she dropped a glove and he picked it up. Or, since Ingeborg worked as a cook at the hospital, maybe Alfred Nelson was a patient there and.... No, I reject that possibility, for I'm sure my father would have told me that, and I don't remember him ever saying, "And that's where I met your mother."

But they did meet. He was tall and handsome, with broad shoulders. She was beautiful and lively. He was living in bunkhouses and tent camps, thirty-seven years old, and in need of a wife. She was living with her uncle and aunt, twenty-five years old, and in need of a husband and her own home. They shared a common culture: on the one hand, the stern strictures of the Church, learned in childhood from the Lutheran Catechism; on the other, the release in seasonal celebrations from the hard life of servitude and poverty, celebrating midsummer and the midnight sun with feasting and dancing around the midsummer pole; on Christmas Eve, steamed dried cod and rice porridge with fruit sauce. They shared a Norse history, a northern landscape, a northern climate. They could quite easily talk with one another, for Swedes and Norwegians, each speaking their own distinctive language, can understand one another. "I love you" sounds almost the same in Norwegian as in Swedish. They fell in love. It was inevitable. She became pregnant. That was inevitable too – contraception was not an option in those days.

They were married in Prince Rupert. In their wedding photograph, Alfred stands erect and soldierly in a dark suit with a white bow tie, a gardenia in his lapel, and Ingeborg's arm is lightly linked with his. He has nice ears, a strong, straight nose and a generous moustache curving kindly around his mouth. His hair is slicked down on either side of an almost-centre part. Ingeborg is wearing a plain, high-waisted white gown with rusching gathered at the neck and sleeves with a flounce, and she does not look pregnant, even though the dress is straight-cut with no fullness at the waist. She wears long, white gloves, the fingerless kind, and little white shoes with laces. She has a corsage of roses and a gardenia in her hair. They both look composed and serious. Her brother Bernt and her cousin Mary signed as witnesses. Family and friends brought splendid gifts of wedding silver: they were starting life together with silver cutlery monogrammed with an "N."

A son, Arthur Ingemar, was born in June of that same year. By that time they had already found a lot where they could build in Prince Rupert, and on November 25 Alfred took out a building permit. He could afford to do that because he had family now – Ingeborg and her uncle and aunt, her brother Bernt, and younger brother, Johannes, who had arrived earlier that year – without Inga. It must have been decided that it would be better for Inga to come later, when the new baby would be a little older. If necessary, Alfred could borrow to eke out what he had saved. He had friends in town, and one of them, a Swedish carpenter named Snickar Johnson, helped him build the house. It was located at 209 West Seventh Avenue, where it ended on English Hill, a name that must have pleased my father, who had transferred his national loyalty quite easily from the Old Country to Canada. Within a few months, in 1914, they were living in their own two-storey wood frame home with a wide verandah decorated with that fancy turned-wood trimming called "gingerbread." In fact, the house is still there and is listed in the Prince Rupert Heritage Inventory as being in good condition for its age. "Of course it is," my father would have said. "I built it myself, with Snickar Johnson." *Snickar* means "carpenter" in Swedish, and the name of this carpenter who was the adviser-cum builder of the House on English Hill thereby became memorialized in family history.

My father might have added that he and Snickar Johnson secured the foundation beams of the house by attaching them with cables to boulders still remaining in the basement after excavation. "But how did they do that?" I asked my brother Art, who remembered the cables and boulders. "They drill a hole in the rock, near the underside, insert an expansion bolt, and the cable's attached to that bolt, see? And the other end to the house beam." Yes, I do see, and I see also that Alfred's house was to be a permanent home, where this new Nelson family would live and work and prosper, securely cabled to English Hill, their home in Canada.

At the beginning of the next century, with a Prince Rupert archivist as my guide, I went to see this house on English Hill, where I was born. I knew it only from family snapshots, for I was too young at the time to remember it. But my brothers had vivid memories: you could see Hays Mountain from the kitchen window, and there was a big boulder in front of the house. How big? Oh, huge, a real landmark, ten, twelve feet high at least, unforgettable!

Through the years this big boulder gave us our bearings, so that in later life, reconstructing our family from its beginnings at 209 West Seventh Avenue, we thought of our rock as part of the street address of the house. When I visited Prince Rupert nearly a hundred years after the house was built, I found the verandah with the fancy gingerbread was gone and a family from Thailand living at this address, in our house-with-the-rock. So it was their house now. It was certainly a big boulder, about four feet high, but not nearly as big I'd imagined it. They invited us in. I was surprised to find that the house, too, had shrunk in size; the rooms were quite tiny, too small to have housed all the big living stored in family memory. The original kitchen was not much bigger than a large closet, but yes, you could see Hays Mountain from the window. The father was a fisherman, and he showed me how he had enlarged the bathroom by removing the adjoining kitchen wall and moving the kitchen to a larger space. A teenage son was working at a computer in his bedroom.

Alfred and Ingeborg's second son, Verner Eric, was born in 1915, and that spring, on the day of his christening, the family went outside on the verandah to have a picture taken. In that photo my father stands tall and proud, pleased with himself and his family. And why shouldn't he be pleased and proud? He was now not some poor, ill-treated, pick-and-shovel railway stiff. Not anymore. He started out in the railway construction camps of the Grand Trunk Pacific, but now he lived in Prince Rupert with his beautiful wife and two sons – he, Alfred Nelson, a labourer and a Swede, in his own house on English Hill.

Ingeborg looks happy too, and serene. It had been only four years since she arrived, and now she was settled in British Columbia with her Norwegian-Canadian family in a little community of Norwegians and Swedes. They played bridge and whist and drank coffee together. All of their wedding silver – a coffee tray with cream jug and sugar bowl, a covered vegetable dish, a handsome silver cake stand, cutlery monogrammed with the initial "N" – well polished, and the bone-china cups and saucers, would in a few years, when their house was fully furnished, be neatly arranged on the shelves of a tall china cabinet with glass doors.

The cake stand occupied the central place on the top shelf. It was an ornate silver salver, delicately cantilevered from a long, slender stem. Two little silver baskets for cookies hung from beneath the salver with offerings of *mandelkaker* and *spritsar*. At family gatherings, birthday celebrations, Christmas, and Midsummer, the traditional whipped-cream cake, handsomely decorated with slivered almonds, slices of banana, strawberries, or other fruit in season, was presented on the stand. That was how cake must be served on special occasions – with the ceremony so dear to Scandinavians. Even in this rough frontier town there could be formality, solemnity, civility.

There was music in that house too, Ingeborg and Alfred singing the songs of their once-upon-a-time lives in Norway and Sweden, he strumming his autoharp. In later years they bought a wind-up gramophone and listened to jolly songs like "Out in the Great Northwest," in which a "Scotsman" calls a house a "hoose," just like Swedish/Norwegian "hus." And, rolling his Scottish r's, much to Alfred's delight: "Now what the deuce / you say you call that thing a moose? / I'd hate to see a rat get loose / out in the Great Northwest." They listened to Enrico Caruso, that famous Italian tenor, by then a household name, singing Verdi's "Celeste Aida," and John McCormack, the Irish tenor: "Ramona" and "Girl of My Dreams." I remember Mama had a favourite record. She played it often, and sang it herself: "Beautiful Ohio, in dreams again I see / Visions of what used to be." Perhaps these words evoked for her tremulous memories of the Old Country, of *"gamle norge,"* of Kristian and Inga, of her mother and father in the house on the fjord where she was born.

But she was happy with Alfred and her family in their house on English Hill. They had postcards made of the snapshot taken on the day of Verner's christening, and she wrote about her happiness on one she sent to her brother Anders Aarvik and his wife Anna. *"Vi are alle well,"* she wrote. Four years after she left Norway, English was already coming unbidden to her Norwegian pen. Then, proudly, *"Vi har to sønner allerede"* – We already have two sons. Back home in Norway, the family would have been pleased to know that Ingeborg was so well settled in Kanada. Her daughter Inga was now seven years old, still living with the grandparents in Viggja. Soon the war would be over and Ingeborg would be able to send for Inga.

When Ingeborg married Alfred, though, she had also taken the Grand Trunk Pacific Railway for better or for worse. Worse would mean moving to another country and starting all over again. It would mean leaving Prince Rupert and the life unfolding in the house on English Hill. Under Yggdrasil, the ash tree of Norse mythology, the Norns were spinning the web of her fate. As it turned out, they ordained for her a far different saga; it is not hers to write, after all. Indeed, who would think the Norns would have known about the Grand Trunk Pacific Railway?

Main Street, Smithers, c.1920.
(*Courtesy Bulkley Valley Museum, Smithers*)

Ingeborg and Alfred Nelson, with (blurred) baby Edwin, Mullan, Idaho, 1918.
(*Author's collection*)

FOUR

THE NORNS, THE GTP, AND HER BEAUTIFUL BLACK HAIR

The July 1912 strike of the Wobblies against the Grand Trunk Pacific Railway workers dragged on for months. The GTP refused to make any concessions. The IWW finally had to call off the strike without any raise in pay; the construction workers were still making only three dollars a day, often less, not much to marry and start a family on. The strike ended on January 9, 1913, which happened to be the day that Alfred and Ingeborg were married in Prince Rupert. They probably didn't know the strike was over, if indeed they bothered to think about it at all on their wedding day, but now, nearly a century later, when their future has become their past, this random bit of chance connecting the two events does resonate with a certain foreboding.

When the strike was over, Alfred got his job "On Construction" back. But even when the Grand Trunk Pacific Railway was completed and Alfred was no longer working for it, the company maintained a hold on the lives of the young couple. The First World War had brought inflation, and wages could not keep up with the cost of living. But large deposits of copper and silver had been found in the mountains of the Skeena and Bulkley rivers, and the whole area promised well for future development. The Hudson's Bay trading post town of Hazelton at the junction of the two rivers had been head of navigation from Prince Rupert for decades, but it was the village of New Hazelton, a few miles farther up the Bulkley, that was confidently expected to become the thriving new city of the north.

New Hazelton was ideally situated to serve the mining claims being developed both north and south of the Bulkley River. Hazelton was on the north side of the Bulkley; New Hazelton was on the south side, on the route of the railway, and the eastward-bound end-of-steel had reached the town by November 1912 – thanks to scab labour. Moreover, New Hazelton was located on terrain with an easy gradient to handle the shipment of ore. The two most promising mines, the Silver Standard north of the Bulkley and Rocher de Boule to the south, had attracted serious capital investment, and Prince Rupert and Hazelton newspapers reported in detail the activities of their local promoters, the visits of U.S. mining financiers, and the discovery of every new rich mineral vein. One such "strike" at Rocher de Boule in 1912 was particularly exciting. The Prince Rupert *Daily News* reported that Rocher de Boule had ore for shipment: "The men are working in solid ore from wall to wall." The *Omineca Herald* printed a photo of four men said to be standing on a solid vein of blue copper, and in an editorial declared, "The future of Rocher de Boule is unlimited."

Alfred and Ingeborg saw their own future at New Hazelton and Rocher de Boule. With the completion of the Grand Trunk Pacific Railway in 1914, Alfred had to look for another job, and in April 1915 he found one at Rocher de Boule. Ingeborg was pregnant with their second child. The baby was due in a month, but her cousin Anna would come over from Port Essington to be with her. Ingeborg remained in Prince Rupert with a two-year old child and the new-born infant, but that was alright because New Hazelton was just up the line, a short rail journey from Prince Rupert. She did not know that the Grand Trunk Pacific would change all their plans.

By 1915 New Hazelton was already a little town with hotel, general store, and bank. And the Grand Trunk Pacific had finally, and only reluctantly, established a station there, though not without a long legal battle that involved the federal cabinet, the Board of Railway Commissioners for Canada, and the president of the GTP, Charles Melville Hays himself, not to mention the local real estate agents, the Hazelton Board of Trade, the New Hazelton Citizens' Association, and, of course, the miners. For even though the Grand Trunk Railway stood to profit by the shipment of ore from the mines and from the passenger and freight traffic generated by a growing community from a site so well situated on its line, it had refused to establish a station there. Its reason was that the New Hazelton townsite lots had already been purchased by a private entrepreneur whom the company could not manipulate to its own advantage. It had therefore chosen instead a station site a few miles farther west, at South Hazelton, where the rail line had to be laid along a curving strip of benchland beside a steep hill. There was scarcely any settlement there at all, but the GTP planned to create one on this steep gradient and forthwith drew up plans for a townsite and embarked on the sale of lots at South Hazelton. Meanwhile, the shipments of ore and transport of other freight from New Hazelton were being held up for lack of a station. For some weeks the GTP even unloaded freight and passengers for New Hazelton at South Hazelton, and from there both were delivered by wagon to their destination. The empty train then proceeded for another three miles to complete its journey to New Hazelton, turned around, and returned to South Hazelton, still empty, to reload for the return trip to Prince Rupert.

This story – incredible, but true, and fully documented by Frank Leonard in *A Thousand Blunders* – is only one instance of the wrong-headed operation of the railway. Leonard studied the documents – and there are masses of them – and concluded that the GTP pursued a policy of "territoriality," aiming to aggrandize its own property holdings and get rid of competing townsites that interfered with its aspirations for a sovereign fiefdom in northern British Columbia. It pursued this policy even though, as in the New Hazelton case, it worked to its own financial disadvantage. That policy also antagonized the townspeople and moved them to organize in protest. The newly formed New Hazelton Citizens' Association immediately sent a petition to the Board of Railway Commissioners demanding that the GTP supply freight and passenger service to their town. Finally, early in 1913 it was forced to comply with an order from the BRC to supply service to New Hazelton. The *Omineca Herald*, in an editorial boosting the town as a tourist attraction, described Rocher de Boule as "a huge mass of cold, hard, defiant rock rising in its towering strength to a height of over 6,000 feet.... The future of Rocher de Boule as a mining camp is unlimited." Unfortunately, no amount of defiance would save New

Hazelton and Rocher de Boule Mine from the stubborn and hostile management practices of the Grand Trunk Pacific.

During this time Rocher de Boule Mine, incorporated by U.S. capital from Butte, Montana, was under ambitious development by another U.S. company. Montana Continental Development had also imagined an unlimited future for the mine, and by 1915 it had created an operation that looked to become a steady producer of copper and a mining camp that would become a stable, permanent community. When Alfred started working there in 1915 he found not filthy, louse-ridden shacks like those he'd lived in at GTP end-of-steel railway camps, but two-storey steam-heated bunkhouses with electric light. There were iron beds with springs. There were two "dry rooms" for the men coming off work, a place where they could shower, change, and hang their work clothes to dry. There was a laundry where they could wash their clothes. There was an electric hoist to carry men back and forth between camp and mine. To encourage a leisure activity that was more wholesome than gambling and drinking, the company provided two large reading rooms.

The company brought in the new compressed-air-driven machines for drilling into rock. These "stopers" would gradually replace the steel hand-drills and sledgehammers that Alfred had wielded when he was drilling coyote holes on Kaien Island for the GTP. Here at Rocher de Boule Alfred started out as a mucker shovelling ore. He used to tell this story: "And one day the boss comes up to me and he says, 'Nelson, do you know how to use one of these?' He's pointing to a new machine. It looks like it could be a jack hammer maybe, but it's on legs. I'd never seen such a thing before, but I answered him, 'Oh yes.'"

My father would be laughing, boasting as he told the story of how, by this smooth bit of bluffing, he advanced from being a lowly mucker with a shovel to a skilled workman who drilled the walls of rock with a powerful machine and filled the stopes with ore. Which only went to show, he'd declare, once again, that "it takes a Swede every time!"

A steam locomotive drew the ore cars from the tunnel exit at the mine's 200-foot level along a narrow gauge track on the mountain ridge to the ore bins at the loading station. An aerial tramway three miles long and equipped with bins carried the ore off the mountain down to ore bins on the railway track, three thousand feet below, not at New Hazelton, which was further southeast on the line, but at a GTP siding called Tramville, created by the company for its own purpose. Here the ore was loaded into box cars to be transported to Prince Rupert. Tramville was not a station on the line: it had no station agent to handle other traffic. It was just a clearing in the forest where the ore was loaded into GTP boxcars. The official GTP station was one and a half miles away at another clearing in the forest, which was where supplies and equipment for the mine had to be picked up. The mine management tried to get the GTP to establish regular train service at Tramville, but it refused.

What did all this matter to Ingeborg with her two little children in her house on English Hill in Prince Rupert? Alfred had a good job and he was sending home his wages. Soon she would be able to send for Inga, who in 1915 was seven years old. Ingeborg did not know it, and she probably would not have believed it if she had been told, but this big corporation, with vast indifference, had their little family in its grip and would change all her plans. By 1916 Rocher de Boule was one of the largest producers of copper in British Columbia, and the price of copper was high. The mine was fulfilling all expectations, and the GTP stood to profit handsomely from the steady transport of copper ore. But individuals in GTP management and operations were still feeling resentful about the New Hazelton standoff and could not tolerate being hampered in their corporate plans by interfering citizens and miners who signed petitions. The GTP felt obliged to retaliate in some way and chose not to provide adequate transportation to move the ore from Rocher de Boule to Prince Rupert and from there to the smelters at Trail or Tacoma. The bunkers at the coast were full, every boxcar was full, and so too were the bunkers and bins at the mine. Even the stopes in the mine itself were full of ore, making it impossible to drill new, rich veins. The drilling had to stop.

Men were laid off, they thought temporarily. Alfred went home to Prince Rupert to wait for a call to return to work, which never came. The GTP made matters worse for the district mines by increasing freight rates for transporting ore. Then, in 1917, when the price of copper fell, Rocher de Boule, the largest producing mine in the district, could not sustain these hits. It closed down in 1918.

Fortunately for the miners, in 1916 Rocher de Boule was still being operated by Americans, who told their men that there were jobs for miners in the United States. Alfred found work at a silver mine in northern Idaho. The family would have to start all over again in the United States, at the Morning Mine in the town of Mullan. They would have to leave the familiar landscape of the west coast, the ocean, the forest, the mountains, for a place that was strange and different. They would have to leave their house on English Hill.

Ingeborg would have to leave her little kitchen that was so *koselig* (cozy), where she could just look out the window and see Hays Mountain. Uncle Thorstein and Aunt Berit had just moved from Port Essington to Prince Rupert, where Thorstein had built a new boat shop at Seal Cove. Ingeborg wouldn't be able to visit them with little Arthur and baby Verner. And where in God's name was Mullan? In Idaho, they said, wherever that was.

She did not know that all this would happen, but it did happen and she could not send for Inga.

Mullan, a little town in northern Idaho, is near the Montana border, high up in the Coeur d'Alene Mountains at elevation 3,277 feet. It was founded in 1884 at the time of the big lead-silver strike in the Coeur d'Alene area and by 1917 had become a small town. After arriving in Idaho, Ingeborg and Alfred, with little Arthur and Verner, took the train all the way across the state to Mullan and the Morning Mine. The journey took them through the Coeur d'Alene forest, a wilderness that, after all, was not unlike that of the Skeena River mountains and forests they had left behind. They arrived in Mullan in February 1917. Ingeborg's brothers Bernt and Johannes also joined them in Mullan.

The Morning Mine, still in operation, is one of a number of lead, silver, and zinc mines along the Coeur d'Alene River, and all belonging to one company. The Federal Mining and Smelting Company had been organized in 1903 under the initiative of an exuberantly enterprising mining developer and promoter, Charles Sweeney. To achieve this extensive merger required millions and millions of dollars, so he approached the man reputed to be the richest in the world, John D. Rockefeller, who viewed the project favourably and provided the necessary millions. In *The Ballyhoo Bonanza*, historian John Fahey describes in scholarly detail the profusion of financial transactions that led to its creation, with, however, a novelist's eye for telling detail. John D. Rockefeller Jr., in August 1903, was on his way in a private railway car to see the Coeur d'Alenes and the properties that his father had favoured with the family's wealth: "Rockefeller sat in the train while it switched in the [Spokane] Great Northern yards, then strode back and forth on the station platform, wearing a dark suit with a white tie sparkling with a horseshoe stickpin of diamonds.

John Finch [a big shareholder] boarded the car for lunch; he and Rockefeller ate bread and milk." Some two years later the Guggenheim corporation obtained the controlling interest in Federal Mining, with the help again of Rockefeller money, though Federal, in the way of subsidiaries in corporate structures, still "owned" the mines. In 1917 Federal was operating the Morning Mine, and Alfred would be working for it.

The United States entered the First World War in April of that year. Soon a wave of patriotism swept the country as it geared itself up for the enormous task of war production and began to search out "the enemies within" that might hinder that effort. The Industrial Workers of the World spoke out against this "imperialist" war, and the federal government and military began taking strong repressive measures against them. Typical of many small towns in the United States, Mullan responded to this perceived threat and called a mass meeting to organize "home defense." On the day of the meeting the *Mullan Progress* ran a story headlined, "Beware of the I.W.W." After urging the authorities to swear in special police deputies against this "spy organization" that was "spreading their treasonable literature among the workers at the mines," it urged in conclusion, "Let us be ready to meet this horde and give them a reception which will forever rid us of that particular class of anarchists."

Whether or not Alfred belonged to the Wobblies, he certainly knew about them, for they had organized the construction workers on both the Grand Trunk Pacific and Canadian Northern railways in British Columbia. Scandinavians were promininent among the leadership in the United States, notably the immigrant Swede, Joseph Hillstrom, better known as Joe Hill. He was the songwriter who inspired workers with his fighting words, which he put to the popular tunes of the day and to the music of familiar hymns. He had composed a song especially for the striking construction workers on the Canadian Northern Railway and had sung about the bosses and "gunny sack contractors" when he visited the railway camps during the 1912 strike. "Where the Fraser River Flows" calls on the Workers of the World to be "true-hearted brave and steady," and to "gather round our standard when the Red Flag is unfurled." It appeared in the little red IWW songbook for 1912, *Songs to Fan the Flames of Discontent*.

Skandinaviska Propaganda Gruppen, an IWW club in Seattle, sought to organize Scandinavian immigrant labourers in the Western states and to provide employment offices and reading rooms. It also published its own version of the IWW songbook, *Skandinavisk IWW Sång Bok*, with songs written by Danes, Norwegians, and Swedes in their own languages. Joe Hill's songs, such as "The Preacher and the Slave," appear in translation, for he wrote in English. The mission statement on the back cover of a Norwegian edition ends with the ringing call of Karl Marx to the Workers of the World: "You have nothing to lose but your chains. A world to win."

Joe Hill was executed in 1915, framed on a murder charge, "murdered by authorities in the state of Utah," said the IWW. By July 1917 the Bolshevik Revolution was well underway in Russia. It was not a good time to be a Wobbly, not in Mullan, or anywhere in Idaho, or in the United States for that matter. Alfred and Ingeborg were neither of them politically ignorant or naive: he knew about "gunny sack contractors" and wage labour from the Grand Trunk Pacific construction camps, and Ingeborg must have learned something about the radical left from her brother Erik, who was politically left-wing. But in the summer of 1917 they were undoubtedly more concerned about finding a decent place to live and getting settled. A new baby was due to be born in several weeks' time.

They lived first in a cabin infested with bed bugs. Right away they had to move once more, an upheaval made all the more difficult for Ingeborg, so heavily pregnant. The baby was born in September 1917. Arthur was four years old and much later on vividly recalled what was one of his first memories: "I was sitting outside on the steps with Lloyd Henderson [his little friend], and I heard this cry and that was Eddie, when he was born." The town had an outbreak of smallpox that year, and schools, pool halls, "picture shows," and bowling alleys were closed and lodge meetings and all public gatherings cancelled. Then came the Spanish flu epidemic. Arthur remembered that the whole family was struck down. Alfred, the least ill, went from bed to bed nursing Ingeborg and the boys – and with baby Nels Edwin, there were now three.

The town had a large population of Scandinavians – miners and their families as well as businesses like Wikstrom's Cash Market and John Rolin, Watchmaker. The *Mullan Progress* even devoted a page to news of Scandinavia. Ingeborg, a sociable person with a lively fund of talk, made friends easily. Arthur recalled how the whole family went to big weekend parties in a place called Finn Gulch, which had a large population of Swede-Finns; that is, Swedes from Finland. There was some difficulty in buying liquor for these parties, for in 1916 Idaho had enacted state-wide prohibition, superseding the county local option law. However, neighbouring Montana was wet and that is where these partying Swedes obtained their liquor. There was, of course, the problem of passing through customs, from wet to dry. The women seem to have helped in this endeavour – Verner saw his mother sewing pockets on the inside of her long skirt, pockets large enough to hold bottles of whiskey and rum. A customs officer would assume that a woman thus expanded across her middle was pregnant. Just the same, Ingeborg must have had some tense moments passing through customs, because smuggling liquor was a dangerously unlawful act, as was simple possession. She would have read regular reports in the *Mullan Progress* of men arrested and fined for drunkenness and possession of liquor, many of them Scandinavians. The law was brutally, even violently enforced. The *Mullan Progress* of March 15, 1918, reported that John Hendrickson, a "Finn" (probably Swede-Finn) who worked at the Morning Mine, was shot and killed when he crossed the border into Idaho with a sack of Montana whiskey on his back. The deputy sheriff had a "16 gauge pump gun loaded with #7 shot." The bullets "entered both legs below the knees," severed the arteries, and Hendrickson bled to death. Alfred and Ingeborg probably knew him. He could have been one of the group of partying Swedes and Swede-Finns at Finn Gulch.

In the summer of 1918, 138 workers at the Morning Mine, led by the IWW, walked out without giving any notice. The strikers wanted travel time from the tunnel portal to the working face and back again to be part of their eight-hour day. They also wanted two paydays a month and better working conditions. They complained that the air was so bad in the mine that they couldn't work a full eight-hour shift. There was a labour shortage because of the war, and the federal government dealt swiftly with disputes that interfered with the production of metals. Two army officers were sent in to settle the strike. They told the workers that they too were soldiers: "You know what would happen if a soldier would disobey an order and leave work.... You might as well have on a uniform." However, the company did concede on the issue of two paydays a month and promised further investigation into working conditions. With this assurance, the men went back to work.

The IWW had been organizing migrant workers for a decade throughout the Western states, inflaming the active hostility of mining corporations, the forest industry, state governors, and town councils. Vigilantes took the law into their own hands in a furore of anti-unionism directed against the Wobblies, who were seized and variously jailed, sentenced to long prison sentences, or deported. Sometimes they were tarred and feathered and run out of town, or worse.

Loyalty Leagues sprang up in support of the war. In April 1918 Mullan declared a Liberty Day. The band played in front of the city hall and two politicians urged increased production for the war. League members canvassed the town "to pick up the few stragglers who have not purchased their third bond." Alfred Nelson had bought his: he was on the published list of subscribers from the Morning Mine. It was prudent to be seen to be loyal and patriotic. After all, the Loyalty League in the town of Jerome in southern Idaho had the year before seized Wobblies and deported them to the California desert and left them there. In Butte, just across the border in Montana, copper production needed for the war had been seriously diminished by a miners' strike also supported by the IWW. Masked vigilantes seized and tortured IWW leader Frank Little, who had been speaking out against "an imperialist war." On the outskirts of town they strung him up with a rope around his neck and lynched him.

Even before the IWW appeared on the labour scene, violence and lawlessness had disrupted the mining industry and spread fear and uncertainty throughout the towns along the south branch of the Coeur d'Alene River. The fragmented unions had come together in 1893 in the Western Federation of Miners. The mine owners had also organized. The Mine Owners Association was opposed to unions and to hiring union workers, and with its support the mining companies either shut down their mines or employed scabs – mostly newly arrived European immigrants, among them Danes, Finns, and Swedes. The companies employed armed guards to protect the scabs on the trains en route to the mines and later, when they went to and from work at the mine. They hired miners according to a permit system that disclosed each applicant's work history and blacklisted those suspected of union sympathies. They hired Pinkerton detectives to infiltrate the unions. To make up for operating losses, they chose to economize by cutting wages. Animosity against the scabs ran high in the towns, where the miners were no longer bringing home paycheques. At the Gem Mine near Mullan, fearing the worst, the management had even erected a barricade around the mine. When the Gem Miners

Union discovered that its recording secretary was a Pinkerton detective re-laying information to the local paper, its members responded with guns and dynamite, which they planted as a threat. The ensuing confrontation with the mine guards ended with a shootout. After that the union men continued on up the river, "occupied" three mines, and posted sentinels on the properties. At one of them, Bunker Hill, they once again planted dynamite. Martial law was declared throughout Shoshone County and federal troops were brought in. For the next five months, 1,500 infantry men were camped along the Coeur d'Alene River to protect the mines, now operating with non-union men. Ac-cording to Fahey's account, some "three or four hundred men from various towns" were arrested for their part in this insurrection and stowed away "in warehouses or an enclosure at Wallace called a 'bullpen.'"

In 1899, when the Wardner local of the Western Federation of Miners, after many attempts at bargaining, once more demanded union recognition and a restoration of wages to $3.50 a day, the mine manager at Bunker Hill refused even to speak to the union representatives. At this the union hijacked a train at Wallace and ordered the engineer at gunpoint to proceed up the line. They stopped on the way to pick up guns and dynamite. At Wardner the ringleaders walked up the hill to the mine, planted dynamite, lit the fuse, and blew up the mill. Forewarned, workers, guards, and management had already fled. Martial law was again declared throughout Shoshone County and the state took draconic measures: "the entire male populations of Gem, Burke, and Mullan" were indiscriminately rounded up and, as in 1892, imprisoned in the notorious bullpens to await trial.

It is not likely that twenty years later the people of Mullan would have forgotten how they had suffered open war that summer, when their town and others along the Coeur d'Alene River became battlegrounds loud with the sound of guns and exploding dynamite, sounds that lingered in their memories as they told and retold the story over the years. Certainly no family whose men had been arrested and jailed would forget the ignominy of that rough attempt at justice, or that it had been delivered in this summary way twice in a decade. In the summer of 1918, when the IWW led the wildcat strike at the Morning Mine, miners and their families and the townspeople too would certainly all have felt alarmed and threatened once again.

This was the climate of fear and hostility that Alfred and Ingeborg were discovering in Idaho. And how did Ingeborg feel about it? Was this the better life she had dreamed of when she emigrated? Was it for this that she had left her child behind in Norway? All the police raids, and the shooting and killing and lynching – no, it was a good thing that Inga was safe in Viggja with her grandparents. This was no place for a ten-year-old girl. From what Ingeborg and Alfred read in the newspapers, anyone in this country might be carrying a gun.

If not that, there were things like that terrible hailstorm when little Arthur ran screaming to get inside the house. Hailstones as big as golf balls were pounding down on him.

Ingeborg was afraid of something else as well: she was afraid that Alfred might be killed at work. Alfred was not just a mucker; he was an experienced miner, and sometimes at night he was called out to go down in the mine to repair a shaft when the timber enclosing it had moved out of alignment. As a result, the cage couldn't run up and down on its guides, and a miner would have to go down into the shaft to realign the timbers or, if it were broken, re-place them. This was dangerous work: he might accidentally release a slide of loose rock and be buried under it. "On those nights," recalled my brother Art, "she was afraid she'd never see him alive again."

My mother had good reason for fear. "Squeezing ground. That's what it was," Art said. The whole underground structure of the mine, with its tunnels, stopes, drifts, and shafts, was supported by a system of timbering that was subjected to pressure from the enclosing rock. It was this pressure, this "squeezing," that damaged the timbers or shifted them out of align-ment. The Morning Mine was notorious for its "squeezing ground," as an Idaho State mine inspector acknowledged in his report for the year 1918, responding to the recommendations of the Federal investigators: "I want to say that the timber never grew that could resist the slow, steady side pres-sure of the walls of the Morning Mine. I would further say that it is one of the best timbered mines in the Coeur d'Alene district and that its operators spend more money per ton of ore extracted in timber actually installed than any other mine in the district." As if in corroboration of Ingeborg's fear for Alfred's safety, he added, "The big cap timbers in the drifts sometime splin-ter into match wood before they have been in position three months, if not watched and eased."

Ingeborg would also have remembered that Ole Strom, a Swede, was killed when he was "barring down" on the 1,200-foot level. The mucker working below cut a hole in the board on the top of the chute to let down the "muck," as the ore was called. Strom was standing above on that board, so when the muck fell, he went through the chute with the muck and was instantly killed.

Alfred's main fear was for the air he was breathing down at No. 18 level, 3,400 feet below the surface. In a letter of July 5, 1919, to Ingeborg's brother Erik Aarvik, Alfred indicated that he did not want to work much longer as a miner: "The wages are good, but it's not healthy." The mine operators were concerned with the problem of ventilation: according to the mine inspector's report of 1918, the company had installed a "modern Sirocco fan" that sent fresh air down to the very deepest levels. The inspector declared, however, that even with the newest ventilation systems, the Morning Mine was difficult to ventilate. However, neither poor ventilation nor broken timbers were reasons for striking. After all, surface working conditions were excellent: "The train [to the mine portal] starts and stops at a modern concrete, steam-heated, fire-proof dry house with accommodations for 300 men, in which the men can wash up and change their clothes and are given separate, cootie-proof, metallic lockers with modern porcelain lavatories and bathing conveniences that are strictly up to date." They have "separate rooms with spring beds ... with janitor work and clean linen supplied." True, stoping contract work, that is, piecework, was "undesirable from a safety and health standpoint," but the pay for those miners did average $6 to $11 a day. He concluded that the 1918 strike was caused by "a few unpatriotic agitators."

In that same letter Alfred wrote that there was going to be another strike: "So then I'll have some time off, unless we [decide] to leave this place." It seems as though he did not intend to take part in that strike, which, led by the IWW, might very well become violent, like the strikes twenty years earlier at Gem and Bunker Hill. If that happened, there would be soldiers camped in Mullan and all the men rounded up and put in the bullpen. As in Prince Rupert in the Battle of Kelly's Cut, when the street workers' strike turned violent, Alfred most likely didn't get involved. "I'll be damned if I get mixed up in that sort of thing!" he might have said. Moreover, in a letter he reported that miners' wages had been raised by fifty cents a day and that he was earning good money. That in itself would be a real inducement to stay, but, like Ingeborg, he shuddered at the reckless lawlessness and the ominous threat to personal safety. "Well, it's no paradise," he wrote. The summer of 1919 was hot and dry, and for a few days the community was in danger of having to flee a raging forest fire. The land was barren: there was no farming in the area, but he was prepared to like this dry climate.

In January 1919 a letter came from Norway with word that Ingeborg's father, Elling Aarvik, had drowned. He was delivering a boat. A storm came up and capsized the vessel in the heavy sea. It was a sorrowful time for Ingeborg. Her brother Bernt had been in Mullan with them but went home to Norway to be with his widowed mother. The younger brother Johannes had also been in Mullan for a time, and used to take Arthur to the movies, for he was a good uncle. And one afternoon in the middle of the movie, Arthur's shrill little voice piped up, "*Skal vi ha ice cream, Johannes?*" ("Are we going to have ice cream, Johannes?"), and the whole audience burst out laughing! Now Johannes too had gone back to Norway and would not be taking Arthur to the movies any more. Ingeborg had reason to feel bereft, despite all her Scandinavian friends in Mullan and Finn Gulch.

A general strike of mines in the Coeur d'Alene district did occur in August 1919, closing all mining operations for two months. The following April a fire started in a drift in No. 6 tunnel, and carbonic acid gas spread throughout several levels. Work in the mine had to stop for several days. In July a timberman was electrocuted on the No. 18 level east when his saw blade accidentally came in touch with a 250-volt trolley wire and he fell over it. He happened to be standing on a metal pipe. Mullan, Idaho, was indeed no paradise for miners.

In 1920 Alfred and Ingeborg decided to go back home, and home was Canada. They returned to Prince Rupert.

They came back to the house that Alfred had built on English Hill. The day they arrived a light rain was falling, but so light you could breathe it, not like the rain in Idaho where it came down suddenly in full force like a punishment. Hays Mountain was still there, with its forest of green. The rock out front was still there. It was their rock. Arthur and Verner rushed over to it as soon as they got out of the taxi. They found their father's drilling steels in the basement and the sledgehammers and started drilling in the rock. Soon all the neighbourhood boys were out there too, taking turns with the drilling. They'd hit the steel, turn it, and hit it again. They'd leave off drilling for a day or two, but they'd keep on coming back to the rock, and they finally did make several holes in it. Years later, when I visited Prince Rupert and found our house, those holes were still there. They weren't very deep, but deep enough to allow me to reclaim the rock as our own.

Ingeborg came back to Seal Cove, where Uncle Thorstein and Aunt Berit now had their boat shop. She came back to whist and bridge parties and coffee with old friends, Norwegians and Swedes and Swede-Finns: the Letnes family, Ungers, Mikkelsons, and Malms; to the china cabinet with the wedding silver; once again she served whipped-cream cake on the handsome silver salver and there was civility and ceremony. She was back in her own kitchen, looking out on Hays Mountain.

One day Alfred came home with some Gorgonzola cheese he'd bought on the way home from work. He was feeling good: he'd stopped first at the house of a fellow worker, an Italian, to drink some homemade wine, and he was even bringing home a bottle of it. He came into the kitchen with his offerings, but as soon as Ingeborg smelled the cheese – and Gorgonzola is famously smelly – "Out," she cried, "Not in my kitchen! Out of my kitchen with that cheese!" Alfred went down to the basement and put the cheese in a little wooden cask. Little Verner followed him, watching, listening. His father placed the lid on the cask and then a rock on top of the lid. With a certain triumph at having confronted an intruder and wrestled him to the ground and tied him up, he said, "Now, stay there, you son of a bitch!" In daily life, civility might take a different form.

Until then the family had spoken a mixture of Swedish and Norwegian at home, and when Arthur started school in Prince Rupert, he was still speaking Norwegian – which brought about a crisis that forever displaced both the mother and father tongues in the Nelson family. Although Arthur could speak English, it was Norwegian mixed with Swedish that sometimes came spontaneously when he spoke. One day he came home from school crying. His mother wiped his tears and asked him why he was crying, but he only cried the harder. Finally little Verner piped up, in Norwegian, "They called him a Finn. The other boys called him a Finn." That was all Alfred needed to hear. He had a very poor opinion of Finns. Oh, he had worked with them – they were hot-headed, they got drunk, they carried knives. He may have been remembering some poor rebellious Finn in one of the railway construction camps who just couldn't take it anymore and went over the edge. Alfred drew himself up to his full six feet and, standing square, struck the table with his fist (you'll understand that he himself was a fairly hot-headed Swede). Decades later Verner re-enacted the scene: "The cups danced on their saucers and he shouted, in his native tongue, "Now there's going to be a stop to this! From now on we speak English in this house." And that's how it was from then on.

The edict presented no problems to the boys. Alfred always read "the funny pages," or "the funnies," in the daily newspaper: *Out Our Way, Maggie and Jiggs, Tillie the Toiler,* and especially *Our Boarding House,* in which one Major Hoople was the main character. He read them aloud, sitting on his tool box at the top of the stairs in the house on English Hill, while Arthur, Verner, and Edwin listened. *Our Boarding House* was launched in 1921, and by the time I came along and was old enough to listen, "Myor Huepel" was a well-established part of the family. Instead of Dr. Seuss, we had "Myor Huepel," a rotund man with a big paunch, big nose, and big ego, who talked big and did nothing. He had no job and was always able to talk his way out of getting one, with many an "Egad!" and "Hrummph," accompanied by the exasperated protests of his wife Martha and the good-natured joshing of the boarders. He was most often employed merely sitting in an easy chair, smoking a cigar and reading the newspaper. On his head he wore what looked to me like a night-cap, but which I later learned was a fez with a tassle.

With the help of Major Hoople and the others, the Nelsons became an English-speaking family. But we children were already programmed for Norwegian and Swedish, because those were the languages we first heard. Even now, after a meal, Alfred still pushed his chair back and said with a satisfied smile, "*Ja, nu har vi spisat igjen.*" We thus didn't need a grammar lesson to learn Swedish/Norwegian word order: "Yes, now have we eaten again." Ingeborg still held us when we were hurt or unhappy and softly crooned as always her words of comfort, words of endearment: "*Stakkars lille venn, det var riktig synd på deg.*" Among themselves and their friends they still spoke Norwegian/Swedish in that lilting singsong that we'd always be able to hear if we wanted to tune in on our other language, even if we ourselves could only speak a few words of it.

Ingeborg made new friends. Just down the street lived Paul and Freda Wicks with their three little boys. Paul was a carpenter and boat-builder, a convivial man with a fund of stories from his earlier days as a telegraph lineman along the Skeena River. Paul and his brother Walter had lived and worked from the time they were children in the fishing grounds and forests at the mouth of the Skeena and had also been part of that army of labourers – the axemen, pile drivers, blasters and carpenters, fishermen and cannery workers – who had built the new city. They were born in Danzig, Germany, and had immigrated to this wilderness on the northern coast of British Columbia in 1900 with their widowed mother, who had arranged to marry a Canadian citizen, Frederick Wicks, a one-time Polish seaman now working onshore at North Pacific Cannery. Paul was eight years old at the time; Walter was seven.

Their German origin was of no consequence until the First World War, when a zealous War Department on the alert for spies and saboteurs threw out a wide net and hauled them in. In *Memories of the Skeena*, Walter tells how he was investigated, made to declare under oath his allegiance to the Crown, and discharged from his job at Inverness Cannery when a military order required aliens to be dismissed so that jobs would go to discharged soldiers. When he tried to enlist he was accused of being a spy and required to report regularly to the authorities. As for Paul, Walter continues, he had been shot at in his boat by soldiers guarding the Zanardi Rapids railway bridge and brought in by special train to the Prince Rupert military headquarters on suspicion of planting a bomb under the bridge. He had been on his way to repair a break in the telegraph line, an essential job in wartime. It turned out that what the soldiers thought was a bomb was a can of milk with a bulge that Paul had thrown overboard because it wasn't safe to use. By the time Alfred and Ingeborg became friends with the Wicks, all this was past history, story material for Paul, an accomplished raconteur.

Freda Anderson was from Norway, a little woman with red hair and a beautiful, big smile. She became Ingeborg's best friend and confidante. She could laugh with Ingeborg about the Gorgonzola cheese. They each had three little boys and used to take turns child-minding. "In and out of one another's houses, and we played Cowboys and Indians, skunk cabbage leaves for shields, lots of skunk cabbage in the marshy areas," recalled my brother Arthur. One of the Anderson boys recalled, at age eighty-seven: "I remember two things about your mother. Her hair, she had black hair. And she was clean. When she polished the boys' shoes, she polished the soles as well." Echoes of Norway? The campaign against TB? "Soap and water, soap and water"?

When Alfred and Ingeborg arrived back in Prince Rupert in 1920, they found that their town could no longer hope to become a major international seaport on the Pacific coast for Canadian trade with the Orient. As the new railway link with Eastern Canada, the Grand Trunk Pacific Railway had planned to build its own hotel in Prince Rupert, twice as large as the Canadian Pacific Railway's Empress Hotel in Victoria. F. M. Rattenbury, designer of the new Provincial Legislature buildings and the Empress Hotel, was to be the architect for the Château-style hotel, rivalling those of the CPR across Canada. The *Daily News*, August 6, 1913, reported that the GTP hotel would be fifteen storeys in height, with a slate roof, 450 bedrooms, a palm room, and a "Turkish bath, both for men and women." Excavation at the hotel site on Second Ave. between Fourth and Fifth streets was started at this time. But in April 1912 GTP president Charles Hays, returning from Europe where he had been studying hotel architecture, had unfortunately sailed on the *Titanic* and was among those who perished, taking with him his inspiring vision for the city. Then came the war. Plans were shelved, construction delayed indefinitely. The GTP gradually slid into bankruptcy and in 1919 the federal government nationalized it, joining it with the Canadian Northern Railway to form the Canadian National Railway. The grand Château hotel with its Gothic roofs and turrets, its palm room and Turkish baths, was never built. When Alfred and Ingeborg returned to Prince Rupert they found the excavation site still there, as it had been when they left in 1917. The big hole had become filled with water, and in winter, when it froze over, people skated on the pond. The CNR forthwith established Vancouver as its Western terminus, abandoning Prince Rupert to become merely the terminus of a branch line.

Alfred decided to quit mining and try fishing instead. This seemed like a sensible decision in a town in which, from its beginnings, the economy had been based on salmon and halibut. But he discovered he was no fisherman and found work instead at Lake Kathlyn near Smithers at a tie-camp operated by a fellow Swede. Olaf Hanson, a tie-and-pole contractor for the Grand Trunk Pacific, invited Alfred to go into business with him. But there was also a silver mine opening up not far from Smithers and men were needed there. Alfred would have liked not to go back to working underground; he'd said as much in a letter to his brother-in-law Erik. Hard-rock mining was an unhealthy occupation, and he knew it. But now Ingeborg was pregnant again – I was born in November 1922 – and he had a growing family to look after. When he was offered the job of foreman at this new mine, he accepted. A future in mining seemed to promise as much as did cutting ties for the Grand Trunk Pacific. Olaf Hanson went on to become a successful businessman in ties and timber, fish, and real estate and brokerage. He was for fifteen years the Liberal Member of Parliament for Skeena; he was Swedish consul for Northern British Columbia; he sat on the International Fisheries Commission. He became an immigrant success story whereas, it might be said, Alfred did not.

The Duthie Mine was on Hudson Bay Mountain, named not for the famous Central Canadian bay but for the Hudson's Bay Company's ranch on Driftwood Creek near Smithers. At the turn of the century, pack mules carrying freight overland from Hazelton on the Skeena were wintered at the ranch. Alfred went on ahead to start working at the Duthie and to find a cabin and make it ready for the family.

Sometime just before the family left Prince Rupert to move again, to another mining camp, this one near the top of a mountain, nine-year-old Arthur came home from school one day to find the house full of women. One of the women was holding a pair of scissors, ready to cut off Ingeborg's long, black hair. "At the first sound of the scissors shearing her hair, Mama cried out as though she'd been stabbed, " Arthur recalled decades later. "When her friend gave her the long ropes of black hair, she took them and held them to her and she cried. She kept them for years. I'd see them from time to time wrapped in tissue paper in a dresser drawer."

In the early 1920s many women were cutting their hair and wearing it short in a stylish bob – wearing short hair was still an event, a daring thing to do. But Ingeborg was not making a statement about being a modern woman. Rather, she had decided that if she had to live in a cabin without running water, with four children to keep clean (and one of them, me, still in diapers), it would be just too much work to have to wash her long hair as well. Short hair was the only thing for a woman in the backwoods. She sacrificed her hair, and her friends all gathered around to give her support.

After Ingeborg had packed the dishes and pots and pans and bedding, and found tenants for the house, she gathered up her children, turned the key in the door and set out with bags and lunch and suitcases, carrying me, an infant, in her arms, to find this cabin in the mountains near the town of Smithers on the other side of the Coast Range in Bulkley River country beyond the Skeena. She left behind the china cabinet.

Ingeborg had bought long pants for all three boys, for she was undertaking this journey with spirit, and her children must be properly dressed. Besides, Alfred had warned her about the mosquitoes. It was the first time the boys had worn long pants, and Arthur was very conscious of them. When we boarded the train for Smithers, he was pleased to see that his teacher was on board and he was sure she noticed his pants. Some eighty years later, that is what he remembered of the train journey.

At Smithers we (for I too am now part of the story) stayed overnight in the Bulkley Hotel, a three-storey wooden building that looked quite impos-ing but rather odd, standing in a landscape of stumps, the desolation of early settlement. In 1913 the Grand Trunk Pacific had against all reason chosen this tract of swamp for a divisional point. By 1923 the swamp had been drained and the nearby forest cleared, but although proper wooden buildings had re-placed the first tents, the stumps remained, waiting to be pulled or blasted out and burned. Another railway town had been built, this one on piles driven into a subsoil of quicksand and clay.

The Bulkley Hotel, built in 1914, and recently renovated, offered every amenity, including electric lighting. This was the best hotel in town, con-ferring a certain status on its guests: local newspapers regularly listed their names. Once inside, the visitors were comfortable enough, if by comfort you did not mean running water and indoor plumbing. Those were the days of the pottery water jug and big, white pottery wash basin in every room. "And there was a white pottery receptacle that slid under the bed," recalled Verner, never loath to call a chamber pot a chamber pot, but enjoying his skill at euphem-ism even more. "This came to be named by some wag 'the thunder mug.'" As for diapers, not disposable in those days, neither of my two elder brothers remembered anything.

Standing on the main street in Smithers on a summer day, Ingeborg could look up and see the two peaks of Hudson Bay Mountain, the bare, grey rock, forbidding and grim, rising seven thousand feet into the sky. She could see the cold, ice-blue glacier between them and below it the dark, green forest covering the lower slopes that fell steeply to the base of the mountain. But she wouldn't have been able to see around to the other side, where creeks rushed down the mountain between high rock walls, or the lakes where moose stood knee-deep near the shore, nibbling on water lilies, or the meadows where deer and elk came to graze and sometimes be surprised by a shaggy, humpbacked grizzly. She could never have guessed, standing on the street in Smithers and looking up at Hudson Bay Mountain, that people actually lived up there. She couldn't see the Wet'suwet'en people camped beside nearby Dennis Lake and setting out to check their traplines. She couldn't see their cabins and tents, or the miners' bunkhouse at the Duthie Mine or the cookhouse where the Chinese cook appeared at the door at mealtime and struck the triangular iron gong to summon the men to breakfast or dinner. Or our eventual home, our cabin, in a little clearing in the forest, the smoke curling up blue and welcoming from the stovepipe in the roof.

None of this could she see; she was starting out into the unknown, for what Alfred was able to tell her was not enough to reassure her that she would indeed find warmth and friends and the bustle of everyday life high up on the other side of Hudson Bay Mountain.

The next morning the Duthie Mine teamster, Al Bannister, came to the hotel with a team of horses and a wagon, though "wagon" is not quite the right word. We travelled to the Duthie in a democrat, which sounds like a classy conveyance. In fact it was so named because it was a serviceable, no-nonsense box on wheels. Its seats had back rests, but the passengers were required to bring their own cushions. Our democrat was even more democratic than this, there being only a front seat with a platform behind for the baggage and extra passengers.

My three brothers sat in the back with our suitcases and lunch. Mama, holding me in her arms, sat up front beside Al Bannister. He was a stocky man, quite husky, with blond hair and a fair complexion. His main job was to haul freight to the Duthie Mine, a distance of sixteen miles from Smithers, and bring back sacks of ore concentrate in five-ton loads. The mosquitoes in that area, he recalled, "were so big and so hungry that the horses were almost crazy from bites and buzzing." He was an expert teamster and so was his friend Bill Leach. They had already hauled a twenty-ton boiler up the mountain to Loon Lake, where it was installed to supply power for the mine. That trip took two days with eight horses. Compared to that job, driving us up to the Duthie with his favourite horses, Major and Topsy, was like going on a holiday: it was easy to manoeuvre around sharp switchbacks with the little democrat.

The way to the mine wound steeply up the side of Hudson Bay Mountain. We would be stopping for lunch at a rough wayside cabin for travellers where Al could build a fire in the stove and make coffee while Mama changed my diaper. But first we would have to follow along the base of the mountain westward through swamp and muskeg and clouds of vicious mosquitoes. It was a wagon road. That great new invention, the automobile, had come to Smithers, of course, and Ford cars and Chevrolets went speeding down the main street of town at twenty miles an hour. But the road to the Duthie wasn't ready for the automobile: nobody, not Henry Ford himself, could have driven along it. The road was passable in those places in which poles had been laid close together across it here and there for a hundred yards or so. Once these stretches of corduroy road ended, the horses had to trudge through wet bog and gumbo. At times the wagon became mired down, and Major and Topsy strained to pull it out.

"Get out and push, boys," Al finally called out. The three boys rolled up their new long pants and jumped out and pushed against the wheels, their shoes squishing with water and mud. Ingeborg stepped out as well to lighten the load and found drier places in the forest where she could walk without sinking into muddy muskeg. "When the horses finally got out of the mud, we ran ahead like deer through the forest," Arthur remembered. "And then we'd run back again to take turns carrying you."

I know what my mother said when she stepped out of the wagon into the mud. She said, "*Uff da!*" I know she did because that's what she'd say later on when we tracked mud all over her clean kitchen floor, or if the cream was sour or if one of the boys had cut himself with the axe when he was chopping kindling. I'm sure she said "*Uff da!*" one time when I was five years old and the car door banged shut on my thumb. "*Uff da!*" for Norwegians is an all-purpose expression of concern, displeasure, or distress. It's a mental twitch of the nose, a pursing of the lips, a concerned wrinkling of the brow and is not so much a word as an exhalation of breath. And yet *uff* actually is a word, an interjection, and the English equivalent is "ugh." The verb is *uffe seg*, to complain or groan. According to my Norwegian-English dictionary, Henrik Ibsen himself wrote "*uff da, hugg han ikke fingeren av!*" (Uff, he chopped off his finger.) In Norwegian-Canadian families, *uff* is one of the expressions that enriches the English language, and in Seattle, where there is a large population of Norwegians, you can sometimes see "*Uff da*" bumper stickers humorously declaring the drivers' proud heritage.

Ingeborg, stepping out of the wagon and feeling her shoes sink into the mud, was not concerned with these linguistic matters, but simply experiencing the struggle and hardship of pioneer life in Canada. Norway had its hardships too, but swamp and muskeg and mosquitoes were not among them, not on the fjord where she was born, where little farms climbed all the way up steep hillsides and white-painted houses and red barns decorated the fields. The hills of Trøndelag, her part of Norway, were neat and tidy. Canada was tangled and wild, the mountains jagged and soaring. True, the coast of British Columbia was like Norway, for long, narrow fjords reached into the land and made sheltered waterways for fishermen and entrances at which people could make their homes along the shores and in the valley clearings, just as her Uncle Thorstein and Aunt Berit had done when he built his boat shop in a little fjord at the mouth of the Skeena River. But she was moving inland, up the Skeena and beyond, into the mountains, away from the Little Trondhjem of her family and friends in Prince Rupert and into a wild, harsh country that would make enormous demands on her strength and powers of endurance.

What was she thinking as she picked her way through the mud, carrying me, nine months old? It had been twelve years since she had left Norway. Inga was now fifteen years old. A mother should not abandon her child, but that is what she had done, though she had not meant to do it. Things had not worked out as she had planned. She shouldn't blame herself, it seemed like fate, an evil Norn intervening over Inga's cradle. Was this the price she had to pay for daring to leave home, for finding a new husband and a new life?

But her hair, her beautiful, black hair! That was her own doing; no wilful Norn had ordained that she cut her hair.

After a while the horses emerged from the mud, the road became drier, and she climbed back into the wagon. My Ingeborg, whom I've re-created out of fragments of memory and out of bits and pieces of historical research and whom I now think I know and understand, my Ingeborg puts her hand to her neck to feel where her hair had been, and the tears come. Whether she weeps for Inga or for her hair or for vexation at the mud and mosquitoes, she does not know, and I do not know, but even as I write I weep with her.

At the cabin on Hudson Bay
Mountain, near the Duthie Mine,
1923. From the left: Arthur,
Edwin, mother Ingeborg with
Irene, father Alfred, Verner.
(*Author's collection*)

School days at the Duthie. Back row,
against the cabin wall, left to right: a
Risdale boy, Verner, Edwin (forehead
only), Arthur, and Katie Ingard (the
tall girl). In the front row, against the
wooden railing: to the left is another
Risdale boy, third from left is Peggy
Northover, and next to Peggy is Irene.
(*Author's collection*)

THE CABIN ON HUDSON BAY MOUNTAIN

It was early evening before Ingeborg and the children finally arrived at the Duthie Mine and teamster Al Bannister handed them over to Alfred, who was waiting for them at the cabin. Although there was still light, the forest was dark and the outlines of the cabin were already dissolving in its shadows. A prospector had built the cabin some years before, and it had lain abandoned to the mice and pack rats after he moved on to try his luck elsewhere. Alfred had bought the cabin for fifty dollars. It was in a forest of jack pine in a little flat space on the hillside, but just outside the door the mountain began its downward slope again, all the way to Henderson Creek. The mine tunnel, mill, office buildings, and bunkhouse were above the cabin, and around them the forest had been cleared in a rough and peremptory way. Higher up, above the mine, the bare, grey rock of the Ice Ages had formed jagged peaks, sudden crevasses, and precipices. If you had been able to reach the mountain peak at seven thousand feet you would have seen the Babine Mountains to the east and the high buttress of the Coast Range to the west; to the north, Hazelton and the Skeena River; to the south, the houses and streets of Smithers and the trains shunting back and forth at the station and the outlying farms with their little houses and barns.

Alfred and Ingeborg Nelson were pioneers, but it was many years before I understood that. For me the pioneers had always been the *habitants* of New France on their narrow strips of land along the St. Lawrence River; the heroic explorers and fur traders waiting out the winter in a tent in the Rockies on a diet of squirrel stew; the stubborn men and women in Red River carts making their slow and difficult way across the empty prairie, choosing finally some place to settle and build a sod hut. It did not occur to me that our rough prospector's cabin qualified as a pioneer habitation every bit as much as a tent in the Rockies or a sod hut on the prairies.

The cabin was built with jack pine logs about thirty feet long, and that more or less determined the length of the cabin. The logs hadn't been peeled: they were still rough with bark. The doorway was narrow and scarcely high enough for Alfred to enter without stooping. Inside he had divided the cabin space with partitions to make two bedrooms. He had made a bed for the three boys out of rough lumber and heaped it with a pile of spruce boughs, fragrant but prickly. What room was left served as kitchen and living space.

There was a little iron stove, serviceable enough for a prospector living on bacon and beans, with a woodbox beside it. There was a washstand with a basin and galvanized-iron water pail and dipper, with a slop pail beneath it – or, taking up the basin full of dirty water, you just opened the door and with one fling of your arm threw the contents outside. There were cupboards on the wall made out of twenty-inch dynamite boxes, a wooden table and chairs, coal-oil lamp on the table. A trap door in the middle of the cabin floor opened on an underground space, not much more than a hole, entered by climbing down a narrow wooden ladder. This was the root cellar, where potatoes, beets, and carrots were stored, buried in sand, and cabbages were hung by strings attached to the bottom of the floor above.

One small window in the front of the cabin looked out on a jack pine forest stretching all the way down the mountain to Loon Lake to the east and Dennis Lake to the west, though you couldn't see either lake because of the trees. Later on that cabin and the window and the trees would be part of a story that Verner would tell again and again. "Just one little window in the kitchen. You looked out and all you saw was trees. The lake was there, farther down at the foot of the hill, Loon Lake, but you couldn't see it for the trees. Trees all around us. Even in summer it would begin to get dark and shadowy before the sun went down. No wonder Mama was getting cabin fever – you know, the way prospectors do when they've been shut up all winter in their cabin with just their dog for company. There weren't any forests in her part of Norway where she came from, just nice little farms and farm houses and she lived right near the water, the fjord."

Ingeborg was a fastidious woman and had kept her house in Prince Rupert immaculate. She polished the furniture with O'Cedar furniture oil and the top of the kitchen stove with stove blacking and a handful of crumpled newspaper. We know that when she polished the children's shoes she gave the soles a good polishing as well. So this rough cabin on Hudson Bay Mountain was a desolation for Ingeborg. *Uff Da!* Pack rats in the cupboards! At least it wasn't bedbugs, as in Idaho. That the family had to move again! And they'd only just got settled back in their house in Prince Rupert, and soon they were going to send for Inga. But now another mining camp, so much drinking, it was no place for a fifteen-year-old girl. And the high school, sixteen miles it was to Smithers. No, after all, Inga was better off in Norway in her grandmother's house for a little while longer until they lived in a proper house again.

After the freight wagon arrived with the McClary stove, the cabin became more habitable. It was still small and dark, with only that one window, and cold and drafty because of outside air coming through the cracks between the logs. At night, lying in bed, you could hear the wolves howling outside. But at least now they had a proper stove, the kind Ingeborg was accustomed to. It was big and square, solid black iron bright with chrome trimming, and it stood on four nicely curved short legs. It had a large firebox and four stove lids that you lifted with a curved wrought-iron stove poker. The stove had a system of little openings or dampers on the side and front for regulating the amount of air entering the firebox, and there was a damper in the stove pipe as well. In addition to an oven for baking and roasting, there was a "warming oven," a metal cabinet above the stove top with a hinged door. The stove pipe rose from the centre back of the stove through the warming oven, which radiated heat and kept food warm until it was served. With the McClary installed, there could be waffles and pea soup, roasts of pork, and rabbit stews, bread and cakes from the oven, and the coffee percolator dozing comfortably on the back of the stove: family life could begin again.

Family life included chopping wood and making kindling, which were tasks that children learned early. In winter the kitchen stove was kept burning all day and night and consumed an enormous amount of wood. Before the large sticks of cordwood stacked outside could be used, we had to split them into smaller pieces so they'd fit nicely in the stove firebox and burn more easily. It was the children's job to keep the woodbox in the kitchen well supplied with firewood. The chopping block was in the woodshed. We went out there and placed a large stick of wood upright on the block, lifted high the big, single-bladed axe and split the wood with a single blow. You had to select the place where you could best avoid meeting a knot. With the big chunk of wood split in two, you had to then slice through those two pieces in the same way. After a few minutes, when you had made a little pile of firewood beside the chopping block, you loaded it neatly in the crook of one arm and, holding it against your chest and steadying it with the other arm, carried it into the kitchen and dumped it into the woodbox. Later in the day, you'd make kindling to start the fire in the morning, for even if it had been banked at night there would be only be a few embers left by morning. We looked for a nice, dry stick of firewood and, holding it upright on the chopping block with one hand, small hatchet in the other, sliced the dry stick lengthwise into thin narrow strips. That was not as dangerous as it sounds. When I was old enough to split wood, I never cut my finger. Kitchen work always proved to be more dangerous, when I used a dull knife to slice, perhaps, a turnip.

In the only family photograph of the cabin, Ingeborg and Alfred are standing in front of it with their three little boys, Arthur, Verner, and Edwin. I'm the baby, not yet a year old, held in the crook of my mother's arm. There's snow on the ground, but she's wearing a short-sleeved cotton housedress, so it must be the first snow of winter, a mild October day before the real winter would come and barricade the cabin with snow drifts piling as high as the door and jagged icicles hanging from the roof. There is no overhang roof to shelter the entrance to the cabin, even though the ridgepole and rafters intended for this use extend at some length from the front of the roof. A large metal box with a lid hangs from a rope stretched high across the front of the cabin, well out of reach of pack rats, squirrels, and wild cats.

The first job was to prepare the cabin for winter by chinking the spaces between the logs with moss. All around the cabin, on boulders and stumps and on the forest floor, grew moss in thick mats and cushions, velvet and green in spring and summer and grey-brown and dry in the fall. In September Arthur and Verner were set to work lifting the moss in big clumps, which they stuffed into gunny sacks and carried to their father. He worked pieces of moss tightly between the logs, tamping it with a thin, flat-bladed wooden tool that he tapped with a wooden mallet. The inside walls were rough logs. Alfred sent to Smithers for heavy building paper to cover them and make the cabin warmer. He and Ingeborg spent a day cutting the paper into floor-to-ceiling lengths, then tacking them into place. The building paper was a beautiful blue, which made the space inside a good deal more friendly.

But it didn't make the living space any larger, and when winter came household activities that could be carried on outside in warmer weather now had to move indoors. Alfred gave the boys their haircuts, and these sessions were always noisy events. And now I sense Verne looking over my shoulder as I write. "We called them 'Papa' and 'Mama,' you know." I did not know, and the words sound strange, for they are not in my memory. But just now I'm writing from Verne's memory, and he remembered sitting perched on a powder box placed on a chair so Papa could work without having to bend over. "Sit still! Sit still! *Djävla trollung*" (devil of a troll kid), he would scold as he worked with the scissors. The clipping finished, he picked up the dreaded clippers for the neck hairs. These were manual clippers, not electric, and the sharp clipping surface was operated by squeezing the handles in and out. Papa was an artist with the clippers, but even he could sometimes pinch, so as soon as he reached for the clippers, Verner would tense up and squirm and get ready to say "Ouch!" Then Papa would let loose his "*djävla trollung*" stream of invective and growl at him to sit still.

Papa was also the family shoemaker. In those days shoes had leather soles and when the leather wore out the shoe was recycled with a new leather sole. Papa had a shoemaker's last with three different foot sizes. It was an iron stand or leg, about thirty-five centimetres high, and the "feet," also cast iron, fitted onto the leg with the bottom of the "foot" facing up. To make a new sole, he would first choose the right size of "foot," clamp it on the last, and fit the shoe over this "foot." Then he'd remove the worn sole, cut a new one roughly to size from a piece of leather, nail it in place, and trim it to an exact fit with a little curved knife. But the sole had to be sewn to the uppers as well as nailed, and for every stitch a hole had to be pierced in the leather with a little sharp awl. He would make a hole and pass the needle and thread down through it;

then he'd make another hole and bring the thread through and up. Recycling a shoe was laborious, time-consuming work, not to be disturbed by *trollunga* fighting one another and bumping into him.

Mama, exasperated and nervous, would be trying to make them sit down and read the funnies and be quiet. Verner remembered: "I can see Papa sitting by the window in front of his last, his mouth full of little nails, going tap tap with his little hammer. When he was finished, he'd say, 'There you are, son. Good as new.'" Not that his work was appreciated. Verne reminded Art: "When you grew out of your shoes, he mended them and passed them on to me. Yeah, I had to wear your old shoes." Verne in old age was still nursing the grievance of a younger brother.

Our father's curved knife and awl and hammer, the needles and strong linen thread, and the ball of dark amber-coloured resin for waxing the thread were all kept in a little, faded red tin box with two interlocking handles. Wherever our family moved in years to come, the little tin box went with us, and the last with its three sizes of foot. He continued to mend our shoes, giving them back to us with that note of pride and satisfaction, until we no longer wanted to depend on him for our footware.

He shaved with a straight razor, and I see him yet. He stands in front of the wash basin, wide suspenders mysteriously trademarked "Police" hanging down over his trousers, the sleeves of his Stanfields long underwear rolled up. He sharpens his razor on a long, leather strap, preparing to shave. The razor blade, about six inches long, is sharpest steel and when not in use resides in its coral-pink handle, which is hinged to the blade. Fold the handle over the blade, and it's safely tucked away out of harm's way. Unfold the handle, and the razor blade is exposed for the dangerous instrument it is.

He pours a little hot water into the basin from the big cast-aluminum kettle on the stove, and I learned early not to use all the hot water for washing the dishes. I must always leave some in the kettle for his shave. He dips his shaving brush in the water, applies the brush to the shaving soap till he has a good lather; then, peering into the little mirror on the wall, lathers his face and begins to shave with long, careful strokes. The steel blade makes a rough sound against his skin, just the sound of the Swedish word "*raka*," to shave. Distant, composed, he concentrates on each slow stroke. Finally he empties the wash basin and with clean water rinses his face, cupping his hands in the water and sloshing it on his face and around his neck. He gropes for the towel, dries himself, puts on his plaid work shirt and pulls up his suspenders. Throughout my childhood, watching my father move through this daily ritual, which was a kind of meditation, I felt secure and grounded in the world.

Over the years the razor became something of a conversation piece and he liked to say that he found it in a trash barrel. Why would it have been thrown away? Had it been used for some sinister, violent purpose and then been guiltily, stealthily disposed of? Had some desperate person held this blade in front of his terrified victim's throat and then to his neck and then . . .? Throughout my childhood, the wicked, bloody history I imagined for my father's razor gave it a special aura, even when it lay quiet and inoffensive on a kitchen shelf.

Verner remembered that shaving ritual too. "That was a lethal weapon, that was. Mama was always so nervous when he was shaving. She was scared to death of the razor." He mimicked her, his voice high and agitated: "Sit down, boys! Sit! Sit!" He said, "We didn't dare get off our chairs till he'd finished shaving. We sat there like little tree stumps and didn't dare move." He whooped with laughter at the memory, transported back to that little cabin, where he's sitting on a chair, a player in the family drama: Papa unperturbed, meditative in front of the mirror, Mama excited, shrill, and the scene so vivid in his mind he has to play it again. "Sit down, boys! Sit!"

However, this is not a funny story. The isolation, confinement within four walls, the high-spirited boys, their constant bickering and shoving, a fretful baby cutting her first teeth: by spring, the stress must have been too much for her, not to mention the physically taxing labour of the daily housework routine, and it must have been even worse in the full force of winter, with its snowstorms and temperatures of forty degrees below Fahrenheit.

Alfred too became stressed out, especially when he was on the graveyard shift, working from midnight till morning and trying to get some sleep during the day. He might have accustomed himself to the routine household noises well enough, but the caterwauling of wild cats in heat right outside the cabin was too much for him. Bears and wolves were no problem at the Duthie: they had their dens, their territories. But the wild cats, or bobcats as they are also called, respected no boundaries. There was a big population of them and they were a nuisance. One sleepless morning Alfred jumped out of bed cursing those *djävlige katter*. He went outside, grabbed the yowling animal, and poured turpentine over its luckless rump. This was a desperate act of survival, and he was always good at survival. He was also good at finding solutions.

When we were first living at the Duthie, Mama couldn't see the lake at the foot of the hill because of the trees. According to family legend, Papa gave Arthur and Verner each a saw and told them to go out and cut down the forest so Mama could see Loon Lake.

Family history doesn't say who made the decision, but Mama was a spirited woman. When she had a problem, she too looked for a solution: if a forest is blocking your view, cut it down. Papa was a practical man. Cutting down a forest didn't seem a difficult task for a man who'd worked at demolishing rocky cliffs that were blocking the construction of the railroad bed of the Grand Trunk Pacific Railway. One day decades later Verne told his version of the story to a group of us.

"Papa had found a job up at the Duthie. A miner has to go where there's work. So we'd moved away from our nice house in Prince Rupert. We couldn't take our gramophone with us in the wagon up that mountain, or any of our records.

"Papa gave Art and me a crosscut saw – a short one, four feet long – and an axe. The trees were quite tall, but only seven or eight inches in diameter, and thick as the hair on a dog's back. We started cutting near the bottom of the hill and worked our way up towards the cabin, so the trees would fall on already fallen trees. First we'd make a cut with the axe on the underside of the tree. Then we'd take the crosscut saw, one of us at each end, sawing from the cut at the back, so the tree would fall forward. It didn't take long – couple of minutes and down she'd come. Sometimes we'd just give it a little shove. If the tree was quite small, we didn't need to use the saw; we could chop it down with an axe. I never cut myself. Art did, a big gash on his hand, that one time. He just walked over to a balsam tree and put some pitch on it and kept on working.

"This was a pretty big job for two little kids. We were out there for months, cutting down trees. We had lots of time because we weren't going to school. There weren't enough children in the camp that year. Eventually we cut a swathe of forest, oh maybe three hundred feet wide and nearly five hundred feet long, and Mama had her view of Loon Lake. Well, we didn't stop there. We proceeded to do the same for Dennis Lake, so that kept us busy felling trees for another couple of months."

Water was another problem that tested my father's ingenuity. At first it had to be carried from Henderson Creek at the foot of the hill. When Alfred was at work and the boys had run off somewhere, Ingeborg took the empty pails and, wearing a wooden yoke across her shoulders, carried the two three-gallon pails, heavy and sloshing, up the hill.

Carrying water from the creek made washday an enormous burden for Ingeborg. So Alfred dug a well on the hillside above the creek. He used a divining rod, a branch of willow that ended in a fork. To locate the underground stream, he walked slowly over the hillside, holding the willow branch in front of him with his two hands, one on each end of the fork until the branch bent down towards the ground. That was where he knew there would be underground water, and that's where he started to dig. When he hit bedrock, he brought out his drilling steels and sledgehammer and asked his workmate, Bob Macken, to drill with him. One turned the steel and the other swung the eight-pound hammer. They drilled a well twenty feet deep, which soon filled with water.

However, the well was a good distance from the cabin and Ingeborg was still walking uphill with a yoke across her shoulders and two pails of water sloshing at her side with every step. So Alfred thought of a way of bringing running water to the door of the cabin. Up the hill about six hundred feet, a spring of pure, clean water bubbled up out of an abandoned mine shaft. His idea was to build a long, narrow trough or flume to carry the water down the hill to the cabin, where it would empty into a barrel. He hollowed out a length of jack pine, and with an axe scored it evenly with single blows every four to six inches. Then, holding the axe almost horizontally, he sliced through the length of the log, peeling off each scored section much as though he were using a wood chisel. When he had finished, the log had a flat top. Next, he cut a v-shaped trough in the log, using the same procedure.

Then he handed Arthur and Verner each an axe and told them to go out and cut down some jack pine trees and hollow them out as he had done. They used a Swedish crosscut saw to cut the logs into lengths of ten or fifteen feet. They had to work at this job for some days, but since they weren't going to school they had all day to do the work. When they had enough hollowed out logs, they carried them to the spring at the mine tunnel and placed the first trough so that it overlapped the second and so on downhill to the cabin, the whole flume supported by short logs laid under the trough sections. They made a little dam at the spring in the tunnel to collect a pool of water to flow into the first trough. When that first water appeared in the trough at the cabin door there was great jubilation. Running water! This was a technological breakthrough! Unfortunately, the water couldn't be used for drinking because it tasted of pitch. They should have charred the inside of the troughs to seal the wood. In winter, of course, the water stopped running, so they had to carry water from the well until spring.

All their lives, Arthur and Verner cherished the memory of building that flume. It became a touchstone against which they measured achievement. They became men who built dams and tunnels and pipelines, dredged and redirected rivers. They had many heroic stories to tell about their work in construction, but the stories of how they cut down a forest and built a water flume at the Duthie Mine when they were little boys was the best story of all.

Ingeborg now had a good supply of water. The Saturday-night bath in the little round galvanized-iron tub in the middle of the kitchen floor was a weekly ritual, as it was for many pioneering families. As each boy finished soaping his head, she poured a pot of warm rinsing water over his head, having first given a supervisory scrubbing to neck and ears – he screwing up his eyes so as not to get soap in them and making little whimpering sounds, anticipating the worst. That same tub of water had to be used three times: it was next to impossible to heat enough water to supply a fresh bath for each child.

Washday started right after breakfast when Ingeborg heated water in a copper clothes boiler on top of the stove and boiled the towels and sheets and pillow cases. Actually boiled the clothes? Certainly the water had to be very, very hot. Diapers she certainly boiled. She used Fels Naptha soap, not a powder in a package, but a bar of soap, from which she made shavings using a butcher knife. From time to time she prodded the clothes with a long wooden spoon so the soap shavings would make good suds. She had to keep building the fire, and the boys had to keep the woodbox replenished. After the clothes had boiled, she lifted them out of the boiler with the spoon and transferred them, heavy and dripping, to one of the two galvanized-iron washtubs placed side by side on two chairs. She transferred the hot, soapy water in the boiler to that tub, using a big dipper, finally lifting the boiler off the stove and pouring off the rest. The cabin was full of steam, the window fogged over.

All this I can personally attest to, for fifteen years later I was washing clothes like this myself, in a different kitchen but just possibly using the same copper boiler, soldered here and there to stop leaks. The round, galvanized-iron tubs and the copper clothes boiler with its lid are cultural icons summing up the history of women's labour in the working-class home.

However, I have questions. Later in our lives I asked Arthur and Verner how our mother managed with me underfoot, just learning to walk, when they weren't around to help and Papa was at work. She'd still have to carry water from the big barrel outside. My brothers shrugged and looked perplexed.

"Well, but think about it," I insisted. "There's a little baby crawling around on the floor, playpens we haven't heard of yet, she's got this scalding water and she's emptying it dipper by dipper into a tub on a chair in the middle of the room ..."

"Women in those days, they just did these things." Arthur was calm and philosophical about woman's lot.

"We did carry water for her." Verne was defensive. "Of course, I carried more than you. You were always away down at Dennis Lake fishing."

But I have left Ingeborg with a tubful of sheets and towels in hot, soapy water and they have to be rinsed. She would fill the second tub with clean, cold water, attach a contraption with two rollers to the rim of the first tub, and, turning the handles of this wringer, feed the sheets and towels between the rollers, which squeeze out the dirty water. The sheets and towels fell into the rinse tub, where she sloshed them around, lifting each piece separately, plunging it again and again into the rinse water.

"The blueing, don't forget to mention the blueing," Verne said in that conversation years later. In the days before powdered detergents with their special whitening agents, you added Reckitt's Blue to the rinse water to make sheets and pillow cases and tablecloths look white. It came in a little cloth bag; you immersed it in the rinse water, which then turned a beautiful blue. But Verne wasn't thinking about laundry when he told me this story about one washday at the Duthie.

"I used to love to make little boats," he said. "Mama came from many, many years of boat-building Aarviks, so I guess I inherited my love of boats from them. One day I carved one with a little cabin on it and a sail. In Prince

Rupert I could go down to the creek or to Cow Bay. But at the Duthie we were too far from Loon Lake, so I had another idea. One day when she was doing the washing as usual in those galvanized tubs, I hung around, but kept my boat behind my back. 'When are you going to put the blueing in, Mama?' I asked. 'Oh, soon, soon.' So I waited, and waited, and kept on asking, 'When are you going to put the blueing in?' And finally she did and I dashed over and put my boat in the tubful of blue water and stood back and looked at it. I wanted the full effect of a boat on the sea. Well, Mama put her arms around me and gave me a big hug and we both laughed and stood there looking at this little boat on the blue water. It really got to her, you know."

I wonder if she was feeling just then a tremor of memory, if she was thinking of her father, Elling Aarvik, drowned in heavy seas on the coast of Norway. The letter from Norway that told of his death was read again and again in our household, and the story of my grandfather's death was told and retold in sorrow and disbelief. *Han druknet*, he drowned. *Druknet*. The word was powerful. When I was a child it was one of the few Norwegian words I knew, but I scarcely dared speak it. For me, it is still, decades later, charged with emotion.

Did Ingeborg, looking at the blue water in the tub, thinking of the child living with her grandparents beside the fjord, hear her own words echo through the cabin: "Soon, soon." She had hoped, promised herself, that soon she would be able to send for Inga. But the time never came.

Thinking of these things, I cannot go on with an account of washday, even though the soapy water still has to be used twice more, for the coloured wash and for work clothes. I feel her grief welling up inside of me. And so I leave Mama bending over the washboard, rhythmically scrubbing heavy woollen work socks, while in the cabin words hover in the air. "*Druknet*." "Soon, soon." But it has stopped snowing, there's a clear, blue sky, and the air is dry and cold. In this weather the washing will dry on the line in no time.

During those years in the cabin on Hudson Bay Mountain, our nearest neighbours were Emily Sam and Bob Macken. Their cabin was in a nearby clearing, not fifty yards away. Emily belonged to the Wet'suwet'en people, and her family belonged to the Wolf clan. They were from Hagwilget, farther north near Hazelton, but her clan had trapping grounds all around Smithers, and as far south as Houston and Morice Lake. Bob was part native Indian, part French Canadian, perhaps Métis, one of the workers at the mine.

Below our cabin, Henderson Creek emerged from between high, rock walls to flow into Loon Lake farther down the mountain. The Dennis family lived on the meadow beside the lake. Like Emily Sam, they were Wet'suwet'en, belonging to the Frog and Beaver clans. They, too, had traplines in the area, and they cut wood for the mine as well. Emily Sam knew the Dennis family: she and Emily Dennis used to pick huckleberries together on the far side of Loon Lake and preserve them in glass jars for the winter.

Emily Sam had lost sight in one eye – it is not known how – and was known throughout the Bulkley Valley as "One-Eyed Emily." So that is what we called her, insensitive of being unfeeling. She is remembered in the local history of the area for having saved the life of a lineman on the old Telegraph Trail. She had come upon Lem Broughton on the trail. He was too ill to reach his house at Deep Creek, so she took him back to her camp and looked after him. His house was a stopping place for travellers, and for a while she was cook and housekeeper there. (Another stopping place was Popcorn Kate's boarding house in Aldermere, now Telkwa, where the menu was mostly beans.)

At first Ingeborg was afraid of Emily because of the shooting. According to my brother Art, this is what happened. Emily suspected that another woman had stolen Bob's affections. This woman lived down by Henderson Creek, below Emily and Bob's cabin. One night in the late summer of 1923 Emily took her thirty-thirty, her grizzly bear gun, and started shooting across the canyon at the other woman, who in turn took shots in the direction of Emily. Alfred was on night shift and Ingeborg was alone with us children. Arthur was ten, Verner eight, Edwin six. I was nine months. The bullets came zinging past the cabin as Ingeborg, shielding me in her arms, and the boys cowered inside, terrified, expecting any minute that a bullet might come crashing through the window. That is Arthur's story. Emily's version I do not know.

There had been another violent incident. The Indians had saved a little bear cub, which then was said to have been sold to Mr. Duthie, who passed it on, presumably as a mascot, to the men in the bunkhouse. So the story goes. The little cub became an amusing pet to fondle and feed. My brother Art remembered that some of the men used to put it on a leash and walk with it down the hill to the little store, where they would buy chocolate bars and feed them to the bear. Unfortunately, as the cub grew to maturity it became hard

to handle and too dangerous and unpredictable to be given the freedom of
the camp. The men decided to get rid of it, but how? If they simply let it loose
in the forest, it would come back to the camp, where it knew it could feed on
chocolate bars rather than forage in the bushes for blueberries or hunt in the
lake for fish.

Somebody had the idea of blowing it up. Of course! Dynamite! Familiar
as bread and butter and as readily available. Explosions of rock were a daily
occurrence in the mine. One stick would do it. The bear could be penned up
in a crate, and then ...

"Verne and I were over at Dennis Lake when we heard the explosion," Art
recalled. "We said, 'What was that?'"

The shocking story of blowing up the bear, the mindless brutality, must
have been supper-table conversation throughout the camp. Whose idea was
it? Couldn't they (whoever "they" were) just have shot the bear? Then they
could at least have saved the pelt and remembered the bear in that way?
Ingeborg, remembering that the family had returned to Canada to escape the
violence of wartime Idaho: "*Uff da*! How can people behave like this?" She
might have thought of Inga, safe in Norway, in Viggja, on the fjord. This mining camp was no place to bring a fifteen-year-old girl. And then thrust another
stick of wood into the stove to bring the potatoes to a boil, replacing the stove
lid with a peremptory bang.

Ethnologist Marius Barbeau, doing field research for the National Museum of Canada, was even then in the early 1920s visiting the Gitksan villages
of the upper Skeena, talking to the carvers themselves or to the elders who
knew the history of each totem pole. Barbeau catalogued the poles, described
them in detail, with the origin in story of the totemic figures. Among all the
animals represented, after the frog, the bear appeared most frequently – grizzly, black, or "ordinary," sitting, standing, climbing or trapped; whether whole
or in part: ribs, stomach, claw marks; its headdress, its den. There were bear
cubs too. Among the totem poles in Hagwilget at the junction of the Skeena
and Bulkley rivers, "the second from the Canyon," said Barbeau, stood the
grizzly bear pole. "It formerly stood in front of a large communal house, about
sixty feet by fifty, and twenty feet high, the name of which was 'the Grizzly-
bear-house.'"

At the Duthie Mine, who was to know about Marius Barbeau and his
totem poles anyway? The Wet'suwet'en people who lived down by Loon Lake

knew that the plants and animals, birds, fish, flowers, trees, even the shadows of the trees, and the moon and stars too, were honoured in heraldic images on totem poles. However, the white community at the Duthie, as elsewhere in British Columbia, were still generally ignorant of this cultural tradition. The miners had no idea they were blowing up an animal that belonged to a world of ceremony and civility. Ingeborg would have understood this if she'd known what the poles were for. Oh yes, for *høytidlighet*. But it would be fifty years before the 'Ksan Historic Village and Museum would be built where the village of Hagwilget has stood for thousands of years, and Kitwanga, Kispayaks, and Gitsegyukla too, and where Bear continues to exist to this day in his double life.

Ingeborg would have felt more comfortable with a Norwegian family close by, or even an English family like the Ponders, who lived down the road at Blackjack (the owner of that mining claim was Blackjack McDonald), or with Mrs. Lyons down the hill and further along Henderson Creek. But Ingeborg soon made friends with Emily, despite her seemingly strange ways. "Mrs. Nelson, could I borrow a cup of lemon extract? I want to build a cake." The law forbade the sale of alcohol to Indians, so they had to find other ways of getting it. There was a lot of drinking in the camp. The men didn't have anything to do when they were off work; they could play cards and they could drink. They ordered their booze from Smithers, and rum, whiskey, and gin arrived regularly with the freight team, along with groceries for the cookhouse and mining equipment and supplies. The hillside behind the bunkhouse was littered with empty bottles. The Indians bought liquor from the miners whenever they could. If not, they drank lemon and vanilla extract instead. Lemon was best: it contained, at that time at least, more alcohol than any other flavouring.

If Ingeborg had lemon extract in the cupboard, she would fill Emily's cup. She herself, after all, was no stranger to devious ways of getting around liquor regulations. Our family had lived in Idaho during prohibition – remember the bottles of bootlegged liquor hidden in the cloth pockets sewn into the waistband of her voluminous skirt?

Arthur and Emily were also good friends. Sometimes when Emily went fishing for chub at Loon Lake, she took him with her. She spread a wide net just where the lake emptied into a large, slow-running creek and let the net sink down to the bottom. Chub are bottom-feeding fish with little, round, sucking mouths, not like trout that jump for flies on the surface. She'd always give Arthur some of her catch to take home. She gave us rabbit too, from her trapline. The forest was alive with rabbits, actually snowshoe hares. The Indians needed them for food and also for the clothing they could make from their skins and fur. Emily showed Arthur how to set snares and how to tap the rabbits on the neck to kill them when they were caught and still struggling and squealing in the snares. He was learning from her how to live on the land in the way that she and her people had always done.

Emily had her own traplines and sold marten and lynx and fox pelts in Smithers. She could read the forest like a book, knew the footprints of the animals and could say how long ago a deer or bear had passed along the trail. She never took chances with grizzlies, not since the day she and Bob had gone after one on a mountainside. Emily had all four pack dogs tied to her waist, and when they heard the first shot, they all started running uphill towards the grizzly, dragging Emily along with them.

Once Emily and Arthur had a near encounter with a grizzly. "One day we were just walking along in the woods," he recalled. "We were bringing back the rabbits caught in her snares. Suddenly, Emily stops. 'C'mon Artu, le's run.'" She had seen the fresh droppings of a grizzly. So we got out of there quick."

When I was about one year old, I became ill with a high fever that brought on convulsions. My little body stiffened and went into contortions. Mama plunged me into a hot bath, but in her panic misjudged the temperature of the water, so that my abdomen was scalded. She sent Arthur to fetch Mrs. Lyons, who was a nurse, and shooed Verner and Edwin out of the cabin, sending them off to Emily and Bob's. Emily went up to the mine office to telephone Dr. Hankinson in Smithers.

Meanwhile, Arthur and Mrs. Lyons were climbing the steep hill from Henderson Creek. Mrs. Lyons was a very big woman, so heavy she could scarcely bring up one foot after the other as she struggled uphill, puffing and panting. Arthur walked behind her, pushing her, and in her anxiety to reach our cabin and be of help she panted, "Push harder, Arthur. Push harder."

Emily stayed with Mama until Mrs. Lyons arrived and then went back to her cabin. Verner remembered what she said that day: "That li'l baby, she gonna die."

I heard that story told over and over again, everyone laughing when Arthur came to the part where Mrs. Lyons said, "Push harder, Arthur." The big woman, the little boy behind her, pushing: it is a comical image. But in fact it is attached to a matter of life and death, and only recently did Verner give me Emily's words, uncensored: "That li'l baby, she gonna die. Her guts is comin' out."

The panic and despair that my mother suffered while she waited for Dr. Hankinson can scarcely be imagined. Was she to lose a second little girl, and this through her own carelessness? Several hours later, Dr. Hankinson arrived, perhaps on horseback rather than by automobile because by that time the wagon road was still probably not passable by car. In any case it was a sixteen-mile journey up the mountain from Smithers, and it was a journey that saved my life.

For I did not die, and Emily wanted to honour my recovery. She said to Arthur, "Gonna make that li'l baby a rabbit paw blanket. You go out and get some rabbits." I learned from Emily's niece Mabel that in fact the women in the Sam family did make these blankets, carrying on a Wet'suwet'en tradition. I would like to think that by making a rabbit paw blanket for me, Emily was adopting me into the Wet'suwet'en nation. Not that she herself said this, nor did our family interpret the gift in this way. It's only now, looking back at that time, that I see she was bestowing on me and our family a great honour.

The rabbits used for the blanket were not the fluffy little rabbits you bring lettuce to in your backyard, and certainly no relation to Beatrix Potter's Peter Rabbit, but rather the snowshoe hare, *lepus americanus*. It has very long ears and large, hairy hind feet. It measures up to twenty inches (fifty centimetres) in length and is similar to the jack rabbit, but of a different species. The snowshoe hare proliferates for seven to ten years, reproducing in great numbers; then dies off for a while before beginning its population cycle again. The Hare People of the Athabaska were so-called because they subsisted on the snowshoe hare and had to endure a period of severe hunger whenever it came to the end of a cycle.

The snowshoe hare is one of those animals that changes colour with the seasons. In winter it is white and invisible against the snow, except for black on the tips of its ears. During the rest of the year it is brown against the forest floor. My blanket was not winter white. It was a creamy brown-grey.

Making the blanket was a huge labour. "Gonna need some more rabbits, Artu," Emily would say. In the morning he would go out into the woods and set snares; later in the day he'd check them and swiftly kill the hares he'd caught by tapping them on the neck with a stick. He helped Emily skin them and chop off the paws. Ingeborg did the same thing when she made rabbit stew. Our family ate a lot of rabbit.

When they had a pile of rabbit paws, Emily showed Arthur how to slip the furry skin off a paw without tearing it, keeping it in one piece. She used a very sharp knife. After she had skinned a few paws, she gave the knife to Arthur: "Here, Artu, now you try." (From Ingeborg, looking on while her little boy performed this delicate surgery, came little gusts of *Uff da*!) Then Emily cut each skin to about three inches in length and sewed them together, about thirty skins to a row, until she had nine rows, the brown fur uppermost, the tan-coloured sole making the underside of the blanket. I know how she made the blanket from the archival description of a similar blanket collected by Barbeau. That blanket was in the Canadian Museum of Civilization in Ottawa, and came from the Gitskan people along the Skeena River who share the cultural traditions of the Wet'suwet'ens of the Bulkley Valley. The finished blanket was about three feet (ninety centimetres) long and almost as wide. It was a beautiful blanket, and I wish I could say it was ours. But no, Barbeau found his blanket in June 1923, just before we arrived at the Duthie.

North American Native peoples believe that between the animal and the hunter there is a certain bond: the hunter kills the animal but takes the flesh and hide as a gift. As many as seventy-five snowshoe hares, three hundred paws, might have been needed to make my blanket. It was a very big gift. Our family had no knowledge of such beliefs, merely accepting the blanket as a testimonial to my happy survival. But whatever happened to my blanket? Perhaps it went with us when we moved back to Prince Rupert, used as a lap robe on the train journey. Or perhaps it was discarded when we moved out of the cabin, tossed in a heap in that immense upheaval, no longer of consequence. The gift of the snowshoe hare dishonoured, we would no longer have been worthy of it. And yet Emily's blanket has been honoured in memory these many years, and I write this story to remember the big-hearted woman who made it especially for me.

Emily became a person to whom our family could turn for help, as we did when our mother Ingeborg needed a cow to provide me with fresh milk. We did have a cow, inherited from an American family who had quit the mine and the camp and couldn't take it with them. It was pastured in the nearby mountain meadow, and Ingeborg milked the cow, morning and night.

Where had she learned to milk a cow? In Norway every summer, cows were brought to the *seter*, the alpine pasture, where some members of the family, perhaps the older children, lived in little mountain huts, milked the cows, and made butter and cheese. It's possible Ingeborg had spent some summers at a *seter* and learned to brush a cow down before starting to squeeze and pull the udder, the sound of milk squirting into a pail with that fast, hard sound. She would know how to strain the milk through a cloth into a pan, then store it in a cool place, wash the pail and straining cloth, and hang the cloth out to dry. It's just as possible that she simply learned because she had to, because there was nobody else to milk the cow and if she wanted to have fresh milk for her child, she would have to learn to milk.

Alfred cut the hay in the meadow with a scythe, just the way he used to do in northern Sweden. Here on Hudson Bay Mountain he had no hayloft for storing the hay, so he piled it instead under the high branches of spruce trees, safe from the winter snow. He also built wooden racks for the hay and set them up in the open meadow. The top layer of hay would become wet and soggy from rain and snow, but underneath would remain dry.

Arthur and Verner cut some trees to build a barn, got the logs ready. They had become expert little loggers. Verne remembered, "And Papa got a bunch of miners down on a Sunday for a barn-raising. They had a little beer, a bottle of rum and the women came from down below the creek and helped Mama make lunch for them. The barn, it went up in a day."

One day the cow died, and Mama could have changed me over then to canned evaporated milk and saved herself the labour of milking twice a day. But no, she would not do that. She would have a cow. She would have a cow because she had lost one daughter by leaving her in Norway. She had almost lost her second little girl. Canned evaporated milk would do for a cup of coffee, but only fresh milk would do for this child. They had to buy a cow.

But a cow was expensive. So, maybe half a cow? Later on nobody remembered who came up with the idea of applying to Emily, but she agreed to share the cost of a cow. Not only that, but she would also take the front half and our family would have the back half and give Emily and Bob all the milk they wanted. Scotty Aitken had a cow for sale out near Canyon Creek, and it was soon arranged that Emily and ten-year-old Arthur would go to the Aitken farm, seven miles from Smithers, to fetch the cow.

So one morning Arthur and Emily travelled to Smithers on the freight wagon and stayed overnight in the Smithers Hotel, owned by Mr. and Mrs. Mackenzie. Arthur made friends right away with their son and they went to the Smithers Moving Picture House. Emily went out drinking. She had many friends in Smithers, and they had a party.

"She went out on a bender," Arthur said. "That didn't bother me because I was at the movie, *Tarzan of the Apes*. Me and their kid, the Mackenzies' boy. It was a silent film and I thought it was pretty wonderful."

Next morning Emily was ready, even with a hangover, to start out after breakfast on the seven-mile walk to Scotty and Nora Aitken's farm, where, presumably, Nora Aitken gave them lunch and money changed hands. The cow's name was Bluebell, and that is all Arthur remembered of the transaction, except that Scotty Aitken gave him a puppy, a collie.

"I'd never had a dog, and it scampered along beside me as we walked along. Bluebell had a rope around her neck and Emily walked beside her. But the road was muddy – thick, sticky gumbo. In that part of the country after a rain, you sink right into the mud and it sticks to your shoes. It's like walking with snowshoes on your feet, you have to keep stopping to kick the mud off your shoes. My puppy couldn't walk at all in that gumbo. So I had to pick it up and carry it. And I did that for three or four miles, but I couldn't manage to walk in that gumbo and carry my puppy. It was too difficult. When we were halfway back to Smithers, we came to an Indian encampment beside the road and I gave my puppy to a little Indian boy there. I cried. That was the only dog I ever had."

At eighty years of age Arthur was still grieving for the collie puppy he lost. Arthur Nelson was never a sentimental man. Of the pain of loss he had experienced his share and borne it stoically. But that puppy was dear to him, had been dear to him for a lifetime, and he had grown old with that cherished, poignant memory.

It was slow going along the road to Smithers, and sometimes Bluebell just stood in the gumbo and mooed with vexation and fatigue. Late in the afternoon the muddy threesome walked into Smithers. Emily took Bluebell to the livery stable, wiped her down, and fed and milked her while Arthur presented himself once more to Mrs. Mackenzie at the Smithers Hotel.

In the morning after breakfast he went to the livery stable where Emily had already fed and milked Bluebell and hired a horse for them to ride on the journey back up the mountain to the mine. Emily mounted easily and was quite at home in the saddle. Arthur climbed up behind her. He had sometimes ridden Cap, one of the mine horses, when the bullcook hitched up the big wooden sled, the "go-devil," to carry away garbage from the cookhouse.

They set off, Emily holding the reins, Arthur holding Bluebell's rope, and Bluebell following behind. No gumbo now, but swamp and corduroy road. Bluebell balked at walking on the logs and Arthur had to keep jumping off the horse and pulling and coaxing the cow to move. Once on the upper part of the mountain road, she walked more easily. From time to time, whenever a good patch of grass appeared, she stopped to graze. In this leisurely way they made their way up the mountain, around switchbacks and across little streams, and were home before dark. They had been gone for three days.

That is a story straight out of folk tale. A Wet'suwet'en woman goes on a journey with a little boy to fetch home a cow that provides fresh milk for a little child. They have various adventures along the way. But the story needs an ending, and I have not been given one. Ingeborg, Alfred, and Emily are long dead, and Verner and Edwin remembered other stories in which they played a part, but not this one. Only Arthur remembered the story of bringing back Bluebell, and over the years he told it again and again, about the Smithers Hotel, Emily going out on a bender, about *Tarzan of the Apes*, the puppy, and the gumbo.

But a folk tale needs an ending, and since Arthur, the family historian, did not provide our folk tale with a proper ending, I take it upon myself to spin the homecoming for him.

I know what it must have been like for Ingeborg, anxiously waiting in the cabin on the third day. Arthur was a sensible, reliable boy, but he had never undertaken a journey like this before and stayed by himself in a hotel for two nights – and supposing Emily got drunk? Around three in the afternoon on the third day, Mama sends Edwin and Verner out to see if they're coming: "*Du, Verner; Du, Edvin*, go up to the road, maybe you can see them." "*Du*" means "you," and among Norwegians, at least in those days, was characteristically used in this way to summon attention. I can hear my mother still, calling me to come for dinner, "*Du, Irene, kom nu, vi skal spise.*"

By suppertime Ingeborg is really anxious. Finally she hears the sound of a cowbell and opens the door to see a triumphant procession: Edwin out in front, then Verner with Emily leading the horse and Arthur leading Bluebell, who switches her tail and moos her impatience to be milked. "*Du, Edvin*" fetches the milking pail, Bob Macken walks over from his cabin, and the whole gang goes down the hill to the newly built barn to witness the first milking, Mama leading the way with me on her hip. She hands me over to Papa, brushes Bluebell down so the cow will be free of dust and dirt, sits down on the milking stool, and begins squeezing the cow's udder in her practised way, the sound of the first squirt-squirts hitting the empty pail with a hard, sharp sound.

It had to be like that. There is no other way for this story to end. When Arthur and Emily arrived, tired and hungry but jubilant, mission accomplished, do you think Alfred just raised his head for a moment from behind his newspaper and then went back to reading the Major Hoople comic strip? And Bluebell – can you stop a cow from switching her tail and mooing and wanting to be milked? Could even the taciturn Bob Macken refrain from coming over and proclaiming Arthur a pretty skookum kid, which he was. He did feel pretty skookum and all his life remembered how sturdy and brave he'd been. As for Emily, she couldn't feel anything but pride and satisfaction at having successfully brought home a cow, both ends, front and back, through gumbo, swamp and muskeg, around switchbacks and through the timber up a long, steep road. There is only one thing she could have said as she watched Ingeborg milk their cow.

"That li'l baby, she not gonna die."

Only two years later the mine would close down and Bluebell had to be sold. We would move back to Prince Rupert, where there was a plentiful supply of fresh milk. We moved back to the company of Uncle Thorstein and Aunt Berit and the Mickelsons and Johnsons and Ungers. Emily found work in a cannery in Prince Rupert and we lost touch with her. But Emily and the shooting spree, Emily and the rabbit paw blanket, Emily bringing back Bluebell: I heard these stories again and again. She became a presence in our family history, and even though I was too young to remember her, I hear her voice: "Gonna make that li'l baby a rabbit paw blanket."

Our family was always offhand about the connection, savouring the stories for their humour and pioneer realism, with Emily as a rich, exotic character. That is not a true picture. She was not just comic relief in our family drama. She actually entered into our lives. I understand now that when we were living in the cabin on Hudson Bay Mountain, Emily was not just a kind and helpful neighbour. She was an unacknowledged aunt, but one of a different kind.

Bobby McEwan and Freddy (Roy) Nelson, in
front of the bunkhouse at the Duthie Mine, 1930.
(*Courtesy Greta Nelson*)

SIX

THE SAGA OF INGEBORG-OLINE AARVIK

Ingeborg Nelson finally did get her wedding silver moved to the Duthie, and the china cabinet with the silver cake stand, but little did she know that her hopes and plans for a proper house and a comfortable settled life were bound up with the hopes and plans of the Guggenheim family of financiers and industrialists in the United States. This syndicate had monopoly control of the mining and smelting industry in North America through the American Smelting and Refining Company, which, by 1907, controlled the silver production of the North and South American continents. It had been exploring mineral properties throughout the Western hemisphere since before the beginning of the century to obtain metal ores to supply their smelters and refineries. In 1922 Seattle shipbuilder John F. Duthie, developing his Henderson claim on the south side of Hudson Bay Mountain, found a promising vein of silver and in 1923 sold a 55 per cent interest in his Henderson and adjoining Mamie claims to a subsidiary company in the vast Guggenheim mining and smelting empire. Duthie Mines Ltd. was created at that time.

This subsidiary was Federal Mining and Smelting, the same company that owned and operated the Morning Mine in Idaho, where Alfred had worked a few years earlier. It was now once again his employer. Federal Mining and Smelting were the new owners of the Duthie Mine. They also operated the mine, so although Alfred and Ingeborg had moved back to Canada, their lives were still governed by that company. In 1924, after developing the Duthie for a year and making several shipments of silver-lead ore, the company suspended operations and laid off, until further notice, seventy-five workers, among them Alfred Nelson. As explained in the *Annual Report of the Minister of Mines*, "The decision by the Federal Company to close down operations was in part due to the unsuccessful development of the property and in part to a desire to arrange different terms with J.F. Duthie for continued operation." And what terms would those be? Did Duthie, the U.S. shipbuilder, make demands that challenged the Guggenheim-Federal ownership of this small stretch of North American mountain?

It was not for Alfred and Ingeborg to know about corporate financial dealings. The family had to move back to Prince Rupert. But scarcely had they unpacked and settled into their house on English Hill, when, only a year later, the mine reopened. It is not clear from the *Report of the Minister of Mines* whether in 1925 Federal still owned the controlling interest in Duthie Mines Ltd., but we do know that in 1926 the actual operation of the mine was under the direction of J.F. Duthie, whatever the change in controlling interest. Duthie needed a mine foreman, and Alfred needed a job, so once again he left Prince Rupert and went on ahead to help reopen the mine while Ingeborg stayed behind to do the packing and prepare for the rest of the family's move. In any case, she was pregnant, and the Duthie Mine was no place to have a baby. Roy Alfred was born in April 1926. He was the fifth child, a tiny, mewling little thing, and was scarcely recovered from the pangs of getting himself born when, that summer, he was bundled up to make a long, strenuous outing, the family's second trip to the Duthie.

At least on this second move to the mine, Ingeborg and the children didn't have to travel by horse and wagon as they had done in 1923. By 1926 the road from Smithers to the Duthie had been made passable for trucks and automobiles. But this time at the end of the journey there was no sturdy log cabin; there was only a tent. True, it was a large tent, and it did have shiplap walls, and Alfred assured Ingeborg that they would only have to live in it over the following winter. By next summer there would be a house. The company had promised him that.

And now my very first memory allows me to see what it must have been like for my mother when she arrived with her brood of five children at the Duthie Mine in the summer of 1926. I was wearing a blue coat. We were all to walk up the hill to the cookhouse for supper, but I refused to go. I stood against the wall of a building, maybe it was the wall of the tent, and cried. That much I remember (I was nearly four years old), but I can imagine the rest of the scene on the hillside: Arthur, Verner, and Edwin have run on ahead, Ingeborg is holding Freddy in her arms, he's whimpering and probably needs changing again, she's exhausted after a long car trip, and now little Irene has become *en trollung*, stubborn and unmanageable, a little brat. Probably my father picked me up and carried me up the hill, screaming and kicking and pummelling him until with a tired sob his troll child fell asleep on his shoulder.

To a woman like myself, wife and mother for a good part of her life, housekeeping for a family of seven in a tent seems like an unremitting labour, so impossibly taxing, both physically and mentally, that it can scarcely be even imagined. The task of keeping everyone clean and fed would be akin to that huge boulder that Sisyphus was destined to roll up the steep mountain, almost to the top, only to repeat the labour the next day. Yet pioneer women like Ingeborg Nelson performed such labours as a matter of course, and neither they nor anyone else thought they were heroic.

It helped, of course, that this time at the Duthie she wouldn't have to carry water: there was a cold water tap in the tent, connected to a pipe that supplied the mine office just up the hill. She still had to heat the water for washday, and begin each week with copper clothes boiler, galvanized-iron washtubs, and scrub board. Of course, washing diapers was a separate labour.

There were actually two tents, placed end to end, creating a kitchen–living room and a bedroom. This long, double tent was in the shape of a real house, with a wooden frame supporting the canvas structure. The floor was also wood and there were scatter rugs on the floor. A canvas fly over the whole of the two tents protected against heavy rain, and as for snow, the heat from the kitchen stove circulated in the air space between fly and tent roof, melting the snow before it became too heavy.

When winter set in with its below-zero temperatures, the wood stove was kept burning day and night. There was no stove in the bedroom, but the kitchen stove circulated plenty of heat. Alfred set the alarm clock and got up several times a night to stoke the kitchen stove, so that Freddy and I wouldn't become chilled if we kicked our blankets off. Arthur, Verner, and Edwin slept, three in a bed, in a third tent nearby. No stove in their tent! They would run out of the warm kitchen into the freezing night, sometimes into a blizzard, screaming, even laughing hysterically with the shock, and when they complained Alfred would say, "Oh , jump into bed and shiver awhile. You'll be alright."

There were only nine children of school age in camp; one more was needed to make up the required minimum school population, and I was that child, even though I had barely turned four. Arthur remembered that we all sat around the table at night doing our homework by the light of the coal oil lamp, and that he and Verner helped me to read and do arithmetic. He also remembered a time when his homework was Sir Walter Scott's *The Lady of the Lake*. Robert Bruce Wallace, our excellent teacher, was himself a Scot. "Don't you see, Art?" he persisted. "'The antlered monarch of the waste / Sprung from his heathery couch in haste.'" "No, I don't see," was Art's helpless reply. That line about the stag at eve drinking his fill, that was easy enough. He'd seen lots of deer, though maybe not in moonlight on Monan's rill. They came down to drink at Henderson Creek, where we got our water. But One-Eyed Emily didn't go hunting with a pack of bloodhounds. She just had her grizzly bear rifle and her trapline, and what kind of animal was this antlered monarch of the waste? To the end of his days, Art was still laughing about *The Lady of the Lake*. It became family history. "Don't you see, Art?" "No, I don't see."

What I remember about the tent is that Edwin was my storyteller. He invented a character called Ham 'n Eggs, a rascally little boy whose mischievous adventures kept me enthralled night after night. The name of this character derived from our father's oft-told story about how, when he first arrived in Canada, he knew so little English that the only meal he could order in a restaurant was ham and eggs.

The way Arthur and I remember life in the tent sounds quite cozy. Memory is kind to this rigorous exercise in physical survival, but now, not remembering, I think diapers, colic, teething; I think crying, whining, yelling, and little boys scuffling and punching. I think toothaches, fevers, coughs and mustard plasters, and, a sudden flash of memory, those two children's laxatives, Castoria and Syrup of Figs, both sweet and delicious. Memory, too, has little to say about Freddy, except, perhaps, for the fearful words "blue baby," which hovered tentatively, anxiously, around him.

Little Freddy survived the winter. He wasn't a blue baby after all: his heart functioned normally. The following summer the company fulfilled its promise and we moved into a real house. Ingeborg could have her china cabinet and silver cake stand and all the wedding silver and the porcelain china coffee cups. By now the camp was home to a community of families, generating a little hum of social activity, with Ingeborg, as wife of the mine foreman, in a favoured position, especially among the Scandinavian and Norwegian wives who came for afternoon coffee and comforting talk and advice. I was allowed to polish the dining-room table and chairs with O'Cedar Furniture Oil. The shift boss came to the house to receive instructions from Alfred about the drifts and stopes where the night shift was to work. John "Happy" Turner, the mine manager, was a regular visitor. He was a jovial man with a fund of good will, and one Christmas Eve Ingeborg served him pickled herring, which he had never before eaten. He proclaimed it, memorably, "Mighty good junk, Al."

I remember lamb with cabbage, the gravy seasoned with whole black peppers; and a potato dumpling, *palt*, with a bit of salt pork at the centre. You took a bit of hot *palt* on your fork and dipped it in a glass of milk to cool it before you ate it. There were Christmas concerts in the new schoolhouse, where Santa's imminent arrival was always heralded with reassuring updates from the stage: his ski plane was delayed because of a snowstorm, or he'd had to touch down in Smithers to have the propeller repaired. There was Eaton's catalogue. The order form said, "Be sure to state size and colour." If you did that, big boxes came in the mail with whatever you wanted, most of all a doll called "Eaton's Beauty," with a choice of either blonde or brown hair, and both of those models arrived in the mail for me, one Christmas at a time.

In the beginning was work; but my brother Verne, as his stories attest, remembered that child labour was fun – as in the time when he and his brother cut down all those trees at the Duthie.

The work that the boys did "was heavy work, men's work," Verne said. "I refused to do any other kind. I remember a few years later we had a party at school – big pot-bellied stove in the middle of the room, all the grades together, one to eight. I was fourteen and noticing girls – Lily and Gerda Hanson, especially Lily. After the party, Mr. Wallace, the teacher, said, 'Verne, I want you to wash the dishes.'

"I said, 'No, I'm not washing dishes.' You see, I'd been brought up to regard that as women's work and I'd never washed a dish in my life. That's the way it was in those days. I chopped wood, dug ditches, shovelled manure, cut hay – didn't wash dishes. It was segregated in those days. There was women's work, there was men's work. So I was firm about that.

"'You're not the boss of me,' I told Mr. Wallace. He gave me a cuff on the ear. There was a school trustees' meeting that night to talk about my insubordination. Next morning, Mr. Wallace arrives at school. 'Verne,' he says, 'you cut the wood. Lily, you wash the dishes.'

"Lily gives me a look: 'My hero.' She was so full of admiration.

The boys quickly became experts in their main job at home, cutting cordwood. "Every day after school my brother Art and I had to chop a rick of wood," Verne said. "The cook stove was the only heat in the cabin, so in really cold weather our father had to set the alarm at bedtime and get up in the middle of the night to stoke the fire. Stove wood was sixteen inches long. We piled it eight feet long and four feet high, and that was called a rick. Three ricks make one cord. Frozen wood splits real easy. You take a hefty swing and it splits neat and straight with a nice cracking sound.

"Later on, we cut wood for the mine too, wood to feed the boilers to make steam for the compressors. The drills in the mine were run by compressed air, you see. There were three boilers, and they needed a huge supply of wood.

"Art and I felled trees and cut wood on our strip to feed those boilers. With the men. I was eleven when we started working Saturdays and after school; Art was thirteen. Thirty or forty men and us two kids.

"The forest was marked off in strips one hundred feet wide. Two shifts a day, two men on a strip, felling trees, cutting them into firewood. Art and I had a strip, you bet.

"We used a Swedish Sandvik saw, a little over three feet long with a blade an inch wide. You had to drive in a wedge when you were sawing to keep from pinching the blade. Jack pine contains a lot of pitch, so we'd use coal oil on the blade to soften and dissolve the pitch. In later years when the new, improved blade came along, the sawing was much easier. The newer Sandvik blades were what they called 'razor backed': less than an inch wide, with the back edge very thin, so that when you cut into a log it wouldn't pinch; you could saw right through a log and it wouldn't bind. It was a steel-framed bow saw with a lever on the back that you could pull for tension.

"A saw-filer came around to the strips to sharpen saws. He charged one dollar, but it was worth it, because when he'd finished your saw would cut through a tree easy as cutting through cheese.

"It was forty below one time when we were out there on the strip. We were pulling on the same saw, one at each end. And Art said, 'Keep working, keep working.' You had to keep moving to stay warm. Your hands and face, your feet would freeze in no time. So we kept working, pulling on the saw. But we didn't build a fire. Art just kept saying, 'Keep working, keep working.' The man on the next strip was alone; he pulled on his saw all by himself. After a while he made a fire. Art says, 'Aha, he's not gonna cut any wood. He's gonna sit by the fire all day.' And that's what happened. We cut two cords of wood and went home, and he was still sitting there by the fire.

"Pine. Beautiful pine. Flagpole jack pine. The waste of wood! For years and years men were cutting that wood to feed the boilers.

"We were paid three dollars a cord. I guess I never really knew what money was in those days. I just cut wood and ate and slept. We gave Dad most of the money we earned and he used it to help pay for his first car – a 1929 Chevrolet.

"But the cheques were made out to me and I felt pretty pleased when I was fourteen and drove down to Smithers to cash my cheque. The officer at the police station wasn't going to give me a driver's licence. But another police officer said, 'C'mon kid, let's see what you can do.' So he tried me out, up and down the main street, backing up, left turn, right turn. When we got back to the police station, he said, 'Give this kid a licence. He can drive better than me.'"

At the family gathering decades later when Verne told this story, he hooted with laughter, reliving the memory, enjoying his young bravado once more, and we laughed with him. Then it was time for a little music. He picked up the accordion, placed it on his knees and arranged the straps comfortably on his shoulders with big, broad hands that early on learned to do men's work. We would say now that those were children's hands, but the way he remembered child labour, it was fun. His fingers rippled over the keys as they found the opening rousing chords of "The Beer Barrel Polka."

Duthie Mine prospered, at least for a while. A 50-ton concentrator had been constructed, and other new machinery was installed. A two-compartment shaft one hundred feet deep had been put down. A ball mill from Sheffield, England, with three-inch and four-inch balls, milled 5,500 tons of ore in the last five months of 1927. By the end of 1928 a whole new camp had been constructed, with an assay office and testing laboratory, a new bunkhouse, and an emergency first-aid room. A townsite had been cleared, and homes built for families. They would be sending their children to a new one-room school within hailing distance of where they lived and not in some old abandoned log cabin like the one where I started school.

All this development led to the doubling of share capital to finance more exploration and further development. One million new shares were issued to Atlas Exploration Company, which became the new owner with J.F. Duthie as president, head office in Vancouver. Alfred continued to be the mine foreman throughout these years. On average, the mine employed ninety-six men. I remember some of their names: C.F. Hoff, the mill superintendent; J.D. Boulding, assayer; Jack McEwan, office manager, A.G. Hattie, superintendent; and, of course, John "Happy" Turner, the manager who thought my mother's pickled herring was "mighty good junk." Among the miners and other workers I remember these names: John Frane, Bob Macken, Lars Dahl – and Dick Cusack with his handsome handlebar moustache. Gunnar Braaten, who became a particularly close family friend, was another.

But 1929 was the year of The Crash. The *Annual Report of Mines* for 1930 noted the fate of the Duthie in a single sentence: "Owing to depressed metal-market conditions, operations were suspended entirely by Duthie Mines in March." What these neutral words meant was wrenching upheaval in the lives of the miners and their families, who packed their belongings and left the community they had built.

Alfred found work at the Planet Mine, further south and on the other side of the Coast Range, near Kamloops at the junction of the North and South Thompson rivers. It was one of those hopeful mining ventures that never did develop beyond the first eager tunnels and drifts, and would soon be closed down. In 1930, though, it seemed to be a promising mine, and Alfred was willing to be the foreman in charge of its handful of workers. The mine had a bunkhouse for the men, with no accommodation for families, but was conveniently located only nineteen or twenty miles south of Kamloops on the south shore of Stump Lake. Ingeborg and we children would live in Kamloops, and Alfred would stay at the mine. He would drive home frequently along the Stump Lake Road.

Once again Ingeborg started packing the wedding silver – the cake stand with its two little cookie baskets suspended from it, the silver and enamel coffee tray decorated with a design of pink fuchsias, the sugar bowl and cream jug wrought with a wreath of flowers. Alfred arranged for a company truck to have the china cabinet crated and with other furniture, boxes, and barrels delivered to Smithers, where it was sent in some miraculous way to our new home. One day in May 1930 we all piled into the Chev and set out for Kamloops, a journey of nearly six hundred miles that would take several days. Our route went beyond the Skeena and Bulkley valleys to Prince George, then south along the Fraser River through Quesnel, Soda Creek, and Williams Lake, where the road took a turn to avoid the sudden deep canyons and cliffs of the Fraser. Eventually we found our way through more friendly terrain to 100 Mile House, 70 Mile House, Clinton, Cache Creek, and finally east and on into Cariboo cattle country, then into the dry brown sagebrush hills of the Thompson River. We had travelled from the Coast and the Skeena through the Coast Range and into the Interior, as it was called.

I have one distinct memory of that trip. We were going to picnic along the way, and my mother had cooked a ham. When she unpacked the ham at our first lunch stop she found maggots on one part of it. She quietly cut that bit away, and whispered to me, "Don't tell Papa." I never did. I was her little co-conspirator.

In Kamloops we settled into a rented two-storey house. Arthur, at age seventeen, left school to work as a shepherd for a few months and then joined his father at the mine. After a few months the mine owner didn't pay them their wages, and the family had to live precariously on savings. The only income was from a paper route that Edwin had. In Kamloops we did not send away to Eaton's and state size and colour. The house was big and bare, even with the china cabinet and the dining-room tables and chairs that had come by freight train and truck. That winter my mother took me to see a doctor. It was whooping cough. I escaped scarlet fever, however, which was also going around: many houses had quarantine signs hanging from the doorknob. Kamloops was not, in memory, a happy place.

One afternoon my mother and father are standing in the living room facing one another, and I am there too. She is telling him that she is pregnant. She doesn't know that I understand what she's saying. I'm looking at my father's face. I think he looks angry. My mother reaches out and holds me to her.

But he wasn't angry. I know that now. What he was feeling was utter dismay and helplessness at the turn of events: the mine closing and everything they'd built up at the Duthie lost, the family uprooted again, a job that didn't even pay wages, and now this, another child.

What did Ingeborg and Alfred know about contraceptives? The dissemination of information about birth control was made illegal in Canada under the Criminal Code of 1892. That law forbade, as "an indictable offence," the manufacture and sale of "obscene matter," in books, magazines, pictures, and "any indecent show," such as, presumably, girlie acts on the vaudeville stage. Included among these obscenities was "any medicine, drug or article intended or represented as a means of preventing conception or causing abortion." Violation of the law was punishable by two years in prison, unless the defendant could prove to have done it for "the public good," but "the motives of the seller, publisher or exhibitor shall be in all cases irrelevant."

The Comstock Act (1872) in the United States was equally punitive, but it did not deter feminist Margaret Sanger. She kept right on reprinting and disseminating *Family Limitation*, her little pamphlet of practical advice on contraception. Eventually, however, Sanger fled to England to escape imprisonment on charges of corrupting public morals. The birth control movement throughout the Western world was similarly defiant, for these were the decades early in the nineteenth century of the New Woman demanding the right to vote, to be a person in her own right. Supported and encouraged by new philosophical inquiry into the nature of human sexuality, in Canada as in Britain, Scandinavia, and Germany this New Woman was refusing to be the Angel in the House, confined to domestic duties, which included the sexual needs and pleasures of her husband, without much regard for her own. It was her duty also to bear his children, to reproduce and multiply. Unfortunately, she could not fulfil this duty and remain altogether morally immaculate, for if she herself were sexually aroused, her very nature would be changed and, in the view of some prominent medical men of the time, would even become that of a monster. A woman could only be redeemed if she conceived and bore a child: hence the laws forbidding the dissemination of information about birth control, and "dissemination" becomes a word pregnant with meaning.

In British Columbia, an ocean and a continent away from this ferment of ideas, a little group of socialists was actively advocating birth control, led by Vancouver school teacher, poet, and journalist Alexander Maitland Stephen. He believed sex education should be part of the school curriculum, that sexual intercourse was not immoral and should not be so reviled. The enemies of the birth control movement were, he said, "ignorance and inertia of those ... still living in the dark ages of medieval priestcraft and superstition." In 1923, under Stephen's leadership, the Birth Control League of Canada was formed, the first such organization in this country. It was a branch of Margaret Sanger's American Birth Control League. When Sanger visited Vancouver that same year and gave a public address, she told her audience, "We have kept sex in the gutter too long, causing widespread ignorance and fear of discussing it. Instead, sex should be sacred and beautiful."

"*Allas! allas! that evere love was synne!*" exclaimed the Wife of Bath, telling her companions about her fifth husband. It was "sin" before and after the poet Chaucer's time in the fourteenth century, and even in twentieth-century Canada. However, the Wife of Bath went on to say, "*I folwed ay myn inclinacioun.*" And, literary exemplars aside, that is just what women did. For centuries they had been trying on their own to prevent unwanted pregnancies. Bearing a child may be "natural," but it is also dangerous, and women were, and still are, very much aware that they could die in the labour of giving birth.

In the days not too long ago, before the pill and condom were legally and readily available at the pharmacy counter, before pamphlets and books were available to inform them, women resorted to their own folk pharmacy of contraceptive measures, collected through the maternal generations and passed on, mother to daughter, friend to friend. The most obvious method was to block the passageway into the uterus with a plug of some kind, like a ball of cotton. A peasant, or perhaps a fourteenth-century cloth merchant like the Wife of Bath, might soak the ball in some herbal solution; in later centuries a woman might soak a sponge in an antiseptic solution containing carbolic acid with some lubricating glycerine, or she could insert a suppository of cocoa butter that would melt pleasantly during intercourse but would not, alas, kill the sperm.

Quinine was said to be good too – five or ten grains dissolved in a hot drink, especially if you took a laxative like castor oil a few days before your period. A cold-water douche immediately following intercourse might or might not be effective, and was commonly advised and used. You could add table salt for more protection, or a little potassium permanganate, or perhaps vinegar, preferably cider. Or Lysol – one teaspoon in two quarts of cold water. You had to put your faith in something. But it required self-discipline to get out of a warm bed and douche your loving body with cold water, and who would want to sleep with a woman smelling of Lysol? As for "coitus interruptus," that method required not just great self-discipline on the part of the man but also a woman's complete trust. Moreover, withdrawing just at the right moment and not a moment too late was thought to be harmful to a man's health.

Collecting the semen directly from the penis in a little rubber sheath was obviously the most practical and efficient way of preventing its passage into the vagina, but the condom was only available where the druggist was willing to ignore the law and sell under the counter contraband. Buying a package of condoms was a purchase that was made quite discreetly, and no respectable woman would ever be seen or heard doing such a thing.

Many couples simply relied on the guesswork of the rhythm method, which depended on a woman's supposed monthly "safe period." It was also quite mistakenly believed that a woman would be safe if she were nursing or if she lay on her left side. If she had the money, and if she could find someone who knew someone, she might even arrange to have a backroom abortion. Otherwise, she might try for a miscarriage by jumping off a table or taking very hot baths. So desperate might a woman feel in the knowledge of an unwanted pregnancy and of its ultimate strenuous and fearful delivery, that she might even try to abort herself by untwisting a coat hanger and thus providing herself with a sharp instrument.

"Delivery" is a clinical term in obstetrics. I've used the wrong word. It is the physician or midwife, in the capacity of the professional helper, the woman's co-worker, who is said, quite appropriately, to deliver a baby. But for others to suggest that a mother delivers, as one would a parcel or a service, is a cold way of honouring the labour of a woman who is straining to release the child she has harboured in her womb for nine months: a new life, a gift to the world. "Bear down," they are urging her. And she does bear down and she bears a child. A little child is born.

It seems incomprehensible that a woman should have been required to perform this miracle over and over again; to bear, to bring forth, in sickness as well as in health, for richer, for poorer; denied information about how not to bring forth if she so wishes; and that in many countries, including Canada, such a ban should have been at one time the law of the land.

But so it was for my mother, Ingeborg Nelson. Between 1920 and 1930 Ingeborg and Alfred had moved the family five times, from one mine to another, because of "metal market conditions" and corporate financial manoeuvres. Moving is hard physical work and emotionally exhausting too, and often during these times Ingeborg was carrying a baby, either in her arms or in her womb. Sometimes she had to manage the move by herself, with Alfred going on ahead to find a place to live or to start work in his new job. By 1931 she was worn out and in no condition to have another child.

Who can know the turmoil in her mind those last weeks of her nine months when she no longer felt the child moving, kicking in her womb? And knew that her child had died. And entered Royal Inland Hospital in this knowledge. Fortunately, Alfred was able to be in Kamloops when, eleven days later, on January 28, 1931, the baby, a boy, was born – though Alfred could not be with her during labour, for in those days family members were not allowed to be in the delivery room with the mother. In those days, after the birth mothers were treated as invalids and at first kept lying down and later only permitted to sit up before finally being allowed to get out of bed. Alfred could not be with her during that time. He had to go back to work at the Planet Mine.

Mama finally came home from the hospital in a taxi and lay down on the sofa in the living room. Our good friend Anna Braaten was there to look after her. Mama asked for some water with baking soda, thinking the pain in her chest was heartburn. Freddy and I were there, watching, listening, from across the living room. I heard her call "Verner." Then there was a rush, and somebody called the doctor, called Papa at the mine. Freddy and I were shooed into the kitchen.

A few minutes later, Ingeborg, our mother, died: February 8, 1931, at 10:30 a.m. The pain in her chest was not heartburn; it was a heart attack caused by a blood clot, an embolism. "Milk leg," it was called, because it sometimes occurred after childbirth. She had been in the hospital for twenty-one days, most of the time in bed, a regimen that might very well have contributed to the formation of the blood clot.

With her death my mother qualifies as an example of maternal mortality as defined by the World Health Organization: "death while pregnant or within 42 days of the termination of pregnancy, irrespective of cause." She also claims a place in Canadian statistics: in 1931 in British Columbia the ratio of deaths to live births was 6.3 per 1,000, the second-highest rate in Canada (5 per 1,000). The B.C. government did not have this information when in 1929 it appointed its Royal Commission on State Health Insurance and Maternity Benefits. However, the inquiry did find substantial evidence that too many women were dying because they had not received any pre-natal care. The families simply could not afford to pay a doctor with money they needed for food and rent; moreover, the fee for having a baby in hospital was $25, or more if there were complications. The Commission's *Final Report* recommended for the province a system of compulsory health insurance that, in addition to its basic provisions, especially addressed this need. Women would receive maternity insurance for childbirth. "But," the report observes rather touchingly, "the mother should, in addition, be placed in possession of a little extra cash the better to provide the comforts of life, which everyone will admit to be most desirable at this critical stage."

The provincial Liberal government in the hard economic times of the Great Depression was not willing to undertake so bold a financial adventure as compulsory health insurance. Universal Medicare for all the provinces would have to wait for legislation under the Canada Health Act of 1957. But it is comforting to know that the men who drew up this report, so compassionate in intent, had a special regard for women in childbirth, women like my mother.

At the funeral service the coffin was open and I knew Mama was in it, there at the front of the church. When the minister had finished speaking, he signalled Papa that the family could now come forward to "view" the body. And so we approached, each in turn to stand there for a moment. But I was wise: I didn't look. I closed my eyes and turned my head before I opened them again. I couldn't bear the thought of her lying there in that box.

I've always been glad I didn't look at her then, because I would have carried that image with me for the rest of my life. Instead I see other images, feel impressions, hear echoes from a happier time when we lived at the Duthie in a real house with a sink and hot and cold running water and a living room with our china cabinet and oak table and chairs. In memory, Mama fills this space, and it is suffused with warmth and with the bustle of a woman in the kitchen and a small girl helping, feeling important and pleased to be a part of the bustle, part of the triumph of the next meal, Mama finally overcoming the fire that wouldn't burn, the kettle that wouldn't boil. I see miners sitting around the kitchen table getting instructions from Papa for the next day's stopes and drifts and shafts. There is a smell of sweat and wet carbide and a little stir of activity as he boils a kettle to make hot rum. I hear the noisy traffic of my older brothers running in and out, but on tiptoe when the bread is rising in the warming oven. I feel the excitement of opening the mail-order parcel from Eaton's, coming all the way from Winnipeg with my new winter coat.

I see the china cabinet, for it was always there, having arrived with the silverware and china cups and saucers carefully packed in those big round stout barrels so deep I would have to stand on a chair to reach very far into them. The round oak table, I see that too, spread with a white cloth, and the pretty china cups and saucers and knives and forks and spoons with that fancy letter "N" on each handle. In the middle of the table on the silver cake stand there is a lovely cake deliciously covered with whipped cream and decorated with slivered almonds and bits of fruit. There are *pepparkakor* and *spritsar* in the two little silver baskets hanging underneath the cake and I am allowed to take one cookie from each basket while I'm helping set the table. There are plates of open-face sandwiches: cheese, herring, and anchovy-with-a-slice-of-hard-boiled-egg-on-top.

I see visitors arriving in a gust of talk and laughter, leaning over me, exclaiming, their lilting voices filling the room with that other language that I do not understand but which is like a familiar melody. Mama is in the middle of it all, vaguely in my mind's eye, always there, the same slim woman with dark hair and a face remembered from photographs who says those comforting words, "*Stakkars lille venn, det er riktig synd på deg*" – poor little friend, that's really too bad. And drifting around this Mama there is the soft aroma of fresh-baked bread and the rich fragrance of coffee, all mingled with little whiffs of O'Cedar Furniture Oil.

Papa gave me her golden wedding ring set with three opals.

Miss Nixon, my Grade 4 teacher, wanting to check what she'd heard, wanting to reach out in some way, asked me kindly, "How is your mother?" I didn't know what to say. I said, "Fine."

Alfred bore the guilt of Ingeborg's death all his life. When I visited him in hospital during his last days and told him I was going to be married, his first thought was for my safety, and he did not offer me words of fatherly approval until he had talked to me about how not to become pregnant. That was in 1948, when the birth control movement had become respectable, even though contraceptives and dissemination of information about them were still illegal and would remain so until 1969. He didn't use the word "contraceptive." He probably didn't know the word. He didn't know that doctors were quietly fitting women for diaphragms, if indeed he knew about them at all. He didn't know that I would be receiving a diaphragm and condoms in plain brown envelopes from A.R. Kaufman's Parents' Information Bureau in Kitchener, Ontario, as did all my friends. With that flair for finding ingenious solutions that was so characteristic of him, he explained how I could take a rubber ball and cut it in half . . .

Many years later, when I met my Aunt Kristine in Norway, she told me about the day she heard the news. Her brother, my Uncle Johannes, was walking up the hill. He had a letter in his hand. He said, *"Ingeborg er död."* When Aunt Kristine repeated those words to me, tears came to her eyes and to mine, and we wept, no longer strangers. We grieved for Ingeborg, who had left her family in Norway and worked so hard to make a new life in Canada. She had promised Inga that she would send for her soon. But soon never came.

Tante Kristine didn't tell me Inga's life history. We didn't have enough time together, and the wonder of our meeting was enough then. But I have since visited Inga's children and they have told me how Inga's life unfolded after her mother waved goodbye to her on that July morning in 1911. Inga grew up in Viggja with no memories of her mother, who was replaced by grandparents, uncles, and aunts in a close-knit family. She was, after all, only three years old when Ingeborg left. All the memory and hope and longing were with her mother across the ocean, on the west coast of Canada. When Inga grew up and left home she worked as a waitress in a restaurant in Trondhjem. In 1926, when she was eighteen, she married a young man who was also an orphan, though not through death or emigration. The parents of Otto Reidar Lunder had in their separate ways simply abandoned him, and he grew up in foster homes. He had to fend for himself at an early age, a young boy alone and penniless, but resourceful and enterprising. He probably met Inga when he was working as a farm labourer near Viggja.

At that point, for my mother, there could be no more talk of "soon." Ingeborg, living in a tent in a mountain mining camp in British Columbia, now knew that her Norwegian daughter would never be joining her Canadian family. Inga was beginning her own family in Norway. By 1930 Inga and Otto Reidar had three children: Thora, Odd, and Rolf. They were settled in a middle-class residential area of Trondhjem. The children's grandmother in Canada would have been like a storybook character, enriching family history.

An overwhelming tragedy soon struck this little family. The second child, Odd, born in 1928, died in infancy, not yet two years old, scalded by an upset pan of boiling water. More than that I do not know, nor can I find words to express their grief and sorrow or the agonizing guilt that Inga must have felt over this terrible accident. She was pregnant at the time with her Rolf, born a few weeks later in October 1930.

Another great misfortune occurred. Inga had a heart malfunction, which was complicated by asthma. She was often in pain, had trouble with her breathing, and from time to time had to go to the hospital. Her son Rolf remembered the time the ambulance came and he ran and hid under the table. But Inga was a practical, strong-minded person, like her mother. Because of her asthma, she wanted very much to have a vacuum cleaner to keep the house as dust-free as possible. To earn money to buy one, she knit *lusekofter* (sweaters with the traditional Norwegian patterns) for a shop. Gradually she had to spend more and more time in bed. Her family, and especially her husband Otto, provided strong support. Ingeborg Lunder, Rolf's wife, remembered Otto fondly. He was "a wonderful man" and "a good, kind husband."

Hard times came to Norway now: the Depression of the 1930s brought mass unemployment and hardship, as it did throughout the Western world. It was Inga and Otto Reidar's further misfortune, as it was for her brothers in Canada, to be young in that decade, to be denied education and opportunity just at the time when they were beginning to make their way in life and ready to offer gifts of body, mind, and intellect to community and country. In Trondheim, Otto Reidar was the neighbourhood milkman. Since he delivered milk in the morning, he was free to take another job for the afternoon and evenings as a salesman selling books door-to-door for a publishing company. Otto and Inga were both hard-working and thrifty, and soon they even managed to build their own house. But three years later, in 1938, the factory that had loaned them money for building materials went bankrupt. Inga and Otto could not repay the loan and had to sell the house.

Then came the war. July 1943: bombs fell in Trondheim, one right next to the house they were living in. They all escaped being killed. Young Rolf was playing with a friend next door, fortunately in the basement room, so he was unharmed. Inga, in her own kitchen, was making blood pudding for dinner. The blast shattered the windows, but she too escaped injury. And Otto? He crawled under the milk truck he was driving and lay there, watching the bombs fall.

For Inga and Otto Reidar, life was difficult, but there were happy times. Inga was musical: in younger days she played the guitar and was a member of a dance band. Otto attended automobile races, bringing little Rolf with him. They enjoyed being parents. Inga made decorations for the Christmas tree and Otto dressed up as Santa. Because of his job selling books, there were always books in the house, and as soon as the war was over, Otto went right out and bought an encyclopedia.

Rolf remembered that his mother read a book by Helge Ingstad. It was about the fur trade in Canada.

"The archaeologist? The one who discovered the remains of Leif Ericsson's habitations in Newfoundland?"

"Yes, he's the one."

"Did your mother read to you?"

"Oh yes." And I still have a book she gave me: *Gulliver's Reisen.*"

"*Gulliver's Travels*? Lilliput?"

"Yes, yes!"

A strange thing was happening to me in this conversation. For the first time I felt connected to Inga, and all because of an eighteenth-century British writer, Jonathan Swift. She was no longer just a shadow, but a person I could have talked to, about our children and household cares, about *Gulliver's Travels*, or even about Helge Ingstad. I could have told her about her mother; she could have told me about Grandma and Grandpa Aarvik. Inga had, indeed, become my sister. My deep regret is that we never met, our families having for so long been out of touch. She died in 1957 when she was only forty-nine years old. Otto Reidar lived on into old age, a much-loved father and grandfather, still reading books.

Delina Noel with the first gold brick, Lorne Mine, 1916.
(*Courtesy Lewis Green*)

SEVEN

GOLD DUST, HOMEBREW, AND CLASS STRUGGLE

In the summer of 1931 our family moved west from Kamloops to the Bridge River Country. It was the time of the Great Depression, but our father was an experienced miner and was able to get a job at the Pioneer Gold Mine, west of the Fraser River and not far from Bralorne, on Cadwallader Creek at the foot of Sunshine Mountain. It was about 120 miles due north of Vancouver. It wasn't just luck that got my father a job at Pioneer. Alfred Nels Nelson was not your ordinary Swede mucker. After all, he was a hard-rock miner who had timbered dangerous, squeezing shafts in Mullan, Idaho, and run the operation at the Duthie Mine near Smithers. Mine managers knew he was a reliable man.

But we weren't really a family anymore, not without Ingeborg, our mother. It was only four months since Mama had died. Alfred was now a single parent bringing up three young adults ("teenagers" didn't exist until after the war) and two small children, and he was fifty-five years old. I was almost nine, Freddy was only five, and we would have cried if we even could have understood that we could never again run to our mother for help when we were hurt or unhappy; that we'd never more feel her arms around us and hear those comforting words, "*Stakkars lille venn, det er riktig synd på deg.*"

At first another family lived with us. Anna and Gunnar Braaten and their little girl Rachel were Norwegian, like my mother. We knew them from the Duthie Mine, which after closing down had scattered workers here and there to look hopelessly for jobs. They had moved in with us in Kamloops after our mother died, and Anna became our housekeeper and surrogate mother. Their daughter Rachel became playmate and sister for me.

The Braatens had emigrated from Norway in 1927, part of a mass migration of Scandinavians answering the call of the Canadian Pacific Railway for settlers to come to Canada and take up land on the Prairies. They were from Rjukan, a small industrial town, site of a large hydro development in the mountains of southern Norway. Gunnar was an unemployed factory worker with no plans to become a farmer but anxious to leave hard times in Norway. He soon found his way to the gold fields of the Bridge River Valley. Father, mother, and daughter were all three typically blond and blue-eyed. Gunnar was amiable and fun-loving; Anna plump, energetic, and bossy. At the Duthie Mine my father was Gunnar's shift boss, and my lively and congenial mother, fifteen years Canadian and a tough veteran of mining-camp life, made the mountain wilderness a little more *koselig* for Anna with coffee and *lefse* and homesick talk about *gamle Norge* (old Norway). Gunnar, however, wasn't homesick. He loved the wilderness, loved to fish and hunt. At some point the family changed their name, anglicizing it to "Brothen."

When Alfred got the job at Pioneer Mine he put in a word for Gunnar Brothen, and Gunnar was hired as well. Thus it was that the two families left Kamloops and the Depression and moved to Pioneer Mine, where there was gold and work and wages.

To get to Pioneer Mine from Kamloops by road meant negotiating more than three hundred rough and tortuous miles, for this was in the years before the interior of British Columbia was connected to the Lower Mainland by a system of paved highways. For this journey up the Fraser Canyon highway, then a narrow, winding road, and into the Coast Range mountains, we had our '29 Chevrolet, but the car didn't have enough room for both families – for the six of us and three of them. It was decided that Art, Verne, and Gunnar would have to get to Pioneer on their own. Ed, who at thirteen was still thin and gangly, was squeezed into the Chev with Freddy and me and the others.

Art and Verne would always vividly remember that journey from Kamloops to the Bridge River Country. With all of ten dollars between them for the trip, the two boys and Gunnar decided to hop a freight train – to "ride the rods" as far as Lytton at the junction of the Fraser and Thompson rivers. Then they would have to strike out on foot – if they were lucky, maybe hitchhike – the seventy or eighty miles to Lillooet, and from there somehow make their way further west into the mountains to reach their destination. They went down to the Kamloops railroad yards, and while they were trying to figure out where to climb onto a freight car without being nabbed by the "railroad bulls," a brakeman hollered at them, "You fellas, there's an empty fruit car down there, go ahead, hop on." They ran down the track, climbed in, and sat with their feet hanging out all the way along the Thompson River to Lytton. This was and still is dry desert country, recorded as one of the hottest places in Canada. Hot and thirsty, they set off on foot for Lillooet. There was only a rough dirt road connecting Lytton and Lillooet, built for wagons, not automobiles. They didn't have a tent, so they slept that night under a big tarpaulin where a road gang had been working. In the morning the road foreman appeared. "You boys know there's a nest of rattlesnakes under that tarpaulin?"

They bought a couple of cans of sardines and a loaf of bread and started walking again. After they had gone a few miles a rickety old car came along and the driver offered them a ride – for seven dollars. That was just about all they had left of their ten dollars after buying the sardines and bread. "Yesus, Yesus," moaned Gunnar, who, as locum parentis, was handling the money. But he handed over the seven dollars. The driver left them at Seton Lake, and again they slept out in the open overnight. Next morning, Art said, "Verne, you gotta shave." He was Verner's big brother, his mentor, and it was incumbent on him to induct his younger brother into this adult ritual. He gave Verne his razor and Verne took one of the empty sardine cans and shined the bottom of it with his shirt tail and used it for a mirror, while Art stood by, supervising the First Shave.

They set off along the railroad track to walk the eighteen miles to Shalalth at the other end of Seton Lake. A locomotive "gas car" came along, headed that way, and the engineer yelled, "Hey, you guys, get up on the coal tender." Feeling lucky once more, they reached Shalalth in no time. But now

Mission Mountain, over five thousand feet at the Pass, loomed over them, and Pioneer Gold Mine, with its jobs and paycheques, lay sixty miles farther into the mountains. More luck: a big Swede from Pioneer drove into Shalalth in his old Packard touring car and gave them a lift up over Mission Mountain to Gold Bridge, then six miles up a mountainside to Bralorne Mine and from there on to their destination, Pioneer Mine. They didn't know that it was situated at the foot of Sunshine Mountain. It was enough to know there was gold here, and that there would be jobs and money.

Pioneer Mine started out as just a camp with a mill on Cadwallader Creek, with a bunkhouse and cookhouse nearby. In the 1930s it became a thriving little town – a mining town fashioned by the company.

The Pioneer claim on Cadwallader Creek was first staked in 1897, and although a mill had been built towards the end of World War I and the first gold brick poured in 1922, the mine didn't really begin steady production until mining engineer David Sloan took it over in 1924. In 1928, with Colonel Victor Spencer, Sloan incorporated a new company, and with renewed capital Pioneer Mines Limited began producing gold bricks in earnest. In 1932 a new mill was built with a capacity of 400 tons a day. Shafts were sunk deeper and deeper: by the end of 1933 No. 2 shaft was down to 2,300 feet below surface, with plans to reach 3,100 feet. Rich veins of high-grade ore were discovered, one of the most promising at 1,700 feet, the fourteenth level. It was two and a half to three feet wide – white quartz with thin bands of gold running through it and averaging seven ounces of gold per ton. In a few places thick bands of gold appeared, and here the quartz was actually 50 per cent gold, an extraordinary yield. This was not your arsenopyrite ore, which had to be put through a cyanide process to release the gold. This was "free gold," quite large flakes in the quartz that could be released when amalagamated with mercury. Discoveries like this soon made Pioneer the leading gold producer in British Columbia. The price of gold in 1932 was $28.34 an ounce.

This high-grade drift was locked in a vault behind a steel door, and several handpicked men were bonded and put to work there. My father, highly valued for his experience, was one of them. They blasted out, but ever so carefully with low-charge dynamite, the precious ore, which fell on a tarpaulin spread on the ground. Then they sorted the pile, gathering up the gold-bearing rocks in wooden dynamite boxes. They loaded the boxes onto ore cars, pushed the cars into the cage, and stayed with those boxes all the way to the surface, where they moved the boxes to the vault and deposited them there. In those days my father was filling that vault with gold.

This cache of free gold ore was used to enrich the regular ore when its value fell. By adding a few boxes of free gold from the vault to the regular ore, the company could increase its production figures. The free gold could also be processed by itself, by amalgamation with mercury instead of being put through the cyanide-flotation process. Mercury or cyanide, the end result was a gold brick, smelted and poured in the refinery beside Cadwallader Creek and mailed to the Mint in Ottawa.

My brother Art helped out in this process. "They might decide to put four dynamite boxes of free gold ore from the vault in with the regular ore," Art explained years later. His regular job at Pioneer was in the sawmill, and the superintendent there, Harry Cain, an American, was a "tough old guy," Art said. "He'd order me to the mill where the crushers were. And he'd put the small chunks of this high-grade ore into the sample crusher. I sat on a chair opposite him with a box on my lap to catch the ground-up ore as it came down the little chute. And some of the dust from the ore fell on my shirt so I was covered with it. And after he'd put through a boxful of ore, he'd say, 'Now, boy, sit still, boy, sit still, don't move boy.' And he'd come with a whisk and he'd whisk my shoulders and the front of my shirt so the dust went into the box. Lots of gold in that dust. And if he had four boxes to put through, he'd whisk my shirt four times." That's how my brother got gold dust on his shirt.

When the gold standard was abandoned in 1931, the price of gold began to rise steadily, and every gold brick in the vault at Pioneer became more valuable for shareholders. In 1933, with gold at $30.39 an ounce, dividends tripled: $735,735 compared with $210,210 in 1932 when gold was still at $28.34.

Pioneer Mines Limited became news on the New York Stock Exchange, and this was in good part owing to the influence of "Sell 'em Ben" Smith, a Wall Street speculator who had adopted selling short as his financial strategy. Smith gained a certain notoriety for contributing to the uneasy bear market of 1930 and 1931. He owned a significant block of shares in Pioneer Mines, and with David Sloan and Colonel Victor Spencer completed a financial mining triumvirate. Under Smith's influence, Pioneer shares traded briskly and the price more than doubled to over $10 in 1934. In that year, on the initiative of President Franklin Roosevelt, the price of gold was fixed at $35 U.S. an ounce, where it was pegged for some years. In 1935 Pioneer Mine dividends totalled $1,401,400.

My father knew that in working at Pioneer he had struck it rich. Economic depression gripped the rest of the world, but in the mountains of the Bridge River Valley in the southwestern part east of the Coast Range, gold-mining camps enjoyed good times. Even though miners struggled with the high cost of living and were often in debt to the company store, they could always put food on the table for their families. Only on the outskirts of the camp was there a reminder of hard times. There unemployed men camped in rude shelters, hoping for the next available job. They existed on handouts from the cookhouse brought to them by the good-hearted mine foreman, Bob Eklof.

At Pioneer, though the company provided bunkhouses for single men it had only just started building houses for married men. It had scarcely any accommodation for families, and during our first winter there we lived in a cabin down the road from Pioneer at Coronation, an abandoned mine that had not fulfilled the promise of its name. Coronation Consolidated Mining Company had briefly developed the Bend 'Or and Countless workings in 1926, only to quit operations the following year. In 1931 the Coronation cabins were still in good condition and quite habitable. Once they were swept out and aired and the stoves stoked with logs of dry jack pine, sticky with pitch so that you could hear the crackling of flames, that abandoned-cabin-smell of pack rats and damp mattresses disappeared.

My three older brothers slept in a bunkhouse down by the creek. The rest of us – our father, four-year-old Freddy and me and Gunnar and Anna and their nine-year-old daughter Rachel – were distributed somehow in the Big Cabin. When I try to recall what it was like inside, as if I were Balzac or Dickens minutely describing each piece of furniture, I find myself thinking instead of the aroma of coffee and cinnamon buns and simmering stews with meat and onions and the sound of a great deal of coming and going and talking and the rush of sudden little gusts of activity. In fact, the cabin was a rough and makeshift dwelling place, and yet in memory, that Norwegian word comes to mind: *koselig*, which doesn't just mean cozy, but cheerful and friendly and comfortable too. With Rachel as playmate and sister, Freddy and I were less lonely for my mother, and I think my father and older brothers must have felt that they were beginning to make a new life without her.

That cabin provided a temporary shelter for us all – seven children and three adults. During that long winter at Coronation, when the washing froze on the line and the men's long underwear and woollen socks hung on clothes lines in the kitchen to finish drying; when the boots and overshoes piled near the door left puddles of melted snow on the floor; when the older boys fought and shouted, and the three little children always seemed to be underfoot and were told to go outside and get out of the way, then tempers flared. Alfred, his blue eyes fierce and angry, threatened the brothers with the strop. Anna banged pots on the stove, while Gunnar looked on distracted and moaned, "Yesus, Yesus."

Not surprisingly, since my father was a miner, I learned about bosses and workers, them and us, early on. Just the same it only recently occurred to me that our family at Pioneer Mine was daily engaged in the Class Struggle. I made the connection when I happened to think of my father's homebrew. An image flashed through my mind of our housekeeper, Anna Brothen, emptying bottles of beer down the kitchen sink. She's a stout woman, comfortably broad in breast and beam, but to me, a skinny little eight-year-old, she seems huge, a veritable giantess. My father is standing nearby, laughing helplessly. Gunnar, her husband, merely looks unhappy and puzzled. They're not angry, or even intimidated. She's the one who is angry.

The men are finally working and the boys, too, are earning wages again, but if the company finds out that any of its workers are making homebrew they'll be fired. She has heard this rumour at the company store and she's not taking any chances. She's getting rid of the beer. All this in singsong Norwegian, her blue eyes flashing, her yellow hair tossing about her face in an electric storm with each bottle she holds over the sink. Neither Gunnar nor my father made a fuss because they figured maybe there was some truth to this rumour. They'd heard that anyone ordering groceries from Vancouver could be sent down the road – fired. The company had built a general store and expected employees to patronize it: there was such a thing as loyalty. The company made the rules, so it was best to play it safe.

I remember that first Christmas at Coronation. In the kitchen right near the entrance the presents were piled high on the big steamer trunk, always a familiar and useful piece of furniture in immigrant homes. Such wealth and bounty after our sad, despairing time in Kamloops! And how cheerful and bright the little candle flames that made the Christmas Tree a warm and living presence.

We'd have felt richer still if we had known the history of the place where we were now finding some measure of hope and contentment. None of our family knew that Coronation had been thus renamed with buoyant optimism in 1910 when King George V was crowned, and that it had a long history of development under different owners. We even called it, in all innocence, "Carnation," after the brand of canned evaporated milk that we used. We didn't know that this abandoned mine site where our family had found emergency shelter had been originally developed around 1900 by one Arthur Noel with his young wife as working partner, and that they had named it the Bend 'Or. They might even have slept in this very cabin, eaten breakfast here, and then gone off to their "diggings" together.

Delina L'Italien and Arthur Noel were married on Christmas Eve 1899, in the Sacred Heart Church in Kamloops. He was from Wisconsin, a prospector and miner, thirty-one years old; she was nineteen, from a convent school in the region of Kamouraska, Quebec, though born in Lillooet. This marriage became more passionate as the years went by: the passion then was for gold, and the gold they sought was in the Bridge River Valley on Cadwallader Creek.

Around 1894 Arthur Noel went north to look for gold in the country around Lillooet on the Fraser. His French-Canadian uncle, Fabian Larochelle from Joliette, Quebec, had arrived even earlier in 1858 from California to join the Fraser River gold rush and had been panning gold there for thirty years. Fabian's brother, Frank, was there too, and Arthur's brother Charles and his Wisconsin cousins, Louis Manderville and Joe Russell (Larochelle anglicized).

Delina's father was also French Canadian. He had taken another, longer route to the gold fields. Joseph L'Italien was from Ste.-Hélène de Kamouraska on the south shore of the St. Lawrence. His father Hyacinthe was a farmer descended from a family that came to Canada in the early eighteenth century. Joseph left Ste.-Hélène as a young man and joined the Overlanders, a group of people who in 1862 had set out from Ontario to travel across Canada on foot and by oxcart, raft, and canoe to reach the goldfields of the Cariboo. They encountered many dangers, and Joseph was among those who nearly met their death in the treacherous rapids of the Fraser. When they finally arrived, many were disappointed and left the goldfields to earn a living elsewhere. Joseph too abandoned his dreams of gold and took up land at Fountain, near Lillooet. When he was well established as a farmer, he went back to Ste.-Hélène, married Clara Castonguay on January 7, 1879, and brought her back with him to his farm at Fountain. Delina was born there, on June 17, 1880, and Louise in 1881.

Clara and the children went back home to Quebec for a few years while Joseph stayed behind. Delina and Louise went to the convent school at Rivière du Loup, not far from Ste.-Hélène. In 1896, when they returned to Joseph and the farm at Fountain, prospectors were panning for gold in Cayoosh Creek, which flows north into the Fraser River at Lillooet, and they were climbing the hills to search for the lode deposits that must be its source. They were also staking claims farther west in Bridge River Country and especially all along Cadwallader Creek. The Lillooet *Prospector* proclaimed the area "destined to become one of the greatest mining camps on the face of the earth ... a Klondike near home," and indeed three decades later Bralorne Mine and Pioneer Mine, located in the Cadwallader Range, did become the biggest gold producers in the province.

Arthur Noel was much more than a prospector. After he'd staked the valuable Golden Cache claims on Cayoosh Creek, he went on to manage the mine, for he had not only a keen nose for gold but also the instincts of an entrepreneur, and he wanted to see a promising claim actually become a producing mine. Moreover, he had the skills and knowledge to manage its day to day operation. After the Golden Cache, he was mine manager at the Bend 'Or on Cadwallader Creek. He had the contract to freight in the twenty-five-ton stamp mill coming all the way from a factory in Ontario, a task of heroic proportions, for at that time there were no roads into the Bridge River. Machinery and equipment had to be hauled in by pack horse, sled, and stone boat. It took four months to transport the stamp mill to the Bend 'Or. The *Prospector* reported this epic journey week by week, with Arthur as protagonist, a mover of machinery and of men.

It was he, in fact, who had founded the *Prospector* and hired an editor soon after he arrived in the area. Tall, rugged-looking, energetic, and full of ideas, Arthur Noel was always good copy: he had gone to California for a holiday; he was back in town with the first "cleanup" of gold from the Bend 'Or;

he had bought a house on Main Street in Lillooet; was building a stone wall behind his lawn and painting the fence; his sister Anna had come from Wisconsin to visit.

Delina was eighteen years old, and exchanged visits with Anna. Delina presumably stayed at Arthur's house.

For Delina and Arthur it was probably just your ordinary kind of love – at first. They'd only been married six months when Arthur took Delina and Louise along with him on a pack-train journey to the Bend 'Or, where he made frequent visits to look after the "cleanups" and bring out the gold bullion. This was the first time that Delina had seen a stamp mill, a machine used in those early days for crushing ore; the first time she'd seen free gold adhering to mercury-coated copper plates and molten gold being poured from an iron retort to make a gold brick. She knew about her father's long journey to the Cariboo gold fields. Now she was beginning her own adventures in the search for gold.

The Bend 'Or failed, and the mine closed down, but in 1909 Arthur Noel leased the property and restored operations, bringing out ore once again for the stamp mill. Delina was living at the mine with him, eager to explore and learn about the workings. The men didn't want to have her around the mine and threatened to quit. She, with her strict convent upbringing, would have been obedient to their wishes. But according to her own account, as related by her lifelong friend, geologist–mining engineer Franc Joubin, Arthur insisted that they accept her. He "openly declared that every one of them could quit if he liked; Mrs. Noel was to have every privilege accorded any man in inspecting the working face." Arthur was evidently a man far ahead of his time in his ideas about a woman's place. So Delina used to go down in the mine, "the men delighting to hoist her up on the stulls to examine the lead." She never actually worked as a miner, mucking and stoping, but she superintended the working of the stamp mill. On occasion she herself pushed ore cars along the tunnel track.

Arthur took her hunting with him, and she became an excellent shot. This was grizzly bear country, and she wanted to kill a grizzly. Joubin reported that on one trip they came upon the big one they'd been tracking for some time, and Arthur generously let her shoot instead of him. She got the grizzly in the lungs, and the bear rolled down a slide, where she found him fifty feet away. She fired, he rolled over, she rushed forward and fired again, but he stood up.

He could have attacked her. She and Arthur both fired and finally killed the 800-pound grizzly, one of the largest on record at that time. She also prepared the skin for mounting. It weighed seventy-eight pounds.

Learning from Arthur, Delina was now a prospector in her own right, buying and selling claims, making crafty deals, outwitting competitors. In 1916 Arthur contracted with Lorne Amalgamation to work its Lorne properties just down the Creek from the Bend 'Or. These were the claims that would eventually become Bralorne Mine. As at the Bend 'Or, Delina, though never actually mucking and drilling underground, was in every other way a full partner: she hired men, supervised them, and operated the stamp mill. On one occasion she directed the sinking of a shaft. "In 1909," Franc Joubin recalled, "she carried her own gold brick to the old assay office on Hastings Street in Vancouver, travelling to the coast by horse-drawn BX stage."

Arthur and Delina built a cabin at Lorne and hung the skin of the 800-pound grizzly on the wall. That was their home for the next ten years. An impressive fireplace in the cabin was Delina's idea. She wanted it to represent the rock formations of the Bridge River area. So she herself, with a worker hired to help her, explored the Cadwallader Creek area and chose the different kinds of rocks for the face of the fireplace. (Her helper became her good friend, later known to all as Big Bill Davidson, owner and developer of Minto Mine and the town of Minto.)

Then the war intervened. Lorne Amalgamated faltered and failed, but Arthur and Delina stayed on, doing all the work themselves.

Delina had seven miscarriages. Was her life simply too strenuous? She no less than Arthur had long been driven by the need to dig for gold, to keep the stamp mill pounding and grinding, with the hope of ever richer cleanups.

They finally did get a rich financial return when in 1926 the affairs of Lorne Amalgamated were settled and they were each awarded a one-eighth interest in the property. Their stubborn years working the Lorne paid off financially, but the marriage was over. Arthur had found solace in another woman and Delina divorced him in June 1930. He remarried, after first transferring 8,000 shares of Lorne Gold to Delina. Though no longer a miner, he continued to make mining deals. He was also twice judge for the Lillooet Stampede, which suggests that he was regarded with some respect and affection in the town. He had spent a lifetime working in the Bridge River Valley and helping to develop it.

Delina took an apartment in Vancouver's West End. In winter she led a sociable life playing bridge with her friends. In summer she drove back to Lorne in her Airflow Chrysler, returning to her cabin with the fireplace and grizzly hides on the walls. She kept on prospecting and in 1945 staked claims on Piebiter Creek, that wild, tangled country southeast of Pioneer Mine, where she began to search not for gold, but for tungsten and copper. Her Chalco property, accessible only by a rough trail from the mouth of the creek, was at an elevation of over 5,500 feet. She built a cabin and campsite and worked every summer towards the tungsten mine she knew was there. Surveyor H. Barry Cotton worked for her in the summers of 1951 and 1952. At seventy-one years, he remembered, she was still physically sturdy. When she needed to replenish supplies, she shouldered her Trapper Nelson and walked eight miles to Bralorne and back again on the same day. She seemed not to admit impossibilities. A tunnel through a rock slide to the rock face, and no machinery? Oscar, her seventy-nine-year-old Swede helper, could put one through – and he did, single-handedly in three days, using only hand tools. Cotton also noted what is sometimes forgotten about her: strong-willed and determined as she was, she was also a most charming person.

In 1958 Delina put away her pick and shovel and closed the door of her cabin at Piebiter Creek for a few days. She had been called to Victoria to receive a Centennial Medal from the B.C. government in recognition of her contribution to the mining industry. Arthur should have received a medal too, for he had spent a lifetime pioneering the mining of gold in the Bridge River Country – prospecting, staking claims, buying and selling them, trenching and tunnelling and blasting, hauling, crushing and milling the ore – and it was he who had taught his eager young wife to do these things too. But in his time, such efforts were not regarded as anything unusual in a province founded on the discovery of gold.

Delina did remember him. Arthur's second wife eventually left him, and he was alone in his last years. Who would be his pallbearers? The story is told, and I believe it's true, that Delina sought out six of his old prospector buddies. She bought them new suits and arranged for them to carry Arthur's coffin. She remembered what she and Arthur had shared, and she honoured it – their passion for gold and their years of heroic labour.

Delina died in Vancouver, on October 14, 1960, at the age of eighty. Only two years earlier she had still been working at Piebiter Creek. The B.C.

Centennial Medal did not serve to honour and protect the Lorne Mine cabin as a Heritage Site. It lay abandoned for over twenty years and was then sold and moved to Lillooet, where it was restored and became somebody's house. The mine at Bralorne apparently ran out of gold and shut down in 1971: Lillooet and the Bridge River Country have long ceased to be "a Klondike near home." Arthur and Delina Noel are still there, though, real in memory and living always in its history.

The cabin in Coronation is real in my memory too. That first Christmas afternoon, I went outside all by myself to try my new skis on the road that led to the cabin. It was a gentle slope and just right for me. The snow lay round about, deep and crisp and even, just like in the song we learned for the school Christmas concert. I stayed outside, skiing down the hill, and then up again for a long time. It began to grow dark, but I didn't want to go inside yet. A light appeared in the cabin window. Someone had lit a coal oil lamp. It began to snow, and the big, soft flakes came down and gently kissed my cheeks. And I was not afraid.

The cabin as home, Delina and Arthur's cabin as home – it's a comforting thought.

During that first long winter Alfred, who had laughed helplessly when Anna poured all the homebrew down the sink, was not laughing any more. He knew what he had to do. As soon as the snow melted in the spring, he would build his own house. There was lots of free land. You just had to cut down a few trees and clear a space. He chose a hilltop above the road that followed Cadwallader Creek upstream towards Pioneer Mine.

An abandoned wooden flume, fed by a dam, ran along the valley floor towards Bralorne Mine, two and a half miles downstream, and at one time fed a penstock that supplied water to their turbine. The planks were sixteen feet long and twelve inches wide and offered themselves to my father as a source of free two-by-fours and two-by-sixes for our house. Setting aside the knowledge that the flume was Bralorne property, he mobilized family manpower to help him take it apart and haul the the planks up the road behind our 1929 Chev. Then they sawed the planks into two-by-fours for the rafters. Alfred had to buy the lumber for the siding, but it was easily available from the company sawmill. The new house went up in no time.

High on the hill it stood, on the road to the schoolhouse, which was even further up at the top of the hill. A trail led from behind our house down the hill through bush to the main road, which followed the creek to the mine and the townsite where company houses were now under construction. Our house was wood-frame, painted brown, with a shingled roof. It had steps leading up to a porch, where firewood was stacked with easy access to the kitchen door. That was the only entrance. The house was never really finished inside; the bedrooms at the back remained in a rough state. The living room was scantily furnished. Most of our furniture, including the china cabinet, had been left behind in Kamloops. The outhouse – which was indeed a little house – was out towards the crest of the hill and supplied with the obligatory Eaton's catalogue.

The kitchen was a cheerful room with a big wood stove, woodbox nearby, and from time to time a barrel of homebrew. We even had a sink, though with only a cold-water tap. We got hot water from a big cast-aluminum kettle kept on the stove. At mealtimes we crowded around a big round table covered with an oil cloth printed with a pretty design. It was quite possibly our oak table, freighted in with the treadle sewing machine and the big wind-up gramophone and our collection of records, including Mama's favourite, "Beautiful Ohio."

The back door of the house led to a generous cleared space intended for a garden sometime in the future. I planted calendula seeds along the back wall, expecting to get a row of bright yellow flowers just like the picture on the package. None of them sprouted. The soil was all clay, and I had never heard of compost.

When the house was finished, Dad had a house-warming to celebrate, and the house was crowded with big Swedes and Norwegians and their ample wives drinking homebrew and hot rum. They were having a great time, but to me it was all noise and confusion, and I felt lost and panicky standing in the kitchen down among so many long legs. I cried out, "I want my mother." The talk and laughter ceased. Dad walked outside and stood underneath the clump of jack pines on the crest of the hill. I followed him a little way, until Verne came out and said, "Now see what you've done." So then I felt even worse.

In the Nelson family the three older brothers were always referred to as "the Boys." Art, Verne, and Ed. They were in their teens, demanding, high-spirited, vociferous, still under the parent roof but with lives of their own outside the family. They had jobs and paycheques and girlfriends, and slicked their hair back with brilliantine. Little Freddy and I, we were just little kids trying not to get in their way.

During the time when we had Anna Brothen to cook and make lunches and do the washing and ironing I often worried about when I should change into a clean dress, for I was afraid of violating some laundry quota that she might have established. She ruled over the family with the authority of a mother, which was good, because there was a huge empty space left where our own mother had been and with Mrs. Brothen in charge that space seemed a little less empty, if not warm and comforting. Little Freddy couldn't pronounce either "Braaten" or "Brothen," and "Mrs." was difficult too. He called her Mia Rotten, which was not acceptable, and so she became simply "Mia."

Mia was not a gentle person; she did not persuade or discuss. Direct action was her way, as Ed one day discovered. He was too old for the Saturday-night bath routine in the galvanized-iron tub, and not yet being a mine employee, didn't shower at the company "dry," as did Art and Verne. When he hadn't bothered to wash his neck and ears for some weeks and didn't take heed of her repeated reminders, she grabbed him one day and held him over the big tin wash basin while she dunked and soaped his head and scrubbed his neck and ears.

I don't recall Mia ever yanking me around like that; nor did I find her soft and motherly. Yet I know she felt a certain compassion for this skinny, little motherless waif, so pitiful in contrast to her Rachel, who was round and plump and pink-cheeked, and I was pleased and grateful when for special occasions at school she would curl my duck-feather straight hair with the curling iron. And she always remembered my birthday and baked me a cake.

By 1934 fifty families had to be accommodated at Pioneer Mine. The company cleared away the forest, built roads, created townsites on both sides of Cadwallader Creek, filled them with houses, established a domestic water system, and delivered electric power. It built the general store, the hospital, the church, the skating rink. It built the community hall, with an auditorium upstairs for movies and dancing; downstairs a restaurant, pool room and barber shop and library.

Plans for this new community had been developed in a Vancouver board room by company directors Colonel Victor Spencer and Alfred Bull in consultation with the founder and managing director, David Sloan. Owning both surface rights and mineral rights, the directors had the power to propose and dispose above as well as below ground, carrying out their plans with strict economy. Without utopian intent on their part, the workings of paternalism and the cheerful co-operation of the employees resulted in a community with all the necessary services and many pleasant amenities.

The houses were cheaply constructed – with wood-burning hot-air furnaces cleverly fashioned by machinist Ben Brosseau from oil drums and installed on cement platforms in the unfinished dirt basements – but the lumber was good and resisted the ravages of weather. The company got a good deal on some red paint, so the first houses on the hill near the school were painted red with white trim. Pioneer Mine was no longer a camp; it was a little town.

Men brought their families and settled at Pioneer. Young people got married and children were born. Soon the one-room school built in 1928 (and it actually was a little red schoolhouse) could no longer accommodate the growing school population. In 1933 a fine new three-room schoolhouse was built on a nearby meadow beside a little creek. Everybody had a pair of skis, so there were ski tournaments and an annual ball where the Ski Queen was crowned. Everybody had skates, and the Pioneer Highgraders fought it out with the Bralorne Golddiggers in the Western Canadian Junior Hockey League. The companies actually looked for good hockey players when they were hiring miners. Hockey rivalry was intense. Pioneer was your hometown. The Highgraders were your team.

The gymnasium, library, pool room, barber shop, and restaurant in the community hall were all operated by the Community Club. Members paid dues and volunteered their services for the annual ski tournament and Ski Club Ball, the baseball games, and July 1 celebration. The company well understood the value in dollars and cents of promoting the health and welfare and community spirit of their town. The citizens looked at the distressed outside world and were grateful for the benevolence that gold was bringing them, even though they might have chafed at the company's control over their lives.

Only company-approved businesses were allowed to operate within company boundaries: the Bank of Toronto and a stockbroker, a dairy service, Gus

Flodberg's tailor shop, "Sizzle" Tang's laundry. But not Zada's. Zada Fontaine was the local madame. With her location two miles down the road at Ogden, a.k.a. Pecker Point, she and her girls operated outside the company boundary. The word "brothel" was scarcely even uttered, only "Zada's." The beer parlour at Ogden was also off limits. For Pioneer Mine was not to be a rowdy, brawling gold-rush mining camp. The company was creating a town where families would want to bring up their children, and to their credit the bosses encouraged, sometimes sponsored, family events. Until the community hall and church were built, the schoolhouse did double duty as a meeting place. During provincial elections, politicians would arrive in camp. Even the children went to listen; I remember hearing George Murray, MLA for Lillooet. The campaign meeting wasn't just politics, it was entertainment too. And once a theatre troupe visited with a puppet show. This was a completely new experience to most of the children and their immigrant parents. For my part I was completely entranced by Punch and Judy. When the community hall was built, children played badminton in the gym and learned to skate on the rink outside the hall.

At the library I soon read my way through the children's section, so the librarian, with some hesitation, allowed me to start on the adult books. I chose Charles Dickens's *Pickwick Papers*, signed it out, and took it home. It proved too difficult for me, so I just held it in my hands from time to time and turned the pages reverently.

After a while the Brothens moved next door into their own little house not far from ours. Then Dad answered an Employment Wanted in the Classifieds, and a Mrs. Wilkins came from Vancouver to be our housekeeper. She was a little, sweet-faced woman who entered our lives for a few months, so private and unassuming that she left scarcely any mark at all on family memory. I was nine years old, yet I scarcely remember her, except that she was middle-aged and had rather wispy brown hair. Was she a widow? Perhaps. What nationality? Oh, English maybe. With the benevolence of old age, Art recalled that she was "a lovely little lady." And yet she must have been brave too, and resourceful and desperate to earn her living when she placed that advertisement and came such a long way to take on this unruly household of men.

The Boys would come stomping up the porch steps to be met by Mrs. Wilkins gently but firmly ordering them to walk quietly: she had bread rising on the stove, and if they clattered around in their big boots the bread would fall. Sometimes it did, and Mrs. Wilkins, exasperated, levelled accusing looks and sniffed with what little malice she could command. "Now see what you're going to have to eat."

Ed was a little different from the other two boys. He was an avid reader and spent so much time reading that Dad put his foot down and limited him to two books a day. But Ed got around this quota by stuffing the crack under his bedroom door and the keyhole as well so that no light would show through and he could keep on reading far into the night. He used to borrow books from the fellows in the bunkhouses – pulp fiction about American cowboys riding the range, lassoes, gunfights, Indian wars. We had a hand-powered washing machine, and Ed was the one who supplied the hand that moved the long stick that powered the agitator. He would hold his Zane Gray novel in one hand and work the washing machine handle with the other, back and forth, back and forth. As he became more and more absorbed in the story, he moved the handle more and more slowly until – "Two noiseless bounds! Another, and he was inside the door! 'Howdy, rustlers! Don't move!' he called." The washing machine stopped altogether. "Ed! Ed!" It was Mrs. Wilkins bringing him back once more from the foothills of Colorado. And he would start moving the handle again.

Mrs. Wilkins soon left us: washing Stanfields long underwear and heavy work pants, even with a washing machine and Ed's help, was too much for her. Her place was taken by Evelyn Lunby, a jolly young Norwegian girl whose father, Carl Lunby, was in charge of pipelines at the mine. She was blonde and blue-eyed, quite tall, and shapely in a sturdy way. As for breasts, the word "buxom" comes to mind. She was not much older than the Boys, eighteen or nineteen, about the same age as Art, and they responded to her potent female presence with much joshing around and kibitzing. Evelyn had a wonderful laugh and she laughed often, with a happy sound of pleasure, a welcome sound in our motherless home. We were comfortable with her: she didn't have to learn our ways, having grown up with *kjøttboller* and *geitost* and *inlagt sild* (meatballs, goat cheese, and pickled herring). She used lots of soap and water, but for all that didn't care about Ed's neck and ears. In any case, with Evelyn arriving every morning, bringing good humour and girlish camaraderie, Ed very soon took over responsibility for those body parts himself. In Evelyn he found another person like himself, ready with light-hearted banter and a quick retort to greet the world in an easy way.

Art was twenty years old by this time. After his day's work at the sawmill and on weekends he went fishing. The Boys had all three grown up in the freedom of the wilderness; it was their natural habitat, but Art was the only one who became an outdoorsman. From the time he was a child, he had a passion for fishing. At Pioneer he fished Cadwallader Creek from above the place where the mine tailings emptied into it at the mill, going all the way upstream to Piebiter Creek, bringing back cutthroat and rainbow trout. He was passionate about skiing too, going cross-country up Mount Ferguson to the timberline at 5,500 feet, downhill, slalom, ski-jumping. He won trophies in the annual Ski Carnival competitions, which were part of the vigorous company program to keep the workers happy with more wholesome activities than forming unions and demanding higher wages. Confident, debonair, he posed holding his trophy with the Carnival Ski Queen and with her danced the first waltz at the ball, gliding around the floor . . . guiding her firmly, right hand on her back, as smooth and graceful as Fred Astaire. But gradually another passion took over when he started playing poker and blackjack. Later, when he was working in a Vancouver Island logging camp, he figured he could make more money playing poker than by working for wages. On occasion he would pay one of his buddies to work his job, while he, having hired a plane, flew out to another camp to play poker and rake in the winnings.

Art was good-looking, but Verne was handsome. He had a striking movie-star profile, a sensuous mouth, and our mother's almost black hair. Whereas Art was smooth and equable, Verne was volatile, irrepressible, and irascible, with a flashing wit. He was apprenticed to master mechanic Harvey McKenzie, trained in Scotland. "Smarts coming out of his ears," claimed Verne. With his encouragement and help, Verne learned the language of lathes and drill presses and pipe-threading machines. He studied trigonometry so that he could build and maintain spiral gears, measurements in ten-thousands of an inch (no computer control in those days). He taught himself to play the accordion and the guitar too. When his fingers were rough and sore after a hard day's work, he soaked them in glycerine and rosewater and rubbed and massaged them so he could play with the local orchestra that night. He bought a motorcycle and took off one day for a trip to Vancouver.

Coming to a ditch across the narrow Fraser River Canyon highway, he leaped over it at full speed, scattering a road crew who retreated for safety to the side of the road.

Ed was tall and fair, recognizably Nordic and so blond he was nicknamed "Snowball." He had a broad forehead and a strong, chiselled nose. Actually, all of us inherited this, our father's nose, but in Ed, favouring Dad rather than our dark-haired mother, more Swede than Norwegian, the Nelson nose found its most congenial inheritor. Art and Verne had early on learned to do hard physical labour, for Dad expected them to contribute their share with pick and shovel and axe. As a matter of course they dug the ditch for our water pipe to the source of a spring of fresh water. It was five feet deep, 1,500 feet up the hill above our house. But Ed somehow found ways of sliding away from this kind of work. "He would have just got in the way," Art scoffed. "We didn't want him anyway." Not that Ed felt rejected: he would rather read a book.

Ed was soon earning his keep too. He got a job behind the meat counter at Pioneer's General Store, where he joked with the women customers and charmed them with his friendly ways. He was a little nonplussed, however, when Zada Fontaine, the local madame, came up to the meat counter one day and charmed *him* with her friendly ways. "She said she wanted a leg of pork," Ed recalled, "and she lifted her skirt and marked off with her finger about five pounds worth at stocking-top level."

In the kitchen, beside the mirror on the wall, hung the strop, which Dad used for sharpening his razor and, when they were younger, for disciplining the Boys if they were scrapping and got out of hand. Or he would administer a "chilivink." I don't know how it's spelled in Swedish, or even if there is such a word, but if there is, "ch" surely becomes "k" or "kj," and I know that it means you get your ear twisted until you cry "ouch." I can hear him threatening one or another of the Boys, *"Jag skal gi deg en kjilivink."* Usually the threat was enough, but sometimes he actually did grab hold of the delinquent's ear. Freddy and I were exempt from this rough treatment. I know now that Dad felt a tenderness and a sadness for us two little ones that he couldn't express. But at Pioneer the Boys were too old for chilivinks: they were workers like himself. They brought home their pay and at first handed it all over to him. Later, they paid room and board.

Not many parents in those days, least of all our father, had ever heard of sibling rivalry. Verne claimed that Dad was partial to Art and Ed and always took their side. It's true that Art was more like a young comrade for Dad, because Art had worked with him at the Planet Mine, had chosen to do so to help support the family rather than go to high school. Verne was more like our Norwegian mother in looks, and he had been her favourite. As adults Art and Verne were pals, but when he was eighty years old, Verne still felt aggrieved: "I carried the water for Mama. Art, he was always out fishing." That old sibling rivalry was still smouldering deep down under his breastbone. It's true that Art, being the eldest, took control, and was immoveable, impregnable. But that didn't stop hot-headed Verne from battering at Fortress Art. In these collisions, our exasperated father could no longer intervene with either strop or chilivink, although in desperation he sometimes grabbed the strop and made threatening gestures with it. The Boys answered by shouting that they were going to pack up and leave and live in the bunkhouse. Meanwhile Freddy and I looked on, wide-eyed, from a safe place.

The final dust-up started one morning over a work shirt. Verne said, "That's my shirt." Art said, "It is not. It's my shirt." They argued, Art was coolly adamant, Verne found Art's superior manner infuriating, they came to blows. Verne put a half-nelson on Art and punched his nose. It bled; there was blood all over the kitchen floor. Art punched him back. Dad roared imprecations at them, "*Djävlig förbannade kidungar.*" And brought down his edict: he was kicking them out of the house and they were leaving that night. So they moved into No. 3 bunkhouse, living at first in separate rooms. After a while Verne moved in with Art and they were roommates until Art left Pioneer to work elsewhere.

They ate at the cookhouse with the rest of the crew, except for a few months with Mrs. Gracey, who had the company's permission to offer board to the employees. Her teenage daughter Bubbles helped prepare and serve, and she taught Art how to dance. But it was Verne who seduced Bubbles into leaving the kitchen to sit on his knee. Then Mrs. Gracey, exasperated, would call out, "Bubbles! Bubbles!"

For most people at Pioneer, gold was just everyday life. It was wages and profits and it supported a community. Children went to school, women bought groceries at the General Store; miners and foremen and superintendents put on their hard hats and went down in the mine. Gold quartz was all around them, in drifts and chutes and ore cars. There was nothing to stop any one of them from carrying high-grade chunks home in their lunch buckets; they didn't have to pass through checkout inspection at the end of shift.

But miners generally didn't bother with high-grading. Sometimes, however, the company became suspicious. "They put a box in the General Store," my brother remembered. "There was a sign, 'Drop your high-grade here, no questions asked.' Of course nobody was going to do that. They just hid it in Cadwallader Creek, or buried it somewhere. One night Wally Seretny and I came across manager Howard James down by the refinery, prowling around, so he had his suspicions."

As well he might. Some mine workers couldn't resist the lure of gold, believing that they could sell it to someone like the enterprising young man at Bradeen Café just down the road. He cached it in the tires of his car and drove to Lillooet with it. Or so it was said. How could you drive with rocks in the inner tube? Well, he ground the rocks fine and sluiced out most of the gold. Stories like this went the rounds of camp and were improved in the telling.

One incident in particular created great excitement. The unlucky high-grader lived near us, at the bottom of our hill near the creek. Gerry (not his real name) was a likeable young man. He worked on the belt where the ore came down the chute from the head frame and moved along towards the crusher. So he was working in an ideal location for high-grading. "I was standing beside him one day where he was working," remembered my brother Art. "'That's a good piece,' he'd say, 'I'll take that.' And he'd pick another, and another. I didn't say anything. I kept quiet. That was his business. Then a friend came to live with him, discovered his cache of gold and made off with it. Gerry phones the office: 'I can't come to work today. Somebody's stolen my gold,' and he takes off after the thief. Pioneer sends a pickup truck after him. Ron Smith, he was a former rum-runner on parole at the mine, is standing in the back of the truck, rifle at the ready and they're goin' through camp like hell on wheels and down past the mill along the road to Bralorne. Provincial police were stationed at Bralorne, they nabbed both of them. Gerry was tried and sentenced to eighteen months. When he got out, he went back to Pioneer, asked to have his job back. He didn't get it."

High-grading was risky; not many tried it. But the lure of gold was tempting just the same, and at the beer parlour in nearby Ogden or at Bradeen Café, the talk switched easily from high-grading to the stock market. It was tempting to invest. My father and brother did invest, not in real money-makers like Pioneer and Bralorne – they couldn't afford them – but in other properties promising big dividends once the claim was developed and producing ore.

Art recalled that mine manager David Sloan used to come down to the sawmill from time to time. "He liked to saw lumber. I'd ask, 'What would you like to do today?' 'I'll set,' he'd reply. He'd set the levers at his end, one inch, two inch, whatever we needed – planks, mine timbers. I'd be at the other end controlling the saw, giving him hand signals. Sometimes we'd stop and talk. '$1.16 a share, Pioneer.' He spoke like that. 'Got any Pioneer?' Of course I didn't. I was only making $3.00 a day. 'Get some, Art, rob a bank, do anything, buy Pioneer.' But I never did. I should have. There was no income tax then. Shares went up to fifteen, sixteen dollars. Gene Tunney, heavyweight champion, he had shares, used to visit Pioneer. I met him."

The refinery was just below the mill, near the creek. It was surrounded by a high, heavy steel-wire fence and was understood to be out of bounds. It was a windowless room, more like a shed, but with a concrete floor. By the time the chunks of quartz rock from the stopes and drifts of the mine reached this little shed, they had gone through that central processing building called the mill, where they had been reduced to little bits, ground in crushers and ball mills, whirled in a tank of water with cyanide to make a cyanide-gold solution and treated with zinc dust to gain release from the cyanide. The waste materials were sent back to the mill to be re-processed. At last the gold was released from other minerals in the rock, though still not recognizable as gold. It was a black powder and had to be mixed with a flux consisting of lead, carbon, and sodium bicarbonate, which would combine with any foreign materials during the smelting process.

Now the black powder was ready for the six-foot furnace, fed by oil and shooting flames, melting the gold at 1,063 degrees Celsius. The molten gold was poured into loaf-shaped moulds. It was now a gold brick. As a young girl, Revelstoke artist Wyn Hagerstone saw the molten gold being poured in the Pioneer refinery where her father Frank Holland was then working. Winnie Holland went to school at Pioneer in the 1930s. She was one of my playmates.

"My father had obtained permission to take me to see the gold bricks being poured. There were several men working there, long asbestos gloves up past their elbows, asbestos aprons, goggles. When they tilted the bucket containing the white hot gold, it created a golden waterfall as it slowly poured into the mould. It had colours of white, yellow, orange and red. I was completely spellbound. It was one of the highlights of my life."

After the gold was poured, the brick was cooled in a barrel of water. It still did not look like gold: black tracings and spots of slag, eliminated by the flux, cover the surface. When these are hammered and wire-brushed, the soft, yellow colour of gold emerges, lustrous and alluring – a gold brick.

One of the refinery workers carried it up the road on his shoulder to the vault where it was stashed along with the dynamite boxes of free gold ore. "I used to see him," Art recalled. "Vic Watt, he worked in the refinery. I was working in the sawmill and I'd see him from time to time walking up the hill with a gold brick or two on his shoulders."

At first the bricks were personally delivered to the Royal Bank in Vancouver by Sloan himself, or on occasion by his trusted Swede foreman, Bob Eklof. It was a two-day journey by truck, train, and boat. A Brink's armoured car was waiting at the dock. The Royal Bank took custody from there, intermediary for the Royal Canadian Mint in Ottawa. Later on, the gold bricks were simply put in the mail at the Post Office in the General Store, wrapped and plastered with postage stamps, maybe one hundred dollars worth for a brick.

Those gold bricks were still not pure gold, but only "crude bullion" containing about 80 per cent gold and 20 per cent silver and other metals. At the Ottawa Mint (with branches in Hull and Winnipeg), the crude bullion was further refined in a process called parting, which separated these metals from the gold. All the gold mined at Pioneer is probably still in existence as gold coins, bracelets, teeth, gold leaf decoration, and insulation, or still at the Mint, in bricks credited to the account of some rich investor.

Although the price of shares fell off somewhat after the mid-1930s, Pioneer Mines continued to hold its position as one of the world's smaller but high-producing gold mines. Its solid performance was supported by another lucky strike of high-grade ore, this one discovered in 1937 by Bob Eklof, that stubborn, independent-minded Swede who went on drilling and stoping a low-grade vein in defiance of the boss's orders and was repaid for disobedience with the dazzling discovery of a white quartz vein streaked with free gold. Once again, the locked steel gate, the bonded workmen, the careful extraction of ore, the reserve of high-grade in the vault. And Vic Watt continued to carry gold bricks on his shoulder along the road to the mine office.

And homebrew? In fact, the company turned a blind eye; in any case, my father knew he was a valued employee. Anna and Gunnar felt secure too, nearby in their own house (there were enough two-by-fours from the flume for them as well). The wooden-stave beer barrel soon returned to its regular place behind our kitchen stove.

My father prided himself on his beer. It began with a cloth bag of hops immersed in a few gallons of water in the copper clothes boiler and boiled for maybe an hour. The whole house was filled with a bitter aroma. A can of Blue Ribbon malt syrup was added during this boiling.

The brew was allowed to cool before being transferred to the wooden barrel. A cake of ordinary bakers' yeast was added, and sugar for fermentation, sometimes a few raisins for extra kick. The barrel was covered with a wooden lid and placed behind the stove. Later on my brother said that if you put your ear to the barrel you could hear the beer "working." From time to time my father tasted the beer, dipping into it with a soup ladle and taking slow, reflective sips. When he judged it ready for bottling, he set up his equipment in the cellar – table with bottle-capping machine, metal bottle caps, clean brown bottles – and then siphoned the beer through a narrow rubber hose emerging from a hole he'd bored in the kitchen floor above.

The miners often gathered in our kitchen on a Saturday morning. My father would fill a glass with the latest brew and hold it up to the light. "Clear as crystal," he'd say. "It takes a Swede every time." And then a toast: "*Skål, kamrater, skål.*" When the beer had too much kick and was likely to foam up and make a mess, he'd open the bottles over a washtub placed in the middle of the kitchen floor. The miners – Norwegians, Swedes, Swede-Finns – sat around the tub and drank and talked. They were loud and vociferous, but not drunk, just "feeling good." That was the expression used when a person had had a few drinks. So I never felt afraid. Half-listening, doing my homework in the next room, I didn't understand their talk but I fully comprehended the hostility they felt towards the company.

The company's goal was not just to make a profit, despite the difficult economic times, but to increase profits, and to do this its managers implemented a system, in the words of their accountant, "devoted to drastic cost control." For each area being worked – stopes, drifts, crosscuts, raises, shafts – they kept a daily mine record of labour employed and explosives and other supplies. At the end of the month they totalled and averaged these columns of figures and apportioned indirect costs such as hoisting, pumping, and steel-sharpening. Month by month comparisons could thus be made, as, for example, tonnage mined per shift on each stope and cost per ton. The system worked: manager-director Sloan reported in 1934 that "direct stoping costs have decreased from $2.67 per ton to $1.92 per ton."

Money could be saved on explosives. The drilled hole was often longer than the stick of dynamite, but only that one stick was needed to produce the desired explosion of rock. Art told me that one of his jobs at the sawmill was to manufacture ten-inch sticks of wood, three-quarters of an inch thick, to supplement the dynamite. That meant that the workers wouldn't have to fill the full length of the drilled hole with the explosive. They would insert the stick of wood into the hole first. Art also remembered a machine that produced sticks of clay like sausages, which were then cut into lengths and, like the sticks of wood, used to fill part of the hole. Such creative strategies would have resulted in a considerable saving on explosives.

The company spoke of efficiency. The men called it speed-up. At the sawmill one of Art's crew was a Russian. He was "a hard worker," Art said. "One day David Sloan came by and got after him for standing there, not working. 'I was just taking a chew of snoose,' says the Russian. 'Well, take ten days off without pay and have a good chew.' He said that, Sloan did."

My father knew about speed-up. On nightshift, he'd sometimes been one of the work crew sent into drifts hundreds of feet from any ventilation only two hours after the day shift had blasted a fifty-pound box of dynamite and the dust had not had time to settle. The men breathed sharp particles of quartz dust containing silica, and they were soon recognizing what that did to their lungs. It damaged them so that it became hard to breathe. My father had silicosis, as did others of the men sitting around that washtub drinking beer.

Fred Johnson, a big, husky Swede, had just finished tramming fifty tons of ore from No. 3 shaft to the mill. He was in the hoist room with Pete Jensen and Eklof when Harry Cain, the mine superintendent, came in. Years later Eklof told me what happened that day. He said Cain went up to Fred and said, "You're just sitting around. You're supposed to be getting some muck down to the mill."

"I get fifty tons down there every day," Fred said in response. "Well," Cain said, "We want more than that."

"So Fred, he picked Harry Cain up and held him over the shaft," Eklof told me. And Fred said to the superintendent, "If you say any more I'll drop you." Eklof called out, "C'mon Fred, put the man down." And he did put him down, but not before telling Cain, "You're not my boss. Don't you come in here any more. If you do, I'll drop you down the shaft."

"Harry Cain, he beat it," Eklof said. "Oh yeah, I remember that pretty well."

"The shaft" – deep, dark, and dangerous – was a powerful word for me, doing my homework, listening in the living room. And I heard other powerful words: "fired," "stool-pigeon," "speed-up" – and "scab."

"Scab" was a swear word. You must never say it. So I never did, because it was a really bad thing to say about anyone. Could a Swede be a Scab? My Dad said Bob Eklof was, and the other men said so too. I heard them – one day when they were all drinking homebrew in the kitchen. But my father was a Swede and *he* wasn't a Scab.

Decades later I understand the reason for this hostility. Bob Eklof had worked for the company from its early days in 1928. He had been both a friend and an employee of Sloan's, working in close co-operation with him in those first faltering days of development during the Depression. He was a much-valued foreman, for he knew every rock face, drift, and stope intimately. He knew where his men should timber and drill and muck to bring down high-grade ore. He and his wife, Ina, had started married life in a log cabin beside the creek; there were no houses or townsites then. Many of the miners were Scandinavians, with nowhere to spend Christmas Eve. Bob and Ina invited them all to come to their log cabin for the traditional Christmas Eve dinner of *lutefisk* and even did the *lutning* themselves – that is, soaked the fish in lye according to custom. They didn't have enough dishes and cutlery, so between sittings everybody pitched in and washed dishes. Bob and Ina both had a certain proprietary feeling for Pioneer. They felt as though it were *their* mine. Pioneer was home.

A foreman, though, is always in an anomalous position. He is the worker who connects with management and passes on their decisions about what rock face to drill, what shaft to sink and where. He's the one who passes on the bad news about wage cuts and layoffs. My father had been foreman at the

Duthie, the "shift boss," and in 1929 he had probably been the one who had to tell his fellow workers that the mine was closing down. He was foreman at the Planet Mine too. At Pioneer Bob Eklof was his foreman. Bob Eklof told Alfred Nelson where to muck and stope and timber, and it rankled.

Our kitchen became a sociable meeting place where my father and the other Scandinavian miners complained about wages and hours and quartz dust and ventured to think that maybe they should have a union so they could go to the boss and ask for a raise in pay. Meanwhile, working on my decimals and fractions I heard, uncomprehending, a stream of angry words, guffaws, and mild curses mingled with hoots of laughter. Yet listening to the miners sitting around that washtub drinking homebrew, I learned about the class struggle. It smelled of boiling hops; it smelled of miners, their bodies permeated with fumes of carbide and blasting smoke. The class struggle was Bob Eklof on one side of a fence, my father on the other. It was stopes and drifts and timbers and hoists. It was "scab" and "fired" and Anna Brothen emptying homebrew down the sink, and Fred Johnson holding Harry Cain over the shaft.

It was "clear as crystal" and, to the clink of glasses, "*Skål, kamrater, skål.*"

Vancouver Board of Trade members, with Pioneer Mine gold brick, 1933. Harry Cain, mine superintendent, is second from the left.
(*Courtesy University of British Columbia Library, Rare Books and Special Collections*)

Pioneer work crew. Back row, second from left, Verner Nelson; furthest right, Harvey McKenzie, Master Mechanic.
(*Author's collection*)

EIGHT

CHILDREN OF THE EMPIRE

LIFE AND DEATH AND BITTER STRIKES

On Friday afternoons regular school work stopped early. We tidied our desks and sat up straight for our treat: the next episode of "Enoch Arden," which our teacher was reading to us in weekly instalments. This was the story of a shipwrecked sailor returning to his native English village to find that his wife Annie had given him up for lost and married again. It was a long narrative poem by the nineteenth-century English poet Alfred, Lord Tennyson, and it allowed us to hear cadences of the English language we had never heard before. When had we ever heard such music as "wrathful seas," "the rosy idol of her solitudes"? Or wondered that a ship could slip "across the summer of the world"? However, true love – faithful, noble, unrequited, and in iambic pentameters – was light years away from our own experience. Enoch and Annie may as well have inhabited some distant galaxy. True, their village had a mill, but it ground wheat into flour, whereas our mill at Pioneer Mine ground rocks to produce gold. They had hazelnut trees in or on a "gray down" which they apparently reached by climbing up, and their hazelwood was "by autumn nutters haunted."

"Nutters"? "Haunted"?

We had evergreen jack pine and fir on steep hills, maple trees and poplars that turned yellow in the fall, and as far as we knew there were no ghosts in the forest, though we knew enough to watch out for bears. As for hazelnuts, which we knew as filberts, our parents bought them at the General Store at Christmas along with Brazil nuts and almonds, and it probably never occurred to us that they had to be picked like apples from a tree. Here in the mountains of British Columbia we took our empty lard pails and went up the mountain for blueberries. We were careful to watch out for a bear picking on the other side of the bush. Meanwhile, over there in England, the villagers "with bag and sack and basket, great and small, / Went nutting to the hazels."

We were learning a new language, different from ordinary Canadian English. The Nelson family was by this time long established in Canada. We spoke English at home, so I was fluent enough in English. But the Gronskei children were still speaking Norwegian when they started attending school at Pioneer, almost directly from Norway, and six-year-old Knut just sat and cried the first days he was in school. Lissie Jensen was still speaking Danish when she began in first grade. The Schutz family had at least spent a year or two at the Hollinger Mine in northern Ontario, but they too spoke Norwegian at home. For these children, school was at first a strange, confusing, irrelevant, sometimes even frightening experience.

We were also learning that the centre of our universe was not here in Canada after all, but Over There in England, the Mother Country, which organized all the affairs of her far-flung Empire, even as far away as Pioneer Mine and our little red schoolhouse in the valley of the Cadwallader at the foot of Sunshine Mountain.

The school had two entrances, one of them leading to a mudroom for boots and coats, a pile of wood, and a bucket of water with a tin dipper floating in it. The pot-bellied stove at the back of the room was fed by two-foot logs. The desks were screwed in rows to long two-by-fours so they could be shifted to the side and leave space for Saturday night dances. From the front wall above the blackboard, King George V, bewhiskered, be-medalled, gave his stern, paternal blessing. A map of the world was attached to the top of the blackboard. When unrolled it revealed large, friendly expanses of British-Empire-Pink, as did the globe of the world on the teacher's desk.

The day began and ended with the Union Jack on the flagpost outside. Fourteen-year-old John, son of mill superintendent Paul Schutz, was the janitor and it was John's daily chore to raise the flag in the morning after he'd lit the fire in the stove. After school he would lower it and put it away. At nine o'clock Teacher came to the door and rang the bell; we trooped into the schoolroom, and standing beside our desks recited the Lord's Prayer in unison, then sang "O Canada" and "God Save the King." Teacher took attendance in the big school register, calling our names, to which we answered each in turn, "Present." Then it was time for arithmetic and reading.

Our teacher from 1931 to 1933 was Guy Algernon Johnson, a young man with wavy hair, a broad forehead, and wide cheekbones. He was not strikingly handsome, but pleasant enough in appearance. And he was earnest and conscientious. Under his tutelage we absorbed British culture and the British worldview, and I, for one, became a little British imperialist. He was only following the course of studies laid down for the schools of British Columbia and teaching from the textbooks supplied by the Department of Education. We did read Canadian stories and poems, and several Canadian publishers were indeed offering children the literature and history of their own country. In 1929, for example, Ryerson Press had published *The Story of Canada*, with illustrations by the well-known artist C.W. Jeffreys, based on his own scholarly research and inspired by his nationalistic sense of mission as an artist.

However, *The Gage Canadian Readers* were more British than Canadian. These were the texts through which we learned to read and gather a vocabulary, and we studied its stories word for word so that our thoughts came to arise out of a different world from the one we lived in. In the Grade 3 reader we learned sacrifice and duty. We read that Sir Philip Sidney, dying on the field of battle, gave his cup of water to a poor, wounded soldier lying near him and said, "Drink this. Thy necessity is greater than mine." We read that Admiral Horatio Nelson as a child lived with his grandmother because his mother was dead and that when he grew up he commanded the fleet of British warships in the Battle of Trafalgar, which we won because even though he was mortally wounded he signalled to all the ships, "England expects that every man will do his duty." In Grade 4 we chanted, "Children of the Empire, clasp hands across the main, / And glory in your brotherhood again and yet again; / Uphold your noble heritage; oh, never let it fall / And love the land that bore you, but the Empire best of all." In Grade 5 we memorized

"The Charge of the Light Brigade" and learned to ride even into "the Valley of Death" to carry out orders: "Theirs not to reason why, Theirs but to do and die," even with "Cannon to right of them, cannon to left of them, / Cannon in front of them ... "

I particularly remember a story about a poor little homeless boy who said his father was "a scholar and a gentleman." What was a gentleman? I never did ask. My father was a miner, so I guessed that he wasn't a gentleman. Dagny Gronskei's father worked in the mill. Lissie Jensen's father was a hoistman. They weren't gentlemen either. There were no stories in our readers about boys and girls whose fathers operated a hoist or stoper or tramcar. Even so, this was no problem for me. I made friends easily with Enoch Arden and Annie, and with David Copperfield and his aunt Betsey Trotwood too, even though they did belong to a distant galaxy, and I accepted Mrs. Cratchit's plum pudding as right and proper for Christmas. Our Scandinavian rice pudding with prune and raisin sauce was only a second-best substitute.

But while Sir Philip Sidney and Admiral Nelson were dying in battle, here at Pioneer death came directly to home and school and not through the pages of a reader. One morning I knocked on the Brothens' door to ask for Rachel. Her mother opened it and said, "Rachel can't come out to play today." Those words are locked in my memory, for I soon learned that her father, Gunnar Brothen, had been killed in an accident down in the mine when a rock fell on his head.

Not many people died at Pioneer, because it was largely a young people's town. True, all miners were in danger of developing silicosis in their lungs from breathing quartz dust, but the disease progressed slowly; its victims died elsewhere, years later after they'd had to quit mining. My father had to quit working in the mine in 1935 because of silicosis, and our family then moved away from Pioneer. There were deaths, too, from accidents in the mine: even a careful miner might be crushed by falling rock. That's what happened to Gunnar Brothen. This knowledge of danger and death entered into the hometown feeling, making it even more strongly felt, because it was touched with a poignant regret and sadness shared by the whole community.

Gunnar Brothen was crushed to death by a falling rock one night when he was working his regular shift at Pioneer Mine. In 1934 he was one of twenty-two men killed at work in and about the hard-rock metal mines of British Columbia. I did not know any of these other men, but I knew Gunnar Brothen.

In Gunnar's friendly way, he often took my fifteen-year-old brother Art along when he went camping at Dennis Lake. In August 1934 the Brothen and Nelson families, now living separately in neighbouring houses, went camping together at Tyaughton Lake, some ten or twelve miles from Pioneer. We ran out of food but were well supplied with flour, and the lake was full of fish. Gunnar and my brothers were out on the lake with their fishing rods every day, pulling in the day's catch, so we ended the holiday with lots of pancakes and fried trout. As soon as we returned, Gunnar went to work on the night shift. He was killed that night.

Alfhild Gronskei, who was living at Pioneer with her husband and family at the time of the accident, long remembered what Anna said afterwards. All of them – children and adults alike – had been playing tag after supper. (I must have been there too, playing with Rachel.) Gunnar tagged Anna and called out "last touch," picked up his lunch bucket, and went off down the trail to work. Alfhild had known the Brothens in Rjukan, Norway. She had gone to school with Gunnar.

According to British Columbia's *Report of the Minister of Mines, 1934,* "the fatal accident which occurred to Gunnar Brothen, miner, *Pioneer* mine, on August 16th was due to a fall of ground while deceased was engaged in firing a round of shots; a piece of the rock pushed him back some 10 feet from the face and crushed him against a stull."* The accident happened towards the end of his shift, when he was getting ready to blast. There was no suggestion that he had been careless.

Mining is dangerous work. Miners know that rock can be treacherous. Before they start drilling in the stope, they "bar down," using a heavy steel rod to dislodge any loose rock. "You bar down pretty damn good," one oldtimer grimly recalled. "There's always loose rock." He was thinking of that long-ago day at Cariboo Gold Quartz when he was in the "dry" changing into his Stanfields and workpants. Meanwhile, one of his buddies lay dead there among them – among the miners getting ready to go on the next shift. Some went to look at their dead comrade, but he didn't. It was enough to know that a slab had fallen on him.

---

* A stull is a wooden supporting beam across an opening.

The slab fell on Gunnar Brothen towards the end of his shift, sometime after he had barred down the loose rock. According to form, he had already drilled a round of holes with his stoper into the vein of quartz where the gold was embedded, and he was now going to load them with sticks of dynamite. He cut off a good length of fuse (a white cord that comes in a roll), inserted one end of it into a metal blasting cap containing the explosive charge, and secured it in place by crimping the cap. Then he punched a hole in a stick of dynamite with a spike, reamed it out, and inserted the blasting cap end of the fuse into the dynamite, which was now explosively ready to be shoved into one of the holes he had drilled with his stoper into the vein of quartz. Whatever space was left in the drilled hole, he filled up with more sticks of dynamite. He was going to fill all the holes that he had drilled in the same way. Then he would light the free end of each fuse, which would then burn their way to the explosive charge in the blasting cap at the other end. The length of the fuse was critical. It had to be long enough to give him time to escape to a safe place.

But on this shift, he'd not had time to do all this. That hanging wall he had so carefully barred down was treacherous and let loose a slab that struck him and pushed him across the stope, crushing him mercilessly against the timbered wall. Gunnar Brothen must have died immediately from a force so violent. He would not have lingered and suffered in pain.

I n November of that same year, as John Schutz reminded me much later, his brother Arthur was skating at King Lake above Pioneer and went through the ice. The other boys ran for help, leaving Knut Gronskei waiting at the lake, screaming hysterically. John's brother drowned.

"You don't remember that?" John was surprised.

I suppose I chose not to remember. There had been too much happening right then. Rachel and her father and mother had just come back from a camping holiday with our family at Tyaughton Lake. Gunnar went straight to work on the night shift and was killed that night, August 16, 1934. Then Arthur, November 17, 1934, the school flag at half mast. I was twelve years old. Although I didn't remember that Arthur had drowned, of all the school children at Pioneer, his face, round and full of freckles, is the one I remember most vividly. And his big, buck-toothed smile, and his shock of straight red hair. Winnifred Holland remembered that she and Lissie Jensen and Arthur used to shinny up the alder trees, which bent under their weight, and they were Tarzan, and yelled and leaped from one tree to another. One time, Arthur fell and broke his arm. She also remembered that she learned to skate because Arthur loaned her his skates.

One winter, after a Saturday night dance in the schoolhouse, a man was killed when another man hit him over the head with a peavey* in a quarrel over a woman. I didn't see the blood on the snow outside the the the school, but Winnie and her brother Frank saw it that Sunday morning.

Our world on the outskirts of Empire was harsh, sometimes even brutal, but in school Guy Algernon Johnson taught us to sing and read music. I asked John Schutz what he remembered about our Mr. Johnson. John, at eighty years of age, searched his memory. "School was a waste of time for me," he confessed, and then announced triumphantly, "The treble clef!" Harry Ashby remembered that we lined up outside the school and sang in chorus. Dagny Gronskei remembered that we sang "John Peel."

Of course! "Do ye ken John Peel in his coat so gay / Do ye ken John Peel at the break of day?" I can see, hear us, sixteen children lined up outside a school building in a mountain wilderness on the fringe of Empire singing about fox hunting: "Peel's view halloo would awaken the dead / And the fox from his lair in the morning."

But Mr. Johnson also taught us how to read music from the little black marks on the page. I remember the day he asked us to open our music books at "Flow Gently Sweet Afton." It was written in two sharps. But we didn't need to know that the lines on the treble clef spelled Every Good Boy Does Fine in order to discover the melody. He taught us instead to find "doh." We found it in the space above middle C and we sang "sol doh doh, me re doh doh." (I learned later that doh was the key, or tonic note; that its location depended on the key in which the music was pitched; and that we were being given a solfeggio exercise in reading music.) That afternoon I rushed home from school and opened my music book at "Ye Banks and Braes o' Bonnie Doon." I found doh, I found soh and fa. I found the tune! I learned it all by myself, I was singing "Ye Banks and Braes" from notes on the page.

---

* A long pole used in logging, with a metal spike protruding from its end and, just above that, a hanging hook used to grab the log at a second location.

Sometimes after school Mr. Johnson taught me to make my own music on the piano, and I discovered that if you spread your fingers and pressed C, E, and G at the same time, you would hear doh, mi, and soh separately and together, vibrating and making a beautiful new sound. It was called a chord.

And then I see us at recess and lunch time, playing beside and sometimes actually in the little creek that ran down the hill past the school and over a bed of rocks and little boulders, which we hefted and rolled and heaved to build dams in partnership with a best friend, the girls in shrill competition with the boys for the best rocks.

Meanwhile, Over There in London, Imperial Conferences were deciding the future of Canada and the other British colonies that wanted to be independent countries. In 1931 the Statute of Westminster declared them to be separate entities within the British Commonwealth of Nations. Britain had loosened her apron strings, following the 1926 report of Lord Balfour. Mr. Johnson explained it all to us and had us memorize a key passage from the Balfour Report, which declared the Dominions to be "autonomous Communities within the British Empire, equal in status, in no way subordinate one to the other in any aspect of their domestic or external affairs, though united by a common allegiance to the Crown, and freely associated as members of the British Commonwealth of Nations." We understood that Canada was now an independent country, although the British Parliament was kindly looking after our Constitution. So King George V was still looking down on us from above the blackboard.

I can still recite Lord Balfour's words. Dagny, Lissie, and Winnie remembered them not at all, though they were studious pupils too, so perhaps I was an odd little girl. John Schutz paid no attention to Lord Balfour, and as soon as he could he went to work at Pioneer for one dollar a day. He salvaged old pipes, and down in the mine he mucked and trammed and helped timbermen. "I was put in every location in that mine. This is hands-on. You're working with men now. You're not working with students or kids or schoolteachers. Now you're with men. Now you don't fool around any more because you've got to keep up." Then he went to British Guiana and put in a grinding system for a cyanide plant. There was no telephone: he couldn't call Canada for help. "Like I said, all this stuff at Pioneer came in good stead."

Winnie used to bring her father his lunch. To do this she had to walk the staging around the huge settling tanks of swirling, seething cyanide solution to reach the compressor room where her father worked. And she clerked in the Pioneer Mine General Store. Dagny learned about real life working at the soda fountain in the General Store. Like Winnie, she too walked that dangerous staging to bring her father his lunch. And when her little sister Marion died, she sewed black armbands for the whole family on their jacket sleeves. More than anything in the world, Dagny wanted to continue in Grade 11, but her father said, No, you're going to stay home and help your mother and get a job. So Dagny learned about real life doing housework at home and in other people's houses, then behind the counter, first at the soda fountain in the community hall and then at the General Store. But after the war she found a new and better real life when she married a young man who had survived thirty night trips over Germany in a Lancaster bomber. They had a happy marriage and family life.

Lissie went to work in Vancouver for a company that manufactured diamond drills. She sat in front of a saucer of diamonds and selected those that would make a cutting edge for drills. I picked strawberries and raspberries on Fraser Valley farms, one cent a pound, or maybe even one and one-half cents, for "crate berries," much less for "jam berries," and I kept house for my father and washed the kitchen floor in the morning before I walked half a mile to catch the school bus at eight o'clock. We all learned early about real life, and we married and had children. We did our share of the work of the world, giving not a thought to Lord Balfour, although when I later became a Canadian nationalist I may have been under the lingering influence of his words.

We were among the last Children of the Empire. By 1936 the *Gage Canadian Readers* were replaced by the *Highroads to Reading* series, authorized for the public schools of British Columbia and the Prairie provinces. By that time I was in high school and had graduated from school readers to French grammar and Shakespeare. But I myself would soon be teaching from the new readers. Although hoistmen, stopers, and trammers still did not appear in the books, the fur traders did, and the Mounties and beavers and wolves and bears, and in the Grade 6 *Highroads to Reading* there was a poem about a Canadian Prairie school. "Do you recognize your school in any part of the descriptions given here?" asked the "Helps to Study?" – anxious for children to connect their reading with their daily life. At Pioneer, as elsewhere in British Columbia, "Medicine Hat," "Moose Jaw," and "Okanagan" appeared on the printed page along with "Alexander Graham Bell" and "Sir Wilfred Grenfell, the Good Doctor of Labrador." In the little red schoolhouse the children read

Canadian poet Bliss Carman's "Rivers of Canada" and chanted with him "Columbia and Fraser and Bear and Kootenay."

"Did you recognize how musical the names of our Canadian rivers are?" asked "Helps to Study," appending a list of further reading by Canadian writers.

At Pioneer, as elsewhere in the province, children were still shunted back to England from time to time. In "Vitai Lampada" (The torch of life), they were playing cricket, evidently a game of some kind with a "bumping pitch and a blinding light." They were urged to "play up, play up and play the game." But they came back to Canada with "Pass that Puck," a hockey story especially written for *Highroads to Reading* by a Canadian sports writer. "Goalie," "bodychecks," "sticking," "blue line": here was language that reverberated from the hockey rink in front of a community hall on Cadwallader Creek or from any other hockey rink across the country. Canadian children were learning that Canada was their home and native land, and that it was an interesting and exciting place.

I am grateful to Lord Balfour for his resounding words declaring the autonomy of the Dominions. But I am even more grateful to Guy Algernon Johnson, for it was he who brought the good news about Canada to our classroom at Pioneer Mine, a whole wilderness away from Enoch Arden and Annie, from London and King George.

And he brought us music and poetry too.

I don't believe there is any such power as Fate predetermining one's lot in life, nor do I believe in those goddesses of destiny, the Norns. But there is such a thing as Luck, sometimes bringing good, sometimes bad. When I think of that slab of rock that hit Gunnar Brothen I see a huge monster looming up in that underground cave and overcoming a man going peaceably about his work, unaware of sudden danger. That's how Bad Luck came to him.

In addition to accidents caused by falling rock, miners could be injured or killed during blasting, as when a "missed shot" unexpectedly exploded. They could fall down chutes or shafts, or get hit by a runaway ore car or burned by inadvertently igniting the methane gas that sometimes leaked into the mine atmosphere from the earth and rock. The steel-wire hoist ropes could break and send a cage plunging recklessly to the bottom of the shaft.

Even experienced miners could be killed by a moment's inattention, a careless response, a mistake in judgement, whether their own or another's. At Pioneer one cage-tender heard a disturbing sound as he ascended the shaft. He put his head outside the cage to discover the cause and was dragged out of the cage when his head was caught by a horizontal timber. He fell down the shaft to his death. At Bralorne, two miles down the road, a miner picked up a stick of dynamite that had failed to go off and put it in his hip pocket. It exploded and killed him a few minutes later.

The mine managers, governed by the Metalliferous Mines Regulation Act and their own good sense, held safety inspections. In 1934, the year Gunnar Brothen was killed, the Act was in the process of being revised once again, but some of its archaic provisions were still in effect. It is unlikely that mine owners in British Columbia employed twelve-year-old boys, as the Act permitted them to do (or even fifteen-year-olds, still allowed in the next revised Act, though not underground). However, in 1934 the Act still allowed an eighteen-year-old to be in charge of the complicated set of mine signals that governed the lowering and raising of men and loads of steel and drills and boxes of dynamite up and down a shaft extending perhaps half a mile below surface. In 1935 the Act was revised to require the hoist-man to be at least twenty-two years old and to have had "adequate experience in operating a reversing hoist." He had to have a medical certificate declaring him to be mentally sound and in possession of all his senses.

To carry out the B.C. Code of Mine Signals, a complicated system using bells, the hoist-man had to have all his wits about him. One bell: the hoist signal to surface; two bells: lower to bottom or to working station; three bells: caution – men preparing to ride. Then came the hoist or lower signal, but only after a fifteen-second double pause. Much depended on that pause, and the order in which the signals were given. A certain combination might mean "men on, to No. 5 Station, lower away." A different order of signals, or bells, with the appropriate pauses, might mean "station wants foreman." One of the rules in the code stated, "The BLASTING or ... 'READY TO SHOOT' signal (four bells) must be *acknowledged* by engineer, as described, before it can be considered as accepted by him. Miners must not light fuse before engineer has so acknowledged and *accepted* their signal, as it may not be possible at that moment to hoist." The hoist-man had a very important job, for the safety of the men going up and down in the cage depended on him. At Pioneer, they were fortunate to have Pete Jensen as their hoist man for some years. With him, the men were in safe hands. Of course, they had to observe a few sensible rules themselves.

The 1935 revised Act also required the mining company to vouch for the competence of miners responsible for setting off the blasts, those daily little earthquakes. Blasters were now required to hold a blasting certificate from the Inspector of Mines. They had to know the rules, and the rules were set out in the Act. The size and number of drill holes, length of fuse, counting of exploding shots, marking and blasting of missed-fire shots: blasting was a complicated and dangerous business.

Gunnar Brothen didn't hold a blasting certificate; like most miners he had simply been shown what to do. Valuing his own life and the lives of his fellow workers, and being, as required by the Act, "trustworthy and sober," on that last night he was doing it right. When all the fuses were ready, he would have lit them and yelled "Fire." Then he and his nipper (helper) would have retreated a safe distance down a passageway, guarding the entrance against anyone who might blunder through it at this time. They would have counted the explosions. If any were missing, Gunnar would have reported them to a shift boss so that the missed-fire shots could later be blasted under special supervision.

The blasting completed, Gunnar and his nipper would have walked over to the shaft and been hoisted up to the surface in the cage. Then he'd have walked across the road to the "dry" to shower and change out of his work clothes. He'd have picked up his black lunch bucket and walked up the hill and home for breakfast.

That slab of rock didn't wait for him to light the fuses and finish his shift. Call it Bad Luck and so answer the impossible question, "Why?"

Otherwise, is there any reason for this miner's death? My father thought gold was a useless metal. "Worthless rocks," my father called the ore he sweated to produce. "Profits for somebody else." I can hear the bitterness in his voice, and I doubt that I could have convinced him that gold did have uses beyond mere ornamentation in the form of bracelets and earrings. It is, for example, an excellent conductor because it is soft and malleable and therefore is used in the electronic industry to coat connections. But what would he have cared about computers? About the long history of gold as a symbol of power, a regulator of world finance by a system, now defunct, called the gold standard? Or about the very word itself, evoking ideas of virtue, truth, beauty?

The men killed in mine accidents at Kirkland Lake, Ontario, have been remembered by a Miner's Memorial Stone on which their names are inscribed.

Let me then make Gunnar Brothen's story a memorial to all the men killed in British Columbia mining accidents throughout the years, represented by the hard-rock metal miners who lost their lives in 1934. Here are their names as listed in the *Report of the Minister of Mines, 1934*.

Joe Annett	Gunnar Brothen	Steve Cernak
Joseph Coyle	Marco Dangela	Robert Fornasa
Ernest Fox	Alexander Gillis	Martin Kralj
Carl Lauderbach	Joseph E. Lewis	Ole Loberg
Rasmus Lodome	Norman McIvor	Dominico Morronel
Samuel Perkins	Samuel Popatz	Alexander Rea
Steve Slonsky	Ferdinand Turk	Joseph Umiljenovich
	Robert White	

The miners sitting in our kitchen after the accident stared into their homebrew, silent except for the occasional *"fan ta det"* – "devil take it." They were thinking about Gunnar in that underground cave called a stope, and of themselves, soon to go on shift again and take their chances.

In the town of Pioneer labour strife was just as intense as the annual hockey rivalries. In 1939 the miners organized under the International Union of Mine, Mill and Smelter Workers, but the company refused to recognize the union. The miners went out on strike. In the end the miners lost, but the strike would go down in history.

Some five months after the miners went out on strike the company still wouldn't budge, wouldn't recognize the Union as bargaining agent. Well, by God, they'd take the strike underground. That would make management see that Local 308 of the International Union of Mine, Mill and Smelter Workers was here to stay. That's how Sam Nomland saw it, and the other union members agreed.

On February 27, 1940, at 4:30 a.m. forty-one strikers at Pioneer Gold entered the mine, descended to the 2,400-foot level, over 3,000 feet below the surface, and remained there for nearly three days. They'd stopped by the "dry" to pick up their carbide lamps (the new battery lamps were company property and unavailable), slipped past two Provincial Police sound asleep at their post, and cut through the high wire fence that the company had constructed around the mine.

"The tunnel entrance was padlocked," Charles "Ace" Haddrell recalled. "We just got our hands on them [the padlocks], and 'C'mon,' we pulled and ripped off the locks. The company hadn't shut off the power, but we couldn't go down in the cage. It was locked." The sit-downers instead descended the shaft by the ladders that extended from level to level. In their packsacks they carried blankets, a supply of food for several days, a radio, and some electric hot plates for cooking.

Apprentice electrician Wally Seretny was among the forty-one union men who went down in the mine that morning. His father was Big Joe Seretny, timberman at Pioneer. The Seretny family couldn't afford to keep Wally in high school in Vancouver, so now he too was working at Pioneer. His job was to look after the mine locomotives.

"Jeez, Irene, that was sixty years ago," he told me when I asked about the strike. "I can't even remember the names of all the lovely ladies I've been with in my life, let alone that strike." Then his eyes took on a faraway look, and he began to see himself climbing down those ladders, down and down for over half a mile.

"And it was rough, eh? A couple of areas around there, 500 level, there were a few little underground streams and some of them were going right into the shaft. The water was dripping down on the ladders. By the time we got down to the bottom we were soaked.... And you know, with carbide lamps you couldn't see very much at all, climbing down in total darkness. It was scary." Wally was eighteen years old at the time. He played guitar and sang and was MC at the Saturday night dances. He rode a unicycle and performed his juggling act for delighted audiences.

Ace Haddrell did not recall the ladders as an ordeal: "We were young and tough then." Ace was then thirty-one, with a wife and child. He was born for books and politics and philosophy, but his formal education finished after elementary school. "That was considered enough in those days." During the 1920s he had to scramble for a living, but he finally got a regular job as a miner at Cariboo Quartz. After that he moved on to Pioneer Mine. He said he had this job because his father, a hotelkeeper, was a bootlegger and knew company director Colonel Victor Spencer as one of his customers. "So I was suspect at first among the boys." But Ace was one of the miners who saw right away that Pioneer needed a union and started it going.

The strikers were installed in the hoist room on the 2,400 level at 6:40 a.m. The descent had taken over two hours. The company hadn't turned off all the power: the lights and telephone were still working. The men immediately phoned management and warned them not to use the hoist. "The barricade was my idea," Ace recalled with a chuckle. "I was the instigator." Throughout the five months of the strike, the Provincial Police had been a heavy presence at the mine. Ace figured a posse of baton-swinging policemen could emerge at any time from the cage. The strikers would have to erect a barrier to prevent a surprise attack. They raised timbers into place to stop the descent of the cage, posted four-man watches at the remaining entry points, and ten-man mid-night watches. Now they were safe. It was warm down there, 65 or 70 degrees Fahrenheit, twice as warm as on the surface, and dry. "We slept a lot," recalled Frank Hennessey. "Daytimes too." He'd been among the unemployed young men who rode the rails across Canada and found work only in the federal relief camps at twenty-five cents a day. "Transients" the government called them. He had marched in the Relief Camp Workers strike in 1935. Now he was married and living at Pioneer in a cabin in the bush with Myrtle and their two-year-old son Danny.

Down in the mine shaft the radio and hot plates couldn't operate because the power voltage was so low. The men collected wooden powder boxes and built a fire under the raise (a vertical or inclined tunnel to the level above), where the smoke would go up and out. Then they could at least boil water for coffee and cocoa.

During the 1930s Pioneer Mine, as one of the largest gold producers in the world, paid handsome dividends. It also paid higher wages than most mining companies: $5.65 a day for miners, $5.00 for muckers. The men were now asking for an increase of $1.00 a day, but the main issue in this strike was not about wages. It was about union recognition. What happened was a show-down between a mining company determined to maintain control of its work-ers and an equally determined union whose members claimed the right to meet with management on an equal footing to discuss wages and grievances.

In the 1930s the general attitude of employers to unions was hostile and suspicious. Throughout Canada unions did not exist legally. There was no such thing as collective bargaining, and "arbitration" and "conciliation" were words as yet foreign to the lexicon of labour relations. Workers did not have the right to strike. If they did go on strike anyway, for better wages and working conditions, the response from employers was more likely police truncheons and tear gas than any attempt at reasonable discussion. It's true that after the First World War a National Industrial Conference of labour and industry had been arranged in Ottawa in 1919. It had included on its agenda "consideration of the Labour Features of the Treaty of Peace." The Versailles Treaty offered nine general principles for consideration by the newly formed League of Nations, with the first and "guiding principle" being "that labour should not be regarded merely as a commodity or article of commerce." It also recommended the eight-hour day, and declared in sum that the producers of a country's goods and services, many of whom were at the time returning soldiers, should have a voice in determining wages and working conditions. It concluded quite firmly that, if adopted, these principles "will confer lasting benefits upon the wage-earners of the world."

However, at the conference many industry spokesmen were eloquent in their defence of the ten-hour, even twelve-hour, day and refused to accept employee recommendations for an eight-hour day. Industry did concede the right of labour to organize, without, however, any obligation on the part of employers to recognize unions. And there matters stood for the next fifteen years.

In 1937 the B.C. government of Premier T. Dufferin Pattullo passed the Industrial Conciliation and Arbitration Act, which finally gave legal recognition to the idea and practice of collective bargaining between employee and employer. Industry evidently made known its objections to this, for only a year later, the Act was amended. The new wording did indeed grant workers the privilege of discussing wages and working conditions with their bosses, but still denied them the right to have a union speak for them. The amended Act now declared that if a union had been organized before December 7, 1938, a company would have to recognize it and negotiate with its officers. After that date, bargaining must be conducted by duly elected representatives of the employees. These representatives could be union officials or not; it didn't matter. What did matter was that the representatives of the workers be elected by a majority of the employees. The existence of a union didn't enter into the question of bargaining. So as far as the employers were concerned, unions did not exist.

In 1938, before becoming a local of Mine-Mill, the miners at Pioneer and Bralorne had belonged not to a union but to a Workmen's Co-operative Committee sponsored by management. Since 1917, Consolidated Mining and Smelting at Trail and Kimberley had been bringing management and labour together by means of just such committees, ostensibly providing workers a voice, but in fact attempting to stall the increasingly vociferous union movement. An editorial in the mining industry's publication (which had the confusing title of *The Miner*) explained:

> The system [of committees] is a truly democratic one, the members of the Workmen's Co-operative Committees being the elected representatives of all the employees, but it departs definitely from the union concept in that it was never designed to be an instrument for "bargaining," but rather a medium to promote sympathetic understanding of common problems and on that basis to ensure fair play to all concerned.

However, the managers at Pioneer did not follow this safe and well-established means of control. They weren't interested even in trying a little "sympathetic understanding." They refused to talk with the Co-operative Committee and discuss grievances, even though it had been elected by majority vote and met the requirements of the amended Act.

It was then that men like Ace Haddrell and Sam Nomland decided that they needed to belong to an organization with some clout. They left the Co-operative Committee, bringing with them a number of the men, and joined Mine-Mill as Local 308.

Managing director–mining engineer Dr. Howard T. James was opposed to unions, and especially to the Mine, Mill and Smelter Workers, who were affiliated with the militant, left-wing CIO (Congress of Industrial Organizations). He shared the general view of the mining industry, as expressed by an editorial in *The Miner*, that the aim of the CIO was "obnoxious" and not to be tolerated, especially in wartime. The editorial further warned that "the CIO is not only an alien organization, but a dangerously subversive one," and that to have uninterrupted production the industry must resist "the malign and disturbing influence of paid agitators of the foreign and communistic CIO."

James was a Harvard graduate, an experienced geologist and mining engineer. When David Sloan was tragically killed in a plane crash in 1934, James took his place, and he proved an able manager. But overseeing the mine operation required him to deal directly with the employees, and unfortunately he was better with rocks than with people. He had no easy fund of talk and argument, and his very reserve made him seem cold and unfeeling. Given his position as a major representative of the mining industry and its anti-union views, this confrontation with the union would also show him to be rigid and stubbornly uncompromising. It is true that the Mine-Mill organizer for Local 308, Tom Forkin – tall, pink-cheeked, curly-haired – was a member of the Communist Party. He was one of five brothers, all labour organizers. Everybody knew the Forkins of Brandon, Manitoba, with their Irish love of language and easy ways – Communist and proud of it. But the union leaders at Pioneer, young men who were breathing quartz dust every day and risking their lives underground, who were not miners by choice but by economic necessity, had already been politicized, as were so many young men, in that decade of the Depression.

Local 308 had been formed in April 1939. When a dispute arose in June, it was settled through a conciliation commissioner working with two bargaining agents, William Cameron and Wilfred "Pat" Paterson, officials of the union. The union claimed this as de facto recognition. They'd held a secret ballot on May 26 at the "dry" to let all the employees on all three shifts vote, and a majority did vote to apply for a conciliation commissioner. Although Cameron and Paterson were officials of the union, in this vote they had represented not just the union but the whole community of employees. Supported by the letter of the law, the Pioneer Mine management did not have to recognize Local 308.

In September, when the union requested formal recognition and dues check-off, management refused even to have a meeting with them to discuss these matters. The union sent an urgent telegram to Labour Minister George Pearson requesting a conciliation commissioner. Pearson replied that the application didn't meet the formal requirements of the Act and sent in an investigator instead. Once again, Pearson was right: the telegram did not qualify as legal proof that a dispute existed. The union officials were young and inexperienced and government and management were unbending and sternly legal, although the concept of investigator was clearly outside the provisions of the Act. After more open meetings of employees, more secret ballots, more confrontation, and increasing hostility, the union distributed a brief giving their side of the story and explaining their position. In a formal printed brief, Labour Minister George Pearson addressed the substance of the union brief, point by point. Paraphrasing the 1938 amendment to the Act, he stated that the representatives of the employees "do not have to be employees of this employer and they can be officers of the Union, but the employer need recognize them only as representatives of his employees and not necessarily as officers of the union." The amended Act effectively made unions powerless, for it allowed management to ignore their existence.

The miners felt scorned, affronted not just by James and the management of Pioneer Mine but also by the Department of Labour and the B.C. government, by a whole world that refused to listen when they spoke. What could be more reasonable than that they as workers should have a say on questions of work and wages? They demanded to be heard.

On October 8, 1939, at 3:45 p.m. the union sent an ultimatum to the company ("Scribbled in pencil!" exclaimed James, incredulous), demanding union recognition, dues check-off, and, for good measure, a one-dollar raise in pay (this last a new demand). They gave the company forty-five minutes to reply. They were determined to go out on strike, ignoring that the law required a fourteen-day waiting period after all attempts at conciliation and arbitration had failed.

At six o'clock that evening the men stopped work, leaving some safety and maintenance men on duty. The government declared the strike illegal because, once again, the workers had not complied with the law and in any case, in its view, the union didn't exist. The union officials – Bill Cameron, Alex Penman, Pat Paterson, A.M. Cameron, Sam Nomland, Ace Haddrell – were charged with violating the law. The union hired a young labour lawyer, John Stanton, but despite his able defence the men were found guilty in magistrate's court and ordered to pay fines of $150 to $200 or spend three months in jail.

In an attempt to break the strike, the company embarked on a campaign of harassment. It disconnected steam pipes, turned off heat and light in the bunkhouses, closed down the hospital, locked up the poolroom and library in the community hall, closed the cookhouse. Howard James and his superintendent and foreman were even said to have entered a bunkhouse one night and snatched blankets off the beds while some of the men were asleep – this last outrage communicated in one of Paterson's phone calls to Stanton as well as in the union's brief.

From October to December the accusations and reprisals proliferated, as did the telegrams and phone calls, the court cases and boardroom meetings, the union appeals for money. The union tried again to reach a settlement: it submitted anew its demands in eight proposals. By December the company was fed up and ready to talk with the union. The price of gold was rising, the operation had to get back into production. The dispute reached the floor of the Legislature, where the CCF (Co-operative Commonwealth Federation), led by Harold Winch, formed the opposition and supported the union's eight proposals. Winch put pressure on the minister of labour to intervene. Pearson phoned company director Alfred Bull, who told him that he was instructing James to accept the union's proposals and settle. The company would even provide each family with a free turkey for Christmas.

The government and the company were finally recognizing Local 308, though it was not the legal recognition the men were striking for. But James would not, could not, give in. He only dug the company in deeper. He drew up his own counterproposals and submitted them to the union.

On January 25, 1940, Deputy Sheriff Charlie Cunningham apologetically began evicting men from the bunkhouses. The company charged that, since the strike was illegal, the men were no longer its employees and were therefore not entitled to accommodation.

Another month went by. Families, themselves short of groceries, were feeding the evicted men, sometimes sheltering them. The union was penniless, its strike funds spent. Strikers went out hunting to provide food for their families. They had been out for five months and it was a long, cold winter. They couldn't go on much longer. When Sam Nomland proposed the sit-down, the union grabbed the idea. Thus it was that on February 27, 1940, at 4:30 a.m., forty-one miners took the strike down the ladders right into the mine.

Premier Pattullo had earlier sent in several members of the Provincial Police force. Now he sent in a detachment eighty-strong under the command of Police Inspector John Shirras. After the men had been holed up on the 2,400 level for sixty-two hours, Inspector Shirras and company officials went down in the cage (the men had removed the barricade). "I wouldn't want to harm a single hair of your heads," he assured them. And he meant it. ("He was a good guy," said Ace Haddrell.) If they didn't come up of their own accord, they'd be driven out, "cost what it might." He promised they wouldn't be prosecuted, so they came out: they'd drawn enough attention to the dispute.

Afterwards, Shirras said that forcing the men out "would have taken 100 men at least and no one can say what might have happened." He may have been thinking of the tear gas sprayed on the unemployed who had occupied the Vancouver Post Office in 1938, or the truncheons used on striking Vancouver longshoremen at Ballantyne Pier. The sit-downers, led by Cameron and Paterson and including other union members, marched in a body to the office of Howard James to learn whether or not they still had a job. Only about forty of the miners were reinstated, those who were needed to get the mine in operation again, such as electricians and timbermen. In all, over a hundred were refused a job – fired on the spot or put off with evasive reasons about the need to cut back. They left camp for Vancouver, their way paid by the government.

When Wally Seretny spoke of his interview with Howard James he no longer had that faraway look in his eyes. He told me: "Because I was so damned belligerent, Howard says, 'I'm sorry, Wally, you're not welcome in our employ anymore.' I blew up. I told him, 'You rotten son of a bitch.'" And here Wally became almost incoherent, telling how James had during the strike asked him to come back to work because the lower levels were flooding and they urgently needed an electrician to repair the pump motors. "He wanted me to scab on the others. Look at me, I'm getting mad all over again. And the doorway to his office was open, eh? The guys waiting in the hall were calling out, 'Atta boy, Seretny, give it to him!'"

Some four years after the strike, the miners did get their voice, along with all other Canadian workers. On February 17, 1944, the federal government enacted an emergency Order-in-Council under the War Measures Act to ensure full war production without interruption by labour disputes. PC1003 provided compulsory collective bargaining between employer and employee. Thus, as the Summary of Regulations reasonably concludes, "Resort to strikes or lockouts is accordingly unnecessary and is forbidden during the term of the collective agreement." The word "conciliation" was written into federal law.

After the war the provincial governments again assumed responsibility for labour relations, except, of course, for industries under federal jurisdiction. Since that time, in British Columbia and other provinces governments have been amending our labour laws, most often to the detriment of labour but sometimes in its favour. But now, half a century after PC1003 wrote conciliation into federal law, the Supreme Court of Canada has re-examined Section 2 of the Canadian Charter of Rights, which sets forth our fundamental freedoms. On June 8, 2007, it ruled that freedom of association does indeed include the right to collective bargaining: "Human dignity, equality, liberty, respect for the autonomy of the person, and the enhancement of democracy are among the values that underlie the Charter.... All of these values are complemented and indeed, promoted, by the protection of collective bargaining in Section 2 (d) of the Charter."

So that settles it. Workers have rights. Employers have to discuss wages and working conditions with their unions in an exchange called bargaining. That kind of discussion is good for the country, for, as the Canada Labour Code says, "the common well-being" is served by "the encouragement of free collective bargaining and the constructive settlement of disputes."

Still, after sixty years the Pioneer men were still angry. "I never wanted to see another mine in my life when I left that place," said Wally Seretny. During the war he served five years in the Royal Canadian Engineers as staff sergeant, earning three stripes and a crown. On furlough he'd sing with the Sandy de Santis band at Vancouver's Palomar: "Chattanooga Choo Choo," "Elmer's Tune," "This Love of Mine," a familiar figure in zoot suit and suede shoes. (The pants had narrow cuffs and were wide at the knees. "You had to keep them well pressed or they'd look like hell.") After the war he became one of Vancouver's most valued electricians, and for thirty-two years he worked for White Spot restaurants, playing and singing as well with the Veterans' Memorial Band and the Happyland Dance Band at Hastings Park.

Ace Haddrell was blacklisted and had to move back east with his family to find a job. He joined the Auto Workers' Union, then was accepted in the air force despite his silicosis. In old age he was still interested in ideas and would rather talk about the state of the world than be interviewed about stopes and quartz dust. And gold? "Most useless metal in the world," he snorted. How did he feel about men going down in the mine every day and spoiling their health for gold? "It's ridiculous, just ridiculous.... We've got to have miners for essential things like copper, iron ... but gold!" He gestured grandly: "If I had my way and was dictator of the universe, I'd say, 'No more gold. Too expensive.'" Ace remained a socialist, and as well as his political activities he entered energetically into the discourse of current events, writing letters to the editor and enjoying companionable conversation. He used some of his savings to make legacies for worthy causes. "And he was one hell of an organ player," claimed Wally.

And Frank Hennessey? Like Ace, he too was blacklisted and left mining behind. He became a camp cook in British Columbia's Cariboo Country and lived for hunting and fishing. "He was cheerful and optimistic, a favourite uncle" who took his little nephew David fishing and solemnly explained that "they had to stand behind a tree to bait their hooks because the fish were so eager they'd jump out of the water and snatch the bait." He was the Cariboo Country's champion fiddler and served as a judge in fiddling competitions.

Now they are old and worn out, all three, remembering only dimly what happened sixty years ago. But if you speak to them of the sit-down strike, images come before their eyes. They flare up and see themselves, young and defiant, huddled together on the 2,400 level. "We were bold and brave and fighting for the cause," said Frank, "fighting for the union." Union recognition was such a reasonable request. They weren't slave labour. They just wanted a voice, for when you have voice you have power. Howard James understood that. So did Tom Forkin. You could say they had something in common after all.

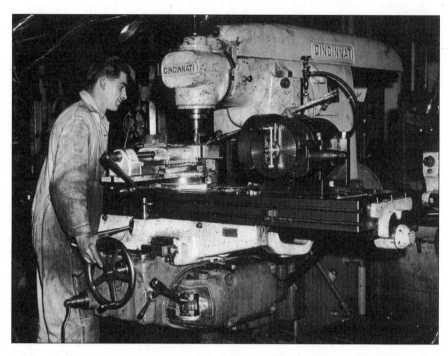

Verner Nelson operating a milling machine, Vancouver c.1950. (*Author's collection*)

Arthur Nelson at the Polaris Taku river landing, c.1950. (*Author's collection*)

NINE

DIAMOND FLUSH AND THE BLOWTORCH SOLUTION

POLARIS TAKU AND OTHER ADVENTURES

One time in the mid-1990s my brother Verne was playing the accordion for a bunch of us while we were reminiscing about the years in the cabin at the Duthie Mine, about our father and mother and the hard physical labour of their lives. "Toil," I said. "That's what it was. A life of unremitting toil. And now economists are predicting a work-scarce society." At this, my eighty-year-old brother stopped playing. If we were going to talk about work, he intended to get his two cents' worth in.

"The end of work, eh? They got that right. The way they're logging now up around Quesnel, I've seen a rig go right up to a tree and hook on to it and – zzzz bonk – down it goes. Some guy just pressed a button. That's all there was to it. And I'll tell you something else. Work began for us kids in a mining camp when we were still in short pants. We didn't sit around all day in front of a computer, playing games, pressing buttons. We were out there working with the men. Axes and saws – that's what we had."

He ran his fingers through his hair, still black without a streak of grey, and whooped with laughter. He was pleased with himself for making Verne Nelson, worker, the measure of your white-collar economists. As well he might, this big man whom I see standing on some mountaintop in British Columbia, arms akimbo, surveying all the mines and pulp mills he worked at. He started out cutting down trees, but he didn't become a logger. He became a machinist-millwright, a skilled craftsman who could do precision lathe work right down to four ten-thousandths of an inch – without your Computer Numerical Control. At Kitimat on the northwest coast he built the first aluminum smelting pot for Alcan. Then he went all across the province – Endako Mines, at Chetwynd, central B.C.; Prince George and Quesnel – pulp and paper; Bull Moose – open-pit coal mining in the foothills of the Rocky Mountains.

But right then, there in my living room, in a family circle of old uncles and aunts and young nieces and nephews, white-collar and computer-savvy, he had axes and saws on his mind and he wanted to tell these youngsters a thing or two about work.

"When I was eight years old," he begins, "I cut down a whole forest. With my brother Art. He was ten." This was always one of Arthur's stories, and we were all familiar with his version of it. But Arthur has other stories too, for he is the family's storyteller.

In the 1940s my older brothers all worked at Polaris Taku, a gold mine in northern British Columbia near the Alaskan border. It was situated on the Tulsequah River but named after the Taku River seven miles upstream, which ran down across the border towards Juneau, Alaska. Planes coming into Polaris landed on the Taku. In winter they had to use an airfield of packed snow. The only way in was by plane.

I have never visited the Tulsequah area, mostly because of the black flies and mosquitoes, so I will let my brother describe it.

"That was wild country up there, and desolate. You'd never know Juneau and civilization were only eighty miles away. The camp was down in a valley in the Coast Range, with high, jagged peaks and ice fields all around. From our camp we looked out on Mount Erickson, which was six thousand feet high. Funny thing though, we called it Erickson's Hill. I guess when you live in that kind of wilderness you find ways of scaling it down so you can manage it.

And I remember George Baker, he was a good man. He'd tell a story, and then he'd laugh, and his laugh would echo in the mountains.

"Some rich Americans owned the mine," Art continued. "Ed Congdon and his family from Minnesota. They were big wheels in Duluth, iron and copper, you know, around Lake Superior. They'd fly up in the summer, spend a few weeks in the manager's beautiful spacious house, have their meals at the cookhouse after the miners had finished eating. It seemed to me the gold mine was more like a hobby for them."

In fact, Edward C. Congdon had been exploring mineral properties in the Taku River area since 1934. Polaris Taku Mining Company Ltd. was formed in 1936, but by 1940, under Walter B. Congdon, 170 men were employed, my three brothers among them. Homes had been built for families. Verne and his wife and child were living in one of them.

"I was a young punk in my twenties, a catskinner,"* Art said. "Trucks couldn't operate in winter so the mail had to be hauled by dog sled, and the powder to the mine – eighteen boxes a day. And then the groceries had to be delivered to families and the garbage hauled away. Sometimes the dogs couldn't handle all the freighting, so I had to help out with the tractor. But one of my main jobs as catskinner was to move the concentrates with the forklift and pile them in the mill. The concentrates were bagged in 135-pound sacks. With the mill working twenty-four hours, it was a pretty big job.

"Moving them was real assembly line. The men lift the sacks onto a conveyor belt, up it goes and drops on a platform. The man there picks it up and throws it down to where they're going to load the sacks onto the sleighs, because they do this in winter. And they hitch up the dog teams and drive them down the road to the Tulsequah River landing. So they unload the sleigh, and pile them, eighteen sacks high, along the side of the road. Every man who worked there lost weight. Even big men. I don't know about the dogs."

This part of the operation had to be done in winter, because in those early days the road out to the Tulsequah River landing from the mine was not developed enough for heavy vehicle traffic. The concentrates had eventually to be delivered to the smelter in Tacoma, but shipping too depended on freeze-up and spring thaw. The bags of concentrates remained piled on the riverbank all winter, waiting for the Taku River to open up again for river

---

* A catskinner is a term for the operator of a vehicle equipped with caterpillar treads.

traffic to the ocean port of Juneau on the Alaskan coast. Art well remembers the loading of the scow:

"Soon as the ice melts and the Taku opens up again, the men have to load the sacks onto sling boards on the bed of a truck, four rows piled six high, twenty-four sacks in each sling, six slings in a truck, that's a hundred and forty-four sacks. Then a crane on shore picks up the sacks from the truck and swings them over to the scow. And a tugboat pushes the scow down the Taku River and then down to Taku Inlet to the border of Alaska. And there's a freighter there, with a crane. It lifts the sacks onto the freighter and dumps them in the hold and the freighter heads off for Tacoma. Only so many months in the year we can do this, so the loading goes on night and day, twenty-four hours. So that was my job. Getting the concentrates out, driving the tractor.

"When I wasn't working I was playing cards. This was just at the beginning of the war and Polaris had only been operating for a couple of years. When I went back there after the war there was a fine new community centre with a bowling alley, coffee shop, and all sorts of activities. But at the beginning there was just the big hall on the second floor of the cookhouse for Saturday night movies and card games – poker, blackjack, whist, bridge. Playing cards was our social life. You could find a card game going any time of the day or night. Everything I know about poker and blackjack I learned from the miners at Polaris Taku.

"The poker was always no-limit: you could bet your shirt if you wanted. At first I always lost my paycheque, though at least I never lost my shirt. But I was playing against the best and I learned fast.

"Psychology John was one of the best. He was a stope-miner, a big rawboned Yugoslav. When he won a pot, his eyes would twinkle and he'd say, 'I play psychology.' I never put any stock in that. I knew he was just a good player who never stooped to any funny business. He was no card shark.

"Handlebar Joe was a Russian sourdough, one of the last of the Klondikers. When he was pondering whether or not to call a hand, he'd stroke his beautiful black moustache. He was the caretaker of the potatoes and carrots and turnips and eggs in the "dry" tunnel, a pretty important job considering he had charge of basic food stuffs for the camp over the winter. Not that anybody gave him credit for that. He had about as much social status as your ordinary mucker. But when he got all dressed up in his brown gabardine suit and flew into Juneau, he was a different man. He'd entertain the mayor or the governor of Alaska in his suite at the Baranoff Hotel, and they'd return his hospitality. He was a great storyteller. His English was broken, he had a heavy accent, but could he ever talk! When he was at a party, everybody crowded around him just to listen.

"Cariboo King was from Switzerland – tough and strong as a mule. He was a mucker. He loaded ore cars and in those days, loading was by hand, with a shovel.

"Soapy Smith was a tall, lean, bearded man, actually related to the *real* Soapy Smith, the American con-man of the Klondike. Our Soapy was just one of the guys. Maybe his name wasn't even Smith. He never said. He was a quiet sort of fellow.

"There were others: Eight-ball, his head shiny as a billiard ball, followed a few months later by his brother Nine-ball, whose head was just as shiny. And Joe Loftus, an Irishman, head of our local. We were all in the Mine, Mill and Smelter Workers' union. I played with these fellows for a whole year. I was easy to beat, but they didn't cold-deck me. They never stacked the deck, I'll say that. Well, we all knew that was strictly out. Any crooked work and you were finished. You'd have to leave the camp.

"Finally, I started to win. I won and I won. I'd play every day, all week, month after month. At the end of a game I could have a fistful of fifty-dollar bills.

"I remember one game of stud poker when I raked in a pot from Joe Loftus. I was dealt a diamond on the first round, Joe got an ace. He was high, so he bet. Some of the players threw in their hands, but I saw him. On the second round he bet again and I raised him because now I had two diamonds and anyway I knew Joe was a bluffer. Of course he didn't know I had another diamond in the hole. On the third round he back-raised me, he went all in, put all his money in the pot and turned up his hole card. It was an ace.

"'Nelson,' he says, 'I've got two aces. Beat that you lousy square-head of a Swede.'

"Now he has nothing left but I've made a pile, so I call his back-raise to give him a play. On the next deal I get another diamond.

"'Joe,' says I, real soft and friendly, 'Joe, do you feel yourself slipping?'

"Joe doesn't look too good. Everybody at the table is getting pretty excited. I turn up my hole card. I've got a diamond flush and he has only a pair of aces.

"'Art,' says Joe in his thick Irish brogue, 'yer too damn lucky. Yer gonna die tomorrah.'

"But I had a weakness and it was blackjack. I'd take my poker winnings to the blackjack table. They'd see me coming. I'd sit down and right away ask, 'How much is in the bank?' It might be as much as two or three thousand dollars. And I'd always tap the bank. Invariably I'd lose. It's hard to beat the bank, because in blackjack the odds are with the bank. The only way to win in blackjack is to make a light bet and wait till you get dealt twenty-one. Then you have the deal and you're in a position to win. But I didn't know these things, so I'd lose all my money and then I'd have to leave. But next night I'd be back to gamble at blackjack with my poker winnings.

"I was an easy mark. When I sat down they'd josh me: 'Well, here's Nelson. Who's gonna be the lucky guy to fly out to Vancouver tomorrow?' Sure enough, next morning somebody would be over at the office, getting ready to take the next plane out – on my winnings. I didn't care, because even though wages were low, I was making lots of money from poker. So I always had enough to fly out to Juneau for a weekend or to Vancouver for a holiday.

"I played blackjack all the time I was at Polaris Taku and I lost and lost. It was years before I finally understood that I wasn't ever going to make money at blackjack – not the way I played it.

"But poker – that was different. I was still gambling hard when I went back to Polaris after the war. I wasn't catskinner any more. I was surface foreman and had a hundred men working under me. Airfield, roads, family housing, freight, shipping – they were all my responsibility now, and it seemed to me like I was running the whole joint. The job got pretty heavy sometimes but that was okay as long as I could keep on winning at poker."

"If hell ever does freeze over, I'm the man they'll ask to come and thaw it out. When the water pipes froze one night, it sure would've been hell if I hadn't thought of a way to get the water running again." Arthur was regaling us with his further adventures at Polaris Taku mining camp, from when he went back there after the war.

"When the water froze in the winter of 1947, they were going to have to evacuate the camp of around four hundred people and fly the women and children out to Juneau. We had about 250 men in bunkhouses – muckers, stope-miners, catskinners, flunkies – and fifteen families in their own houses: Tommy Cox, mechanic, and his wife Mar; Lars Dahl, carpenter, and Louise;

the Belinskis – Bill was the underground-motor-man, drove the tram cars; Tom Skomedal, mine superintendent after Dave Yorston, and Evelyn; Anthony Arnold, radio operator, timekeeper, and Iris.

"And Gordie Phillips, the cook, and Jean. Terrible what happened to Gordie at Polaris – burned to death one night when their house went up in flames. Yeah, so terrible. Jeez, even now, when I think of it. . . . I tried climbing up into the window, you know . . . "

Art stopped to reflect on this terrible tragedy, not able to talk about it, forgetting for the moment frozen water pipes that would leave a community of four hundred people without water for drinking, washing, or flushing toilets. I try now to imagine what it must have been like with the plumbing frozen solid from the "dry house" where the miners changed their clothes and showered when they came off shift, to the houses where the women were washing dishes and putting kids to bed. I can just hear Evelyn Skomedal – our housekeeper at Pioneer, Evelyn Lunby then – and I remember her jolly laugh, but I'm sure she wasn't laughing this time, when she turned on the tap and got nothing but a sputter.

So why did the water freeze this particular winter? Surely the water system was built to handle temperatures of 30 below?

Art explained: "The camp was down in a mountain valley and a nice little creek flowed through it. We got all our drinking water from higher up the creek where the water was collected in a big tank on the hillside. It was a wooden stave tank with a capacity of 50,000 gallons. The pipeline from the tank ran deep underground down to the bottom of the mountain, where it came to surface and entered the snowshed.

"Now this snowshed was a wood plank walkway five hundred feet long, ten feet wide, and it had to cross the creek. We built a roof over it, pitched so the snow would slide off, with side walls. The miners walked through the snowshed on their way to work at the mine, which was on the mountainside on the other side of the creek from the camp. Without this snowshed, the miners would've had to shovel a path every day. I'll tell you how much it snowed up there. All the houses had steep roofs made of corrugated iron. The snow piled up so high the kids could slide off the roofs right onto the snow in one long, unbroken slide.

"Of course, we had to insulate the pipeline when it emerged from underground. So here's what we did. Inside the snowshed, running the whole length, we built a long box filled with sawdust. We ran the pipeline, buried in sawdust, through the box, and the water wouldn't freeze even at 50 below. But this particular winter, 1947, the water did freeze. The sawdust had been changed and the new sawdust was a little damp. So the water froze just where the snowshed crossed the creek and didn't have the protection of ground underneath.

"So all the big wheels got together for an emergency meeting – manager, mill superintendent, mine superintendent, head accountant. I was only surface foreman, but I came anyway to listen in. They were pretty worried. The manager, Robertson, figured they'd have to close the camp down. He was a mean old cuss, the kind of guy who could make you squirm, but he was okay. I remember one time we met head on. I wouldn't do what he wanted.

"So he threatens, 'Nelson, I could fire you.'

"He didn't scare me. 'Go ahead, start firing.'

"And then he says, 'Oh, shut up, Nelson. C'mon home with me and have a drink.'

"And now, because of a frozen water pipe he was figuring on evacuating the camp! I listened for a while, the others weren't saying much, and I didn't say anything either, but I thought to myself, 'Goddammit, that's crazy.' and I left. I knew right away where the trouble was and I knew what to do.

"I called out my crew. It was just after supper. Everybody was settling down for the evening.

"'Jimmy,' I said – that was Jimmy Weir, drove the pickup truck. Liked his booze, but he was a good worker – 'Jimmy, take half a dozen men up to the mine portal and get a load of fourteen-inch fan pipe. We'll need five hundred feet in all. And Charlie, Joe, Tommy, you gather up the fire hoses. Make sure they're good and dry.'

"There was a fire hydrant at the far end of the snowshed, and the water in it wasn't frozen. The valve at the other end was in the 'dry house,' which was close to the snowshed. My idea was to construct a bypass to bring that water through and over the creek where the pipe was frozen. The water could run through the fire hose. That part was simple enough. The main problem was to prevent the water in the fire hose from freezing. That's what the fourteen-inch fan pipes were for. I was going to run the hose through those pipes and heat the air around it with a blowtorch.

"Well, the crew just stood there at first. They thought I was crazy, said my plan wouldn't work.

"'Never mind if it won't work. Just do it.'

"But how was I going to heat the bypass without burning the hose? Even an ordinary propane torch reaches temperatures of a thousand degrees Celsius, and this was a fuel oil torch, the kind that's used in doing asphalt road work. It had a big tank, maybe fifteen gallons. With a tank that big, you can pump up a lot of pressure, and the more pressure the longer the flame. A torch like this can shoot flames two or three feet long. It could frizzle a fire hose in a couple of seconds.

"No problem. I just fitted a forty-foot length of steel pipe to one end of the fire hose. Then I stood back a couple of feet, lit the torch, and there was a big roar of blue and red flame as the cold air got sucked in and mixed with the hot air rushing down the line.

"'OK boys,' I yelled, 'Turn 'em on.' They opened the valves and the water went rushing through the hose. My men cheered, water sputtered in the taps of the houses, women came to their kitchen doors calling to one another.

"We kept the torch running for three weeks, twenty-four hours a day, hot air shooting down those fan pipes and keeping the fire hydrant hose warm. At the same time we were working on the regular pipeline, repacking it with dry sawdust, and that was some job too. But we got it done and finally turned off the heat.

"Another time at Polaris Taku, I used a blowtorch to thaw out a plane. The pilot was an American who had flown flat-tops in the war in the South Pacific. Now he was flying passengers and freight in and out of Polaris Taku for Alaska Airlines. The landing field was packed snow, about four miles from camp on the Tulsequah River. It was about thirty below and windy and he couldn't get his twin-engine started. Right away I thought of how I'd used a blowtorch to keep the water running.

"I phoned camp and told them to send over two hundred feet of fourteen-inch pipe, a couple of the heaviest canvas tarps and the fuel torch, the same one I'd used to thaw the frozen water pipes. We covered the engine cowlings with the tarps. They hung all the way to the ground, making a little tent over the enclosed engines. We laid down two hundred feet of fan pipe with the end just inside the canvas tent. I turned on the torch, and blasts of hot air went shooting down the pipe and up under the covered engines. In two or three minutes black oil started dripping in the snow.

"'Good enough,' yells the pilot.

"We pulled the tarps off. He climbed into the cockpit, started the engine and taxied down the airstrip.

"That was one happy bush pilot. I can still see him looking at that dripping oil and then at the blowtorch shooting flame, and he's saying, 'I never seen that happen before.'

"It was old stuff for me. In my job I was always dealing with emergencies – never knew what might happen next. But a blowtorch helped me out a lot of times. Of course, it helped to use your brains, I can tell you that."

Art phoned one day in the late 1990s to tell me about his dream. He was walking with a woman beside a river where they found rocks full of gold on the shore, glinting in the sunlight. They found kidney beans among the rocks, and each bean contained a pearl. The kidney beans have an easy explanation: his neighbour had brought him a bowl of chili con carne for dinner that night. The golden rocks also have an explanation, but it goes back to when he was a young man working at Pioneer Gold Mine in the Bridge River Country.

Remember the gold dust on my brother's shirt? The scene transforms itself in my mind. My eighty-six-year-old brother, battered by age and industrial accident, becomes a Golden Youth holding a box of gold on his knees, and Harry Cain at the crusher is there too, the whole scene hammered out in a bas-relief panel as by some Egyptian goldsmith in aeons past for the young Tutankhamen in his tomb. It's my own archaeological find, an offering to a continuing history that goes back to long before even the treasures of that pharoah or of Croesus, back even to the Neolithic Age, and it commemorates our veneration of this precious metal and our fascination with it through the ages. It also commemorates the place of gold in the history and economy of British Columbia.

After the mining camps Art became a logger and a dredge-foreman; Verne a master mechanic and milllwright; Ed a high-school teacher and Member of Parliament in Ottawa, representing the New Democratic Party.

The Boys were among the thousands of young men dispossessed by the Great Depression of a formal education. In a later decade, they might have gone on to have professional careers in science, medicine, technology, the arts. Instead, they were forced to take whatever work came their way and make the best of it. It was all arbitrary, and a good many of the workers at

Pioneer Mine were young men like my brothers. Then the Second World War came along, and shunted them about again.

Workers in essential industries were frozen in their jobs. Lumber was needed for construction, loggers were needed, and Art had been a faller on Vancouver Island. "Any of you men loggers?" barked the recruiting sergeant. Art didn't respond, but one of his buddies piped up, "Art Nelson, he's a logger." Art was summarily pulled out of the lineup of recruits and sent to the Alberni Canal on Vancouver Island to fell sitka spruce to make ribs for the Canadian fleet of Mosquito bombers. Built by de Havilland Aircraft, these were unarmed wooden speed planes used to carry out air raids over Germany. Verne was working as a machinist at Burrard Drydock when war was declared in 1939. Ships were needed. Shipbuilding was designated an essential industry and Verne remained at Burrard, but now he was one of 14,000 workers turning out at peak production one-third of all the cargo ships produced in Canada. "Victory Ships" they were called. Ed had been a flunky in the cookhouse at Polaris Taku gold mine before he joined up, and what with his experience behind the meat counter at Pioneer General Store as well, it only made sense to make him quartermaster and send him to the training camp at Harrison Lake to be in charge of stores.

At a morale-building concert for troops, Ed sang "Rose O'Day," the "Filla-da-Gusha Song," which Kate Smith made famous. He did this with a Swedish accent, and performed with such spirit and comic mimicry of the Swedish vowel sounds that he brought down the house. The men cheered and clapped and whistled and stomped their boots in a storm of applause. They rushed the stage and lifted him up on their shoulders and paraded him around the hall. Well, after that he'd probably have been sent overseas to help Bob Hope and Vera Lynn entertain the troops in Sicily, if it weren't that one day, opening a bottle of Coca Cola, it broke and the jagged glass cut the tendon of his right hand. Henceforth he was unfit for active service despite his best efforts at squeezing a little rubber ball with the injured hand. But he was philosophical and claimed modestly to have been wounded on active service at the Battle of Harrison Lake.

That story is vintage family anecdote. It says nothing about the thoughtful, serious Ed, the high-school principal and English teacher, Member of Parliament representing Burnaby-Seymour for the New Democratic Party, stout Canadian nationalist who in 1973 introduced a private member's bill to establish February 15 as Canada Flag Day. This was the day in 1965 that the Maple

Leaf flag was first raised. The purpose of Bill C136, as proposed by Ed and thus described in Hansard, was to provide a holiday to "emphasize Canadian unity and to commemorate the ideals of the Bill of Rights and Late Prime Minister Pearson." The Bill found general approval in the House, for these were the years when Prime Minister Pierre Trudeau was fighting for a strong, united Canada. The Canada Flag Day Bill passed into law, February 5, 1973. The Monday after February 15 is now Heritage Day in some parts of Canada. Although not always celebrated as such, it's legal to take a mid-winter break in February, to go skiing for the weekend, and to think about Canada and Lester B. Pearson.

In the 1972 federal election, Ed had campaigned for the New Democratic Party on the question of the pollution of the oceans, and this long before the plight of the planet and our continued existence on it became of general concern. There was no Law of the Sea at that time, the word "moratorium" had not entered the language of fisheries, and governments were only that summer planning to meet and draw up protective legislation. As NDP member for Burnaby-Seymour, in question period he urged the government to get the conference to rule on the size of the supertankers that were endangering marine life. Some countries, not signatories to the NORPAC fishing agreement, were overfishing on our west coast. He urged the government make an effort to have those countries included in the agreement.

And Freddy? He turned eighteen in 1944, and after a few months of training at Camp Borden in Saskatchewan was ready to be sent to the Pacific theatre of war to fight the Japanese. Dad was desolate at the prospect of little Freddy holding a gun and urged him to try to be placed in some housekeeping department of the army, peeling potatoes maybe in a cook tent behind the lines. But suddenly the war ended. Freddy used his Department of Veterans Affairs Allowance to apprentice as an electrician and announced that he was no longer Freddy, he was Roy, and he would be known by his rightful, birth-certificate name, Roy Alfred. He bought a property at Ruth Lake, deep in the Cariboo, at the end of a road that he and his neighbours built. He moved his family there so his children wouldn't grow up hanging around on city streets, but would ski and skate on the lake in winter and in summer take the rowboat and go out and fish for rainbow trout. He transformed the old log cabin into a Swiss chalet, and he and his wife Edith generously allowed the rest of the family to visit on holidays, so that it became a family tourist resort where of an evening one would sit around the kitchen table, drink apricot brandy, and eat licorice allsorts while playing Trivial Pursuit. He was head electrician at Weldwood Forest Products near the town of 100 Mile. In winter he got up at three a.m. to plough the three miles of Ruth Lake Road, then went back home with the plough, grabbed his lunch box, and drove the fifteen miles to work. He was expert at rewinding electric motors, and he listened to the CBC as he worked. He was staunchly New Democrat, but admired Pierre Trudeau. He was a strong union man too in his local of the International Woodworkers of America. He was a faithful member of the local branch of the Canadian Legion.

Art never made any money on Bridge River gold, but he continued to invest in gold mines. He always was a gambler: win some, lose some, that was his way of looking at both cards and the stock market. He never gave up on gold, even in old age. When he was eighty-five years old, he and his friend Joe the Prospector, both crippled with osteoarthritis, went prospecting for gold, with Joe's dog Para in the back seat. Art knew just where to look. In 1930, when he and his father were driving to Planet Mine, Art had spotted an excavation in the hills, and they stopped to explore. His father said, "It's no use, son. The price is too low. Cover it over." But Art was excited about it and planned to go back some day. Some seventy years later he went back with Joe. They couldn't find the excavation.

"The countryside had changed," Art later told me. "There was a new road into Stump Lake, and there were summer homes, and the government had stocked the lake with fish. That ore body was on the old road, higher up. I said, 'Joe , we've got to go back there again.'"

They would take Para, of course. "He's smart," said Art. Then, laughing, "Maybe we can teach him to smell gold.

"I dreamt two or three men were shovelling gold dust into a truck. Worth countless millions and millions," Art told me later. "It was a big truck that could stand the weight. And then it was going to a new place for gold. There was a windstorm and gold blew out the back of the truck. People behind it were picking up gold. It was raining. The gold was pouring out of the truck, lost half of it in the street."

And then he laughed in a wondering sort of way. "It was so real that when I woke up I had to think about it for an hour to realize it was a dream."

My brother is no longer the Golden Youth with a box of gold on his knees, hammered out in bas-relief like a young Tutankhamen on a golden throne. I've made a new archaeological find, another gold bas-relief: Art and Joe with pickaxe and Para, above them the peaks of the Cascades. And just as in the gold panel behind the young king's throne, there's a big, round sun shining down. It shines on these two gallant, old prospectors who hope they're going to strike it rich some day.

The Boys, and Freddy too: they became Men, good, decent, hard-working like their father. But unlike him, never administering the chilivink to discipline their children. Like their spirited, fluent mother, they were talkers, seldom at a loss for words, having her easy gift of language. They were, I think, gently amused by, but proud, yes, proud, of their intellectual sister, washed up on the Shores of Local History, scratching out messages with a quill pen fashioned from a seagull's feather she found on the beach.

The mill at Pioneer Mine, with the shaft house above, c.1934.
(*Courtesy Charlie Cunningham and Beverly Orgnacco*)

The vault (left) and office (right) at Pioneer Mine, 1997.
(*Author's collection*)

TEN

SEARCHING FOR
MY HOMETOWN

PIONEER AND BRALORNE MINES, 1997

The mill was a pile of rubble. You could still make out the outlines of the cyanide tanks where they'd collapsed, but the mill building that housed the tanks and the ore crushers was just a pile of rubble. And the refinery building, too, where the gold was smelted and poured into moulds to make gold bricks. Only the big iron ball mills, stranded there beside Cadwallader Creek for nearly forty years, looked as though they could be put to use again for grinding gold quartz ore.

I was standing on the road above the creek looking at what was left of the Pioneer Gold Mine. I had driven the 350 kilometres from Vancouver into the Bridge River Valley in the Coast Range west of the Fraser River to revisit the place where I had spent part of my childhood. This was where I had first learned to stand by myself, without my mother to guide me. In memory, Pioneer seemed like my hometown. So I wanted to see what it was like there now, and how it answered my kind and forgiving nostalgia.

Abandoned now, Pioneer, true to its name, was the first producing mine among all the properties that made up the Bridge River Gold Camp, and for a brief time it was the largest gold mine in British Columbia. All the other gold mines in this Gold Camp have been abandoned too, all except Bralorne, which became the biggest producer of all. It is now the only one in the Bridge River Valley that is still operating, milling ore, and that only after a long period of inactivity.

But the Bridge River Valley has another valuable resource that took the place of gold: the river itself and the terrain through which it flows. During the postwar years, until the construction of the Bennett Dam on the Peace River was completed in 1968, Vancouver and the Lower Mainland were supplied with electricity from the power stations in the Bridge River Valley. The Bridge River is an unspectacular, meandering river for most of its course, but not far from where it flows into the Fraser it enters a bedrock canyon. Terzaghi Dam was constructed in this canyon, creating a reservoir thirty-eight miles long and flooding the fields and farms, camps, and other communities and even the road that followed the river along its westward course. This reservoir is Carpenter Lake. When the lake is full, at surface it is 2,145 feet above sea level, and can be drawn down to the 2,000-foot level to generate power.

Now Terzaghi Dam is 2,136 feet higher than Seton Lake, which is situated below and not far from Mission Mountain. This is the lucky geological happenstance – besides, of course, the force and fact of gravity – that gives the Bridge River a second claim on history. Water from the Carpenter Lake reservoir flows through two tunnels bored at a slight grade through Mission Mountain and becomes a head of water feeding into steel penstocks and rushing down to the turbines in the power stations below on the shore of Seton Lake, which has an elevation of only about 775 feet above sea level. The B.C. Electric company (later BC Hydro) had been actively developing the hydro power potential of the Bridge River since July 1930, when the first tunnel was holed through, and by 1934 a power station on Seton Lake was supplying electricity to the mines. However, the company deferred its major project until a later time because there was no market for its power in Vancouver at that time. Terzaghi Dam, named for the man who designed it, is still regarded today as a brilliant feat of scientific engineering.

Leaving Lillooet on the Fraser, my route into this historic valley turned west along the Bridge River towards the little village of Gold Bridge. The blacktop soon became a winding, narrow dirt road following the north shore of Carpenter Lake. Highway crews were patrolling the road twice a day to re-move falling rock. You would not know the valley had been flooded unless the level of the lake dropped. Then you might see the outlines of the gold mining town of Minto in the water below, like some legendary Greek Atlantis or Celtic Land Beneath the Sea. From Carpenter Lake, with a BC Hydro Diversion Dam near its western end, the road continues along the Bridge River another forty miles to the little village of Gold Bridge, population forty-three.

It was pouring rain the afternoon I drove that route, and the mud was splashing my red Honda as high as the windows. My friend Norman Grons-kei, who lives near Gold Bridge, urged me to phone him when I was leaving Lillooet. If I didn't arrive at Gold Bridge by a certain time, he'd phone the RCMP and they'd come looking for me. It wasn't that he thought I was a care-less driver. "That's just what we do up here," he explained. "There have been accidents, cars going off the side of the road when they're making a turn." I prudently followed his instructions. After Gold Bridge, it was another six miles up the mountain to Bralorne, where the mine had been closed since 1971 but a small community had hung on through the years, providing stopping places and services for travellers. Pioneer was another two miles along a road that switchbacks east and follows Cadwallader Creek. There was no bed and breakfast there. It was not even a ghost camp now.

But in 1931, when our family, we Nelsons and Braatens, set out from Kamloops for Pioneer, we did not travel this route. For Carpenter Lake was not flooded until thirty years later, and although the B.C. Electric had started work on hydro-power development in the Gold Bridge area in 1926, that work was delayed by the Great Depression and then World War II. Moreover, Bralorne and Pioneer, the two most promising mines, were only just starting to mill significant amounts of ore. We were arriving at the beginning of excit-ing times. The town of Gold Bridge did not yet exist, and Charlie and Evelyn Cunningham had yet to arrive, and Dan Eng and Charlie Hodgins, and all the others whose energy and drive would fuel the Bridge River Gold Rush. And Minto in 1931 may not even have been conceived by the intrepid Big Bill Davidson, mining developer-cum-visionary entrepreneur, who in 1934 created a town complete with streets and houses and waterworks and every other amenity, including the Minto Hotel. Nor had Minto been chosen as a safe place to stow some of the large population of the Canadian Japanese, evacuated because of ill-founded suspicions from the West Coast after the bombing of Pearl Harbor. When we squeezed into the '29 Chevrolet and set out from Kamloops to Pioneer, we were heading for a remote mining camp somewhere near the Coast Mountains and isolated by them in a wilderness of forest, lake, and river.

From the home we were leaving in Kamloops, the fifty miles along the Thompson River to Cache Creek were easy enough, if dry and hot in that desert country. From Cache Creek the route lay west past Pavilion Lake and through Marble Canyon to join the Fraser at Lillooet near the western end of Seton Lake. But here the road came to an end. There was no direct road connection beyond Lillooet, and there would not be one until 1955. Travellers had instead to negotiate Mission Mountain, a formidable barrier at the entrance to the gold fields of the Bridge River Valley. The starting place for this part of the journey was the little town of Shalalth on Seton Lake at the foot of the mountain. To reach Shalalth, at the other end of the lake, we had to load the car onto a flat car towed by a jitney, a gas-powered rail car. If there had not been so many of us, we too could have travelled on the jitney. Instead we crossed Seton Lake on a little ferry. At Shalalth we began the six-mile climb on a narrow, dirt road up Mission Mountain to the pass at 3,000 feet, an ascent achieved by navigating a number of scary hairpin turns, or "switchbacks." The constant intensity of the climb caused radiators to run dry on the trip up the mountain. Norman Gronskei told me that drivers used to stop halfway up the mountain to fill their radiators with water from a creek that ran close to the road. That place on the road became a social stop as well, for there might be several drivers there, all filling their radiators. They also brought along an extra supply of drinking water, carrying it in white canvas bags that they hung "somewhere on the car." My own vivid memory is of the four-mile descent down the other side of the mountain. My father used to put the car in neutral and coast down the road to save gas. The road was narrow and winding, and once again avoided the impossible by switchbacks carved into the mountain. I was terrified.

At the bottom of Mission Mountain the road enters the Bridge River Valley, and follows it for about thirty miles to the place where the Hurley River empties into the Bridge River and where the town of Gold Bridge would be built two years later in 1933 to service the mining camps. But in 1931 there was as yet no stopping place for travellers, so we pressed on another six miles up another mountain to the abandoned cabins of Coronation Mine, near where

Noel Creek empties into the Cadwallader. Pioneer Mine, our ultimate destination, was another mile up the road.

This is grizzly bear country, precipice and canyon country, gold and timber country. The community of Bralorne was located on a sunny bench of land above Cadwallader Creek, but Pioneer was crowded into the narrow creek bottom at the foot of Sunshine Mountain, beyond which the sun disappeared during the winter, leaving Pioneer Mine on the north side in gloomy winter shadow. When I was a child the Cadwallader, rough with huge boulders, was The Creek, pronounced Crick. There was supposed to be a tobacco can of stolen high-grade ore cached among the boulders near the shore. We children searched for it often.

With World War II a change had come in the fortunes of Pioneer Mine. Victory ships and Mosquito bombers, not gold bricks, were the new priority. Production at Pioneer dropped to one hundred tons a day with an underground crew of only sixty. In 1949 the hospital was closed. Gradually, in the next decade, the gold-bearing veins ran out. In 1960 Pioneer Mines, despite amalgamation with Bralorne Mines, ceased production. The tunnels and shafts were sealed up and the town abandoned.

Under recent orders from the Ministry of the Environment, today's owner of the surface rights must demolish any buildings that are still standing and remove all the debris. This work was in progress in 1997 when our party of visitors drove up to the mine site on Cadwallader Creek and was stopped by a No Trespassing sign and a snarling dog.

Our guide was Norman Gronskei, whose family had come to Pioneer in the early 1930s, recent emigrants from Norway. I'd gone to school with his sister Dagny and played with her and her brothers and sisters after school. Alfhild, their mother, took pity on me, a skinny, little motherless waif. She was kind and welcoming and fed me good things to eat, all of which I happily accepted with no sense that I was being mothered or singled out as poor little Irene. Knut Gronskei, the father (his son was also named "Knut"), worked in the mill.

Norman was born at Pioneer, lived there till he was eighteen. A broad, ruddy-faced man with a fund of stories, he loved the Bridge River Valley, and he and his wife Olga returned to live there in their retirement. Pioneer was where he'd stood sorting ore at the picking belt in the crusher building. Pioneer was where he'd played brilliant hockey for the Highgraders, even caught the eye of a National Hockey League talent scout. Pioneer was his hometown, and it was mine too.

The foreman of the wrecking crew gave us permission to enter the mine site. The snarling dogs backed off. Norman walked us around, re-creating the scene: the machine shop, the assay office, the General Store, the Bank of Toronto, where there'd been a robbery in 1935 and another one in 1942. They were all gone, but the crusher building was still there, an ore bunker behind it, and farther along a piece of concrete wall with two gaping door holes.

"That's the office," Norman said. "That there's the door to the vault."

I thought of my father filling dynamite boxes with high-grade ore behind a locked steel door and had a sudden image of him in his hard hat, coming up to surface in the cage and standing for a moment in the sudden daylight to take a chew of snuff before heading to the vault with the boxes of free gold.

We left the mine site and hiked up a steep, rough road on a hill high above the creek and beyond the mine site. "This is where your house used to be," Norman said. We were looking into a large hole, covered with a sheet of plastic.

A man in a cabin across the road, the lone resident at Pioneer, was the garbage collector for the Bralorne area. He evidently had a plan for this hole, at one time the basement of our house. A water cistern? A pond? Norman took a picture of me beside the hole, which was all that was left of the house my father and brothers had built.

"What happened to our house?" I wondered.

"Oh, it burned down. Yeah, a crazy kook shacked up here. One day he left a candle burning when he went to work."

It was a sunny day, but the sunshine did nothing to brighten the melancholy scene. I wanted to shout into the lonely silence, "I've come back! I've read *Pickwick Papers*!" Instead I turned to Norman. "What about your house?"

We walked further up the hill to the School Townsite, where the Gronskeis used to live. Alfhild had a flower garden and a rock garden too. A little bit of her ice plant was still growing there. So was Knut's apple tree, stunted, only about five feet tall, but healthy enough. "My father used to baby that tree," mused Norman.

"Your parents must have felt sad when the mine closed down and they had to leave."

"Well, they stayed on for a while with some other families, but it wasn't the same any more, so in the end my mother was glad to leave. They'd lived in that house for over thirty-five years. The company offered the houses for sale at $100. Some were bought and used for lumber. Any remaining after a year were bulldozed and burned."

"And your parents' house? Did anyone buy it?"

"No."

"So they just closed the door and left."

"It was a company house," said Norman. "The gold ran out."

During my 1997 visit to the Bridge River area I also visited the mining town of Bralorne, just two miles further down Cadwallader Creek. At Pioneer Mine I had found only its sad remains, rusting machinery and a few sagging buildings waiting for the bulldozer. Bralorne was still a town, even though only some eighty people lived there and the mine wasn't producing any gold. But there was a new mill, waiting for ore.

The old ore bin was full of low-grade "muck" – broken rock that may contain a little gold – and that muck had been there since the mine closed in 1971. But now Bralorne Pioneer Gold Mines Limited, the new company, was confident that the new mill wouldn't have to wait much longer. According to its brochure of spring 1997, "With just $1 million, the mill could be up and running within six weeks on a limited basis, tuning up the facility for future production of up to 450 tons per day."

In September 1997 the new mill still wasn't running. It was still waiting for ore. But mine manager J. Wayne Murton, walking me through this vast, high-ceilinged building, could see it in full swing. He could hear it too: the loud crunching of rocks in the primary and secondary crushers, the rackety grinding of the big iron ball mills, the pulsing sound of the jig going up and down, pulverizing the rock until it was almost like flour.

This jig is a wonderful machine. It collects the heavy material – coarse-grained sulphides and gold particles – in a bottom hutch and sends the lighter, floury material, much greater in volume, off to the flotation cells to be made into a flotation concentrate, which is a black powder.

Then comes the task of releasing the gold from one or another of the sulphides it inhabits, like seeds in an orange.

At that point in the process the mining company has to consult its government permit, which demands that gold be extracted with due consideration for the environment. In the old days a mill usually treated flotation concentrate with cyanide, with the waste, or "tailings," going into any nearby creek. But the rules had changed, so there were no cyanide tanks in this new mill. Under the company's operating permit, cyanide was ruled out. Instead, the concentrate would go out on trucks in one-ton sacks to some other mill where cyanide was still allowed, perhaps in the United States, or offshore, where it would be made ready for the refinery.

But the heavy material that remained in the bottom of the hutch presented no problem at all. The gold particles in that black sand could be extracted by using gravity – clean, cheap, and friendly. The black sand went to a shaking table, where the gold, because it's a heavy metal, was separated from the unwanted sulphides. The shaking table worked just like a placer miner in a creekbed shaking a gold pan. This gold could be sent straight to a crucible in the furnace, where it would be smelted, refined, and poured into a mould. Of course, you would want to be jigging good rich ore. If the ore averaged .25 ounces of gold per ton, then a mill with a daily capacity of 400 tons would have to work a full day to produce 100 Troy ounces, at 12 ounces per pound, for 7 pounds of gold. A gold brick usually weighs about 60 pounds.

"A gold brick by Christmas." Wayne Murton was confident, but he added with a laugh. "Of course, I'm not saying which Christmas." He was well aware that the community had seen Christmases come and go without the mine being reopened, that they had been disappointed.

But this community did not depend on the mine to stay alive. It sustained itself on hope and hard work and confidence in the future, based on a knowledge of the town's rich history – going back to the early part of the century, when Arthur and Delina Noel worked their hopeful claims on Cadwallader Creek.

At its peak Bralorne, one of the richest gold mines in British Columbia, supported a town of some three thousand people. In the 1930s, out of one hundred miles of tunnels, from shafts sometimes one mile deep and two thousand feet below sea level, was blasted the milk-white quartz that yielded per ton at least half an ounce of gold, often more. The company's web page in 1997 nostalgically recalled "clumps of gold as big a man's fist."

But eventually the gold-streaked veins petered out at Bralorne, as they had done at Pioneer. The two companies merged in 1959. Pioneer closed down the following year and Bralorne in 1971. The price of gold was still only $35 an ounce, and had been fixed there for decades.

Soon after closure, surface rights to the Bralorne Pioneer Mine property, some one thousand acres, were purchased by the Whiting brothers, John, Gerald, and Frank, and were incorporated as Marmot Enterprises Limited. Bralorne had been a company town, with residential townsites built by the company. The Whitings' plan was to re-create Bralorne with utilities, sewers, and roads meeting government standards so that it could be brought under the Squamish-Lillooet Regional District. They hired a government surveyor, laid out lots. Some houses were demolished; most were offered for sale at bargain prices: from $5,000 to $6,000 for a 6,000-foot lot; $12,000 to $30,000 for a house with lot. "Help build a town," Marmot Enterprises advertised. Its managers envisioned a neighbourly community, not just for holidaying families, but also for retired people.

The 1970s were the Trudeau years: the Whiting brothers applied for and received a $100,000 government grant to establish a mushroom farm in the upper tunnels of Bralorne Mine, where the temperature was ideal for that purpose. They didn't have long to wait for a harvest: mushrooms grow to maturity in two to three weeks. Soon mine cars once loaded with ore were being loaded with mushrooms and brought out of the tunnel along the old tunnel tracks. The mushroom farm, employing six workers, looked to be a success. Unfortunately, the mushrooms turned out to be wormy. They had been fertilized with manure that hadn't been sterilized. That was the end of the mushroom farm.

In any case, under their agreement with Bralorne Pioneer Mine, the mushroom business would have to fold if the mine reopened; and after only four or five months, that is what happened, for when the price of gold was allowed to rise, Bralorne Pioneer Mines tried to get back into production. It failed in the attempt, the mine closed again, and then the town had neither mine nor mushroom farm.

Gold, mushrooms, real estate, tourism – since 1971 all had been tried and all had failed, yet twenty years later this community of only eighty to one hundred people was still supporting one bed and breakfast, two motels, and a pub-with-restaurant.

Trish White and Gerry Onischak bought one of Marmot's houses and turned it into Patchwork Place Guest House. Exploring the Bridge River Valley one summer, they had discovered Bralorne and knew this was home. Trish, an occupational therapist in Vancouver, arranged her summer hours so she could spend time in Bralorne. "I'm a commuter," she said. "Only four hours by the Hurley River road." This is a narrow, rough dirt road with six miles of hairpin turns over a steep mountain pass. Fortunately, she had a four-wheel drive. Gerry, a semi-retired social worker, served the porridge and eggs and saskatoon berry jam when Trish was in Vancouver. He kept in touch with the world by ham radio. When we stopped there they welcomed us with tea around the airtight heater. Then Gerry went outside and hosed down my car, mud-splashed to the windows from the last few miles between Lillooet and Gold Bridge.

The forest industry was the major employer in the community. The fences in front of some houses bear a sign: "This family is supported by timber dollars." In addition to the loggers and tree planters and truck drivers and equipment operators going off to work in the morning with their lunch buckets, logging consultants and foresters come up from Vancouver on special contracts. The mine also needs consultants, and geologists and engineers. They all need a place to stay, and Bralorne is the end of the line.

Nick and Linda Skutnik understood this when they built their fine new Mines Motel in 1997. Business had exceeded expectations: their ten rooms are well occupied. The hotel was a project that looked to the future, to the day when Nick, a logger, would want to quit logging. They later took over the deserted Red Owl Restaurant and Pub, renaming it the Claim Jumper Bar & Grill.

Slim and lithe in her brief summer print dress, Linda was a self-assured, articulate business woman claiming her place in the world. She came from a Lillooet logging family and was sure that when people became better informed they would agree that logging communities had to be protected as well as the forests. Bralorne was where she and Nick wanted to live and bring up their two children to be independent and responsible. Her ten-year-old son was already taking her place in the office when she went home to cook dinner. "A ten-year-old boy here can take a rifle and a dirt bike and go out target-practising," she said. "They go camping by themselves."

Down the street I found Kathleen Doyon in jeans and plaid flannel shirt in front of her Bralorne-Pioneer Mines Motel, raking the soil for replanting. The building was the old Bralorne Mine administration office, originally sold to a visionary purchaser who saw an apartment house with murals, pool, sauna – and an authentic log cabin with loft and skylight located *inside* the building and forming part of one of the suites. Kathleen and her husband Christian had just bought the building and were renovating and carrying on with these plans for the three motel rooms and four suites, one with a mural in black silhouette of Bob Dylan. When we visited, tree planters were renting some of the rooms. The Doyons had 7,000 square feet of floor space, and they could see it all, complete and fully realized, upstairs, downstairs, people coming and going, this historic mine building saved from slow decline and devastation, made beautiful and useful. "I love this building," she said. She and Christian had settled there. They and their two children lived in the former mine manager's house. Christian was working as a logger to support their family to supplement the income from the motel.

Kathleen and Christian were members of a Katimavik team posted to the Bridge River Valley in 1979. She was from Winnipeg, he from the little town of Warwick on the south shore of the St. Lawrence, not far from Montreal. They met during their term of service with Katimavik, which began in New Brunswick and moved on to Saskatchewan and finally to British Columbia and Bralorne. Katimavik was a national youth training program founded in 1978 during the Trudeau years by the writer–publisher–social activist, later Senator, Jacques Hébert. It was funded for eighteen years by the federal government, during which time it sent some 1,700 young people to communities all across the country to develop their national awareness and personal potential as citizens of Canada. They received room and board and a stipend of one dollar a day or $1,000 on completion of a nine-month term of service. Kristian and Kathleen finished their term and married and stayed in Bralorne. The program is still being offered today, though on a smaller scale and not funded by the government.

The Doyons were among the people in Bralorne, certainly the women I met, who really did have faith in their town, even though that faith might sometimes falter. They seem to have absorbed the spirit of Arthur and Delina Noel, especially of Delina – who, after all, believed so strongly in the Bridge River Valley and, even after Arthur left, stayed on, working a claim on her own until she was seventy years old. Delina's stubborn faith was very much alive in Bralorne in 1997. Kathleen and Christian had a photograph of her in their kitchen – the one of Delina with the grizzly bear she had just shot.

I walked with Wayne Murton up the hill to the mine portal. The saskatoon bushes were heavy with berries and he stopped to pick a handful. He had just made a batch of saskatoon jelly. He had worked in other small mines in Alaska and South America. "I like working here," he said. "It's great, and old places are neat – old buildings, the old history. There's still ore to be mined here. We've found promising new vein systems."

Back in the mine office, he put a two-pound chunk of quartz, seven inches long, in my hand. A half-inch area at one end was circled in black. "If you get the light the right way," he said, "you can see the pinpoint of gold."

And I could. I saw the little pinpoint of gold.

In 2004 Bralorne Mine did reopen, and a gold brick was poured, though not from newly mined ore. This gold brick was produced from old "muck" in the ore bin and elsewhere on the property, rock that had been mined thirty-three years earlier, before operations ceased in 1971. The forty-ounce bar of gold was "symbolic," explained Louis Wolfin, chairman of Bralorne–Pioneer Mines Limited, and he was right. For the people of Bralorne this gold brick confirmed their faith in the mine, for by 2004 it was employing forty-two people, sixteen of them from the community. Hopes were high that the next gold brick would be poured from ore that had been newly processed in a fully operational mill.

A year later the mine closed again, temporarily it was hoped, for further exploration, but not without having claimed the life of one of the miners. While working underground, Paul Egan was killed by a fall of rock. He was "scaling" – prying off loose rock from a rock wall – when he happened on "bad ground." He was said to be a careful and experienced miner.

Even if the company had to close for a few months in 2005, it was still able to pour "a doré bar from gravity concentrate for immediate cash flow." So Bralorne did produce a gold brick by Christmas. It was too late for Trish White and Gerry Onischak, who closed the Patchwork Bed and Breakfast and returned to Vancouver, and for Nick and Linda Skutnik, who suffered foreclosure of their Mines Motel and Claim Jumper Bar & Grill and moved away from

Bralorne to settle down in Ladysmith on Vancouver Island. Linda remained in business, but was now working in real estate; Nick was still a logger; he and a partner had their own company doing helicopter logging. They partnered with the helicopter company as well.

Christian and Kathleen were still living in Bralorne and operating Bralorne–Pioneer Mines Motel. When the mine reopened, Christian got a job working underground in the mine. Kathleen became the camp cook, working a ten-hour day on a split shift. She was also the first-aid attendant. Bralorne was still their home. They had invested too much in their community to give up now. Besides, they had almost finished paying off their mortgage.

Mine foreman Alfred Nelson, right,
at Duthie Mine tunnel, 1920s.
(*Courtesy Bulkley Valley Museum*)

Alfred Nelson and his bride,
Ingeborg-Oline Aarvik, 1913.
(*Author's collection*)

ELEVEN

THE PRICE OF FREE GOLD

In my dreams my father always used to wear a blue-and-grey-striped dressing gown – terry cloth, standard issue. But in those dreams he was never at the hospital, sitting up in bed under an oxygen tent. He appeared in his dressing gown, among other people in their workaday clothes, and I always tried to avoid him, wishing he weren't there. Lately, he's been appearing fully dressed like everybody else. Although I'm still not comfortable with him, I'm accepting him. If he'd only say "It takes a Swede every time," the way he used to when he stood back and admired his own clever handiwork, I'd know he's cured of his disease.

What do they mean, these dreams? Maybe by wearing his flannel shirt and suspenders and broad-brimmed felt hat he's telling me I should stop feeling guilty about not being with him the night he died. Maybe I think he comes to me like the ghost of Hamlet's father, and if I write about the silicosis and the TB I'll appease his proud Swedish spirit. Maybe I think he wants me to come to a full rolling boil about the gold and his years of breathing quartz dust down in the mines.

Miners have died before from silicosis and TB, but those men weren't my father. Some fifty years later, as I write this, I sit and cry, and it's not just about the oxygen tent and the desperate last gasps and my not being there that night. It's about the gold, the Christly, useless gold (that's his word, "Christly"), stashed away somewhere – in Ottawa at the Royal Mint I guess, and Fort Knox, Kentucky.

In my childhood I didn't connect the gold with my father's breathing. Yet I knew from my father and the miners who came to our house that there existed a certain malign presence in the world called "They." "They" represented a vague but powerful accumulation of forces, beginning with the bosses, then the mining company and moving on to financiers, capitalists, and finally to Capitalism and the Government. "They" worked in mysterious collusion in a powerful System to produce wealth for themselves in complete disregard for the welfare of the working man. In my arrogant teens, I argued earnestly with my father, for I truly believed what I learned in school about individual effort and aspiration and progress in a Canada secure in the benevolent protection of Britain, our Mother Country. He'd listen for a while, then tilt his chair back, shake his head, and repeat like an old refrain: "You can't win, they'll beat you every time. You can't beat the System." He would smile sadly at my innocence.

He had given up then, given up hope that the world would change. He'd had to quit the mine, but he wasn't ready to die. He bought two and a half acres in Aldergrove, a village in the Fraser Valley thirty-six miles from Vancouver, and established himself as a poultry farmer. What did he know about chicks and incubators and mash and grading eggs? He was a miner, his language was carbide, dynamite, shaft, hoist, mill. From drilling and stoping, blasting and mucking, he went to mucking out chicken houses and nursing chicks.

"I'm just a broken-down mucker / My life in the mines I have spent." That's a mining camp song, and it describes what happens to a miner's body and mind. "The drifting machine done for my hearing / the mine gases dimmed my sight." Those mine gases were fumes of nitrogen dioxide that occurred when a stick of dynamite didn't explode but only burned. They were called "red fumes," and they damaged eyes and lungs. The song doesn't mention the dreaded silicosis that also damages and finally destroys the lungs, but "I know my last days are nearing / I know it only too well." It ends with a black and bitterly mocking flourish: "I'll be working and sweating and swearing / with a pick and shovel in hell."

This song is not one that I remember from my childhood. The one I do remember is "Oh Susannah" – "Oh Susannah, don't you cry for me/ I'm going to California/ to dig gold for you." That's a translation, because it was sung in a rollicking Swedish tongue: *"Oh Susannah, du må ikke skrike för mig …"* The miners sat in our kitchen and drank my father's homebrew, singing this jaunty immigrant song that everybody knew. They were boisterous, mocking, for they had believed in Amerika, and in Kanada, which was part of Amerika. They had forgotten about the Old Country by now and all that wild talk of streets paved with gold. They had long ago discovered that they were digging gold for someone else, and that this was a fair deal according to The System because the gold turned into profits that kept The System going. They were earning a living, that was their part of the bargain. So, *fan ta det!* – devil take it! With this mild oath they dismissed in the same breath the legendary gold fields of California, dismissed the real wealth they were producing that would never be theirs. But they were ready to stand up for wages and working conditions, and they hated scabs. There was, after all, such a thing as solidarity.

Yet these miners clung to that dream of gold in another way. They bought shares in mining companies listed on the Vancouver Stock Exchange. Over homebrew, over coffee, they talked about the latest claims being developed. It was easy to invest. At Pioneer Mine a stockbroker from Vancouver had a little branch office on the porch of the General Store. He was James E. Pollard, associated with a reputable Howe Street firm. Art had an arrangement with Jimmy Pollard, who was to put out a little red flag to signal something promising on the stock market. When the flag appeared, my brother closed down operations for fifteen minutes while he walked over to the broker's office to buy or sell some shares. My father bought shares too. How could he not invest? Gold wasn't just an economic abstraction. He held it in his hands every day. It was there in the rocks he blasted and mucked and trammed to the vault. But the properties he invested in never got beyond a few tunnels in a hillside, never yielded him a nickel. Sheep Creek, Short o' Bacon, Kootenay Belle – all turned out to be just moose pasture.

He kept his share certificates anyway in the little red trunk that had come with him all the way from the port of Narvik in Norway when he emigrated. It was made of wood and had a curved lid with wide metal bands. The lock was opened with a very large key, but only by the Open Sesame known to my father. He'd offer people the key (it weighed nearly half a pound) and challenge them to open the trunk. They'd kneel down and insert the key, turn it this way and that, but the lock wouldn't yield. My father, meanwhile, stood behind, laughing, taunting.

This little red trunk that had accompanied him to Amerika went with our family from house to house, camp to camp, every time we moved. It went with my father when he moved for the last time to enter the makeshift wartime hospital at Jericho Beach in Vancouver.

He had been breathing rock dust for most of his working life, perhaps even in Sweden when he worked at Kiruna, an iron mine in Northern Sweden. Breathing rock dust wasn't what he had planned to do in Canada. After all, the first thing he did when he came to Canada was pre-empt a parcel of land in Kenora. For whatever reason, he was not destined to be a farmer in Northern Ontario, and he ended up moving on west with the railway, and in Prince Rupert working for years drilling with sledgehammer and steel and blasting out the rock cuts of Kaien Island to build the city streets. He breathed rock dust, but he was still young. And he got married to a beautiful, young Norwegian widow. They had a house of their own that he himself built on English Hill – a house with a verandah where he and Ingeborg posed for the camera, his first-born in a sailor suit, holding his hand, a second son in christening robe in his mother's arms. They were part of the Scandinavian community in Prince Rupert, they knew the Norwegian Consul, they played Caruso on their gramophone.

It was when Alfred became a miner that he began learning rock dust, learning quartz dust. He was breathing sharp little particles of silica that bit into his lungs, microscopic particles that didn't settle because ventilation systems and stoper-drilling with water only partially cleared the air. He would have liked to find other work, but he had to earn a living and times were hard. He had to move his family from camp to camp, and everywhere they went my father went down in the mine and breathed quartz dust. He breathed it at Rocher de Boule near Hazelton, in Idaho at the Morning Mine, at the Duthie mine near Smithers, at Pioneer Mine in the Bridge River Valley.

It was at Pioneer that he worked in that special stope bringing down high-grade gold from behind a locked steel door – free gold. Each day before he left the house to go to work he performed a little ritual. At the kitchen door he checked to make sure he had everything he needed. "Lunch bucket, lamp, hard hat, snoose," he recited. The way he intoned the words made them seem to me like a charm, but they didn't protect him from the sharp bite of quartz dust. My father needed more than a charm for protection. He had spent most of his working life drilling and blasting rocks above and below ground – Prince Rupert, the Grand Trunk Pacific, Rocher de Boule, the Morning Mine, the Duthie, Planet Mine, Pioneer Gold. After all those years in the mines, his lungs were nearing their time.

Every time he went down into the mine, he was aware of what was happening to his lungs, and he was worried and anxious about the slow death he was breathing. It was quite usual for the night shift to be sent into a drift hundreds of feet from ventilation only two hours after the day shift had blasted fifty pounds of dynamite and before the dust had had time to settle. Microscopic particles simply remained airborne. When the miners sat around in our kitchen drinking homebrew, they sang "Oh Susannah," but they also talked, complained, cursed the bosses and the foreman and the Christly speed-up, and swore about the dust. Ben Tran was there, a tall, bony Norwegian who lived with his wife and two little daughters in a cabin across the road from us. He was one of Alfred's partners behind those steel doors where they both breathed quartz dust. At the end of their shift they filled ore cars with boxes of free gold. They trammed the day's treasure to the vault.

In earlier years Alfred Nelson may have grumbled privately about working conditions and wages, but he didn't take part in demonstrations and strikes, not in the Battle of Kelly's Cut in Prince Rupert, not in the IWW strike on the Grand Trunk Pacific, or even in the two strikes of the miners at the Morning Mine in Idaho. During that last strike in 1919, he'd found a job in a railway tie camp. When the strike was over he didn't go back to work but started making preparations for the family to return to Canada. He had always been a prudent, cautious man, solicitous of his family's welfare. He and Ingeborg had started out well in their new life in Canada, and he didn't want to risk that by getting involved with troublemakers. But when the Duthie Mine closed down in 1929 and the family was sent adrift once more, he began to feel as though he had nothing left to lose. His sense of failure was the more poignant because of the death of Ingeborg.

At Pioneer, having to start all over again, having even to find shelter for the family, he was ready to join with other miners to take a stand and confront what he called "the System." I didn't understand at the time that our house in Pioneer had become an informal meeting place where he and his fellow workers not only drank homebrew and talked and complained about working conditions and wages, but also, by the spring of 1935, were planning what they could do about it. At this time there was no union, and collective bargaining for management and labour had yet to be become law in federal labour legislation.

Early that May a group of miners went to mine manager Howard James and asked for a wage increase of one dollar a day. I believe my father was among them. The company offered twenty-five cents. With that response, the Pioneer miners went out on strike on May 4, 1935. They sent a delegation to all the mines in the district, urging the workers there to walk out with them.

On May 7 Bralorne joined the strike, and Wayside Consolidated and Bradian and several other small operations – in all, nearly 750 miners. There was no hotheaded altercation or violence. The women saw to that. They went to the five hotels in the Bridge River Valley and persuaded them not to serve liquor during the strike. As for the bootleggers, the miners themselves threatened "direct action" if they too didn't stop selling. The deputy minister of labour, Adam Bell, was sent in to talk with the men. When he failed to settle the dispute, Colonel Spencer flew in to address a meeting with the miners in the Pioneer community hall, supported by Bell and MLA George Murray.

Howard James spoke too, and explained why the company could not afford to meet the strikers' demands. At this, my father stood up. He quoted a few figures from the financial pages of the *Vancouver Province* and reminded the manager that Pioneer was now a leading gold producer in British Columbia. "And now," he asked, "can you tell me one good reason why you can't pay a miner more than $5.00 a day?"

My brother Art was there. "Howard James grabbed his hat and stormed out the door. He was mad as hell!"

Perhaps Swedish maidservant Sara Erika Hansdotter, Alfred Nelson's mother, was there in spirit that evening – she who made that eighteen-year-old landowner's son admit in district court to being the father of her child. Sara Erika knew when she was being exploited, and her son Nils Alfred knew when he was being exploited too.

In the summer of 1935 Alfred had his yearly examination by the mine doctor. He was told he had silicosis. So he would have to quit the mine. He wouldn't be able to work underground any more. But the doctor reassured him that the disease hadn't progressed very far and that in a couple of years he'd be alright. Indeed, some miners with silicosis, once they had changed occupations and were no longer breathing quartz dust, did live on, even to old age. The Pioneer underground miners Charles "Ace" Haddrell and Bob Eklof lived into their nineties.

And so that same summer my father went about the business of being a chicken rancher in Aldergrove, nursing batches of fragile new chicks until they were sturdy enough to be settled into their chicken houses. He mixed their feed, cleaned their nests, collected, candled, graded, and shipped the eggs. He built a second chicken house, and soon he had a thousand chickens. His little wire-haired terrier, Martha, went around with him and kept him company as he made the rounds of the chicken houses. Other Scandinavian farmers in the area had chickens too, and sometimes when they built a new chicken house they would celebrate by arranging a dance in the new building before the chickens were moved in. My father would be there, dancing the *Schottische* and the *Hambo*, as he did at the Swedes' annual Vasa Lodge Ball in the big Agricultural Hall near the corner of Jackman Road and the Yale Highway.

But gradually he began not to feel so much like mowing the hay or milking the cow and feeding the chickens, much less dancing. He was tired, he wasn't breathing right, and it wasn't just old age. He was only sixty-two years old. An X-ray with the Coast Travelling Clinic found "fine nodulation in the upper half of both lungs, which becomes fairly heavy in the lower third on each side." It was silicosis in the second stage.

The X-ray report is dated December 20, 1938, and it wasn't good news for Christmas. Alfred immediately applied to the Workmen's Compensation Board for a monthly pension but was refused: "We have to advise that the Act only applies to persons who have become disabled since January 1, 1936." He had breathed quartz dust for fifteen years, but his old quartz dust didn't qualify under the newly amended Act. He had quit mining on July 24, 1935. If he had worked another five months and three weeks, would he have been eligible for compensation then? It appears so.

He kept on tending the chickens and grading eggs, milking the cow and digging the patch of field beside the barn for potatoes. But he was often out of breath. He applied again for compensation. As he explained to the doctor who interviewed him, "Any time I worked a little harder, like pushing a wheelbarrow, I would be tuckered out." But even then, according to the doctor's report, in physical appearance he was "healthy," "erect," and "well nourished."

In April 1941 he was awarded compensation for silicosis disability, $38.13 per month. It would have been $44.00, but it was reduced by two-fifteenths because he had worked outside of British Columbia for two years and four months, and only British Columbia quartz dust was eligible for compensation. The time limit that he was under earlier, however, seems to have been waived.

His next visit to the Travelling Clinic discovered tuberculosis, not unusual for the silicotic lung. Years later in my archival research on gold mines, I came across an inquest report describing the silicotic-tubercular lungs of a hard-rock miner. The pathologist opens the body "in the usual manner" and finds that "very dense, firmly adherent fibrous adhesions are present in a patchy fashion over the entire surface of both lungs." With his hands he palpates the lungs. They're very lumpy, and when he cuts into the lumps, he finds a "cheesy material" in "caseous areas," which are "grossly tuberculous."

That's what my father's lung must have looked like after being assaulted by needles of silica for twenty years, causing scar tissue to cover the normally elastic lung tissue so that it became difficult for him to breathe. Ben Tran's lung would have looked like this too, and the lungs of the other hard-rock miners who drank homebrew in our kitchen. A lung thus ravaged is predisposed to tuberculosis. That is why it was becoming difficult for my father to push a wheelbarrow: silicosis plus tuberculosis. That is why, as he said to the examining doctor, he was sometimes staying in bed for two days at a time, "too tired and cold and all tight in the chest."

My father was fortunate in being awarded the pension, for in a hard-rock miner's X-ray, the silicotic nodules are often obscured by the presence of tuberculosis, not compensable under the Act. In his case the silicosis was clearly evident from the first X-ray. The TB diagnosis came later. But not all miners had this lucky order of diagnosis of malignancy, with the result that the Workmen's Compensation Board did deny pensions on the grounds that the claimant suffered not from silicosis but from tuberculosis, and they did this sometimes even though the examination by doctors offered medical evidence that silicosis was indeed present.

That was the case with Jack Zucco, whose story made front-page news in Vancouver in the late 1950s. After he'd been working underground for a number of years, his X-rays in 1943 showed a shadow on his lungs. He was told it was tuberculosis. However, in 1949 a panel of doctors diagnosed silicosis and suggested he apply for a pension. The Workmen's Compensation Board refused his claim. He continued to appeal for compensation but was always turned down, and for the same reason: the WCB Act required that the claimant's X-ray show evidence of silicosis and his X-ray failed to show such evidence. In 1956 his wife, Beatrice, began to stage demonstrations with her children, first in the lobby of the WCB office in Vancouver, then on the steps of the Legislature in Victoria, in an attempt to get some help from government. One night, February 28, she found convenient shelter for her three children. They slept in a room in the Parliament Buildings in the care of their fifteen-year-old sister, the youngest hugging her doll. She herself was befriended by a family in Victoria. Meanwhile, "in a nearby room," the Legislature was in session and Labour Minister Lyle Wicks was reporting to the assembled MLAs that "he was studying the situation." To his credit he did consult Ottawa, and he did attempt to set up an inquiry.

For nine years the Zuccos pleaded their case without result, even though sixteen doctors had in the course of those years diagnosed silicosis. The Board refused to accept the doctors' professional opinion and, threatened with legal redress, argued that it could not be sued because the Board was "an emanation of the Crown." This meant that, as in earlier centuries, the King had Divine Right and thus could do no wrong. The Zuccos brought their case to court anyway, and it was argued by Senator J.W. deB. Farris himself, political and legal *éminence grise* and head of the Bar in British Columbia. But to no avail. The judge ruled that the WCB was indeed an emanation of the Crown, and the Zuccos could only sue the Board if the provincial government granted them a Petition of Right. The Zuccos' lawyer duly made application, and then waited five months for an answer.

Meanwhile, Jack Zucco was dying in hospital of silicosis brought on by the quartz dust that he breathed in British Columbia's hard-rock mines. His wife was in Kitimat, where she was earning a living driving taxi. Her children were being looked after elsewhere. Finally, she wrote to Social Credit MLA Phil Gaglardi. He replied, "You are butting your head against a stone wall of your own making." She should really be looking after her children, not driving taxi. But he was praying for her.

The Petition of Right to sue was denied. But the government was setting up a special board to review problem cases of silicosis, and Jack Zucco would head the list. He would be the first to be X-rayed once more, and his body examined not by just one, but by three, University of British Columbia doctors. The examination was duly completed. Once again the Chairman of the Board, J. Edwin Eades, reported that there was no evidence of silicosis shown on the X-rays.

Jack Zucco died a year later, in April 1958. He never did receive compensation from the Workmen's Compensation Board. Beatrice Zucco, however, received a settlement from the Board, though not until she had applied for an autopsy on her husband's body, and a pathologist had cut open the lung cavity and found physical evidence of silicosis that the WCB could no longer deny. Even then, just to make sure, the WCB had requested a second autopsy. It confirmed the first pathologist's report. Jack Zucco did indeed have silicosis. The WCB would pay Bea Zucco a pension of $75 for herself and $25 for each of her four children.

The Zucco case roused public indignation. The *Vancouver Sun* published a stern editorial admonishing the WCB, declaring it had made "a tragic mistake" and that it should forthwith make speedy amends. "She can't be compensated in money for years of grief and misery. But she may derive some satisfaction from knowing that her fellow citizens regard her as a woman of heroic character."

Alfred Nelson too wrote many letters to the Compensation Board and to the government, putting forward his case. He gave them to me to edit, and I used to write the final copy in my school-girl hand. Eventually he did receive the partial compensation and then, after TB was diagnosed, the full compensation, less the two-fifteenths deducted for the foreign quartz dust. In 1945 he wrote the Workmen's Compensation Board to point out that the amount of the deduction, if restored to his pension, would pay for his housekeeper, without whom he would have to enter hospital, which would cost a lot more. They replied: "This reduction was in accordance with Section 8, (6) (d) of the Workmen's Compensation Act. The Board therefore have no power to change the award already granted you." They did always pay for his bus fare into Vancouver for interviews and medical examinations, though once again withholding two-fifteenths from the total fare.

Meanwhile he was writing letters to the editor. He was especially scornful of ignorant radio broadcasters who had never been down in a mine "telling us how well the hard-rock miners are looked after and how well paid they are" and explaining that their strike at Pioneer Mine was illegal. He recalled the stope with only one manway to provide ventilation, the speed-up, the dust still settling as the night shift arrived for work. "That was where I got my reward – silicosis. *That* was illegal too, but they didn't say so over the radio."

These words too I copied for him and sent off to the socialist *CCF News*. Years later, reading microfilm, I happened on this letter and recognized it with a jolt. I was distressed by my editorial changes, constructions I'd have learned in my high-school composition class, but foreign to his way of speaking. I wished I'd exercised a lighter editorial hand. Yet other sentences I'd left unchanged, and when I read them I could still hear his voice:

"What do these low-grade race-of-gold operators expect if they want miners to work all their lives and shorten their life span many years in order to make profits for someone else out of some worthless rocks? Why not close all these low-grade gold mines that can't pay the miners a decent wage for their toil?"

My father, Nils Alfred Nilsson, entered Jericho Hospital in January 1947. He was one of the patients on whom the new antibiotics, streptomycin and isoniazid, were being tested. He himself knew that for him it was a little late for wonder drugs. The nurses were very good and kind, and I know that he would want me to mention especially Miss Ellis, who took a special interest in him.

Nils Alfred Nilsson died at Jericho Hospital in May 1948 of tuberculosis brought on by silicosis. I retrieved from the hospital his little red trunk, released after it had been fumigated, and in it I found his hopeful Sheep Creek share certificates.

Now I know the price of "free gold." Unaccountably, I feel as though I share the blame for what the System did to my father's lungs. I grieve because I didn't know what to say when I sat beside his bed, as he struggled for breath in an oxygen tent and needed his daughter to say some farewell words of blessing. I might at least have said, "Lunch bucket, lamp, hard hat, snoose."

Next time he comes to me in a dream, I'll recite those words and maybe he'll reply, "It takes a Swede every time." Then he will know I was sharing his pain and suffering, as I still do now. I would like Sara Erika to appear, uppity and unrepentant, snorting indignation at the landowner's son and full of stories about the maidservant's life. We will all three laugh and cry together about the System, about free gold and the whole bloody unfairness of life in general. Maybe we'll sing *"Oh Susannah, du må ikke skrike för mig."* My father will shake his head, take a chew of snoose, and Sara Erika and I will allow him the last word: "What did you expect anyway? Hummingbirds?"

The four Nelson brothers and their sister, early 1960s. Back, left to right, Ed, Irene, Roy; front, Verne, Art. (*Author's collection*)

The Norwegian sister, Inga Viggen, with bridegroom Otto Reidar Lunder, 1926. (*Courtesy Ingeborg and Rolf Lunder*)

EPILOGUE

No, they expected more. In 1913 when Alfred bought land in Prince Rupert and built his house on English Hill, he anchored it there with bolts and steel chains. He and Ingeborg expected to bring up a family and furnish their house with tables and chairs, crockery and cutlery, beds and blankets – everything a family must have. So they studied the Eaton's mail-order catalogue. Ingeborg said they must have a china cabinet – they had to have somewhere to put the wedding silver. She wasn't going to put the silver cake stand in the kitchen cupboard. The china cabinet in the catalogue would cost $18.50. Yes, she admitted, they couldn't afford that now, even though they wouldn't have to pay the freight. But soon! Next year maybe!

The T. Eaton Company was mindful of their wishes, if not of their finances: "More than once it has been declared by public speakers that the Eaton Catalogue is one of the big factors in the Canadianizing of the foreign settler. In the study of its pages, he is helped on his way to familiarity with the language, the dress, and all the home-making appurtenances of the country of his adoption."

So goes the True Story of my family. I walk out into the sunshine and up the street. Two little children are kneeling on the sidewalk. They are stroking a woolly brown caterpillar, tenderly, taking turns. I watch for a moment, and then, as I watch, I'm seeing the china cabinet and suddenly I think, "They loved one another. Alfred and Ingeborg." So is it with the human mind, I reflect, that it can make such a leap. But perhaps not so strange, because every time they moved, they had to decide what to do with the furniture – Ingeborg pleading, "We can store it, have it shipped later. We're not going to live in a cabin the rest of our lives," and Alfred, grumbling, but yielding, smiling, "*Ja, ja*" – and arranging for the furniture to follow, eventually, to the new destination.

I walk on up the hill, leaving the children still stroking the caterpillar, and return to my True Story. For I am stern with myself. I call up the image of the china cabinet the last time I saw it, in the living room of our house on the farm in Aldergrove, 1948, the year my father died. By that time it had travelled several thousand miles across the continent from the Eaton Mail-Order Department in Winnipeg over the Rockies to Prince Rupert on the northwest coast, and from then on, from time to time for over fifty years, by truck and rail up and down more mountains, along narrow canyon roads and railways in the country of the Skeena and the Bulkley rivers, the Fraser and the Thompson. It had been shunted around in freight sheds and at divisional rail points. Wherever we lived in British Columbia, the china cabinet eventually arrived, not by some miracle, but by the efforts of Alfred on behalf of Ingeborg, even after she died. The china cabinet is one of my childhood memories. I know further that it is still in the family, in the home of one of their granddaughters. She says there's a T. Eaton label on the back, and she's calculated how far the china cabinet has travelled since 1948, under the care of her family: 1,500 miles. She says that when her father sold his house, he phoned her to come and take it to her house in Clinton, 75 miles away. Thus I reckon that the total mileage travelled since 1914 is nearly 3,000 miles.

I thought it only fitting that I end the True Story of my family with this account of the Sentimental Journey of our China Cabinet, because it was always sent on its way from home to home with much strain and struggle, but in the end with love. And that is a journey worth telling.

NOTES

Note: Spellings of Norwegian names vary –
e.g., Sigurd Ulstreng/Ullstreng; Aarvik/
Orwig; Thorstein/Thorsten.

1. COYOTE HOLES AND BLACK POWDER

GENERAL

For the story of the construction of the Grand
Trunk Pacific Railway along the Skeena River
I have relied on Frank Leonard, *A Thousand
Blunders: The Grand Trunk Pacific Railway
and Northern British Columbia* (Vancouver: UBC Press, 1996); R. Geddes Large, *The
Skeena: River of Destiny*, 2nd ed. (Vancouver:
Mitchell Press, 1958); F.A. Talbot, *The Making
of a Great Canadian Railway* (London: See-
ley, Service, 1912). Detailed information also
came from Prince Rupert and Fort George
newspapers and the IWW newspaper, *The
Industrial Worker* (IW).

p.8

The steam-powered Burleigh rock drill: *The
Evening Empire* (Prince Rupert) (*EE*),
April 3, 1909, p.1. *The Evening Empire*
first published on July 20, 1907. It was
a weekly from then until Nov. 6, 1909;
three issues per week, Nov. 12, 1909 to
Dec. 30, 1909; and daily except Sunday
after that. It ceased publication in the
1940s.

In one blast, 66,250 pounds of dynamite: *EE*,
Jan.16, 1909, p.1; Feb 13, 1909, p.1.
"Explosion Creates Havoc in Hotel": *EE*, Aug.
4, 1911, p.1.
"A huge rock weighing": *DN*, May 3, 1911.
"struck a chair in which Mrs. McLure": *DN*,
June 20, 1908.
In yet another blasting incident: *The Prince
Rupert Optimist* (*PRO*), April 12, 1910,
p.1. The *Optimist*, first published July 1,
1909, was a weekly until April 22, 1910;
then published daily, except Sundays,
after that; it became *The Daily News*,
May 1, 1911.

p.9

Following the precepts of the City Beautiful
Movement: Leonard, *Thousand Blunders*,
p.129.
They were all "sober, industrious workers":
PRO, Jan. 11, 1911.
"Mastilo tried to leap clear": *PRO*,
Jan. 19, 1911.

p.10

In 1909 Local 126 was formed: *IW*,
May 20, 1909.
The Prince Rupert organizer of the WFM,
Patrick Daly: Leonard, *Thousand Blun-
ders*, p.111.
The IWW was an industrial union: Melvyn
Dubofsky, *We Shall Be All: A History of
the IWW* (Chicago: Quadrangle Books,
1969).

The worker who "lies torn and trampled":
IW, Nov. 17, 1910, p.2, from "Queen
Mab," Canto 4, line 202.

They were demanding forty-five cents: EE,
Feb. 27, 1909, p.1; PRO, Feb. 28, 1911, p.1;
PRO, Feb. 6, 1911, p.1.

p.11

"Starve the —— out": cited by Leonard,
Thousand Blunders, p.116.

"When the Union Steamship Company's
Camosun": PRO, March 4, 1911, p.8.

But when this army of some one
thousand strikers arrived: Leonard,
Thousand Blunders, pp.115–17; Large,
Skeena, 145–46; The Omineca Herald
(OH), April 8, 1911; PRO, April 7, 1911,
p.1.

"I watched the marching men": Walter
Wicks, Memories of the Skeena (Saanichton, B.C. and Seattle: Hancock House,
1976), pp.101–2.

p.12

Which said that "paid agitators": Leonard,
Thousand Blunders, p.117.

The cruiser HMCS Rainbow: Leonard, Thousand Blunders, p.116.

The company therefore used its influence:
Leonard, Thousand Blunders, p.119.

"Shoot if necessary": PRO, April 7, 1911,
pp.1, 4.

p.13

Of the fifty strikers arrested: PRO,
April 7, 1911.

Scandinavian Propaganda Club: IW,
Jan. 5, 1911.

p.14

"Give me Swedes and snoose": attributed
to James J. Hill, an early director of the
Canadian Pacific Railway.

"15 Italians and Swedes to report": EE, Sept.
5, 1908, p.1.

Another news item for 1909: EE, March 27,
1909, p.6.

"On the way to Port Essington": EE, March 6,
1909, p.4.

"the men plying the drills": Talbot, Making of
a Great Canadian Railway, p.280.

p.15

One week later five more men were blown
up in a tunnel: OH, Feb. 18, 1911.

Navigating the Grand Canyon: Fort George
Herald (FGH), June 7, 1913, p.3, June 14,
1913, p.3, June 20, 1911.

p.16

"One station-man confessed to me": Talbot,
Making of a Great Canadian Railway,
p.283.

"a Herculean Swede": Pierre Berton, The
Last Spike (Toronto: McClelland and
Stewart, 1971), p.228.

The two lines of steel that moved westward … eventually met: R.A. Harlow to
DN, March 11, 1974 <www.bc.ca/living/
harlow.htm>. I am grateful to Frank
Leonard for suggesting this website.
Some sources give the date as April 6,
1914. However, Harlow was there at the
driving of the GTP Last Spike: "At this
point I came into the picture and with
a small can of white paint and a brush I
inscribed the following on the flange of
that 11-foot last rail: Point of Completion
April 7, 1914."

p.17

"a single ditch started close to the kitchen
door": E.H.L. Johnston, "The Under-Dog:
A Story of Existing Conditions in the
Construction Camps of the Grand Trunk
Pacific," British Columbia Magazine, 7
(November 1911), p.1161. Also Wicks,
Memories of the Skeena, pp.143–44; Leon-
ard, Thousand Blunders, pp.96, 102.

Cases of typhoid and diptheria: FGH, June 7,
1913, p.3.

"And for the love of Mike, send us a potato":
FGH, June 14, 1913, p.4.

On the Grand Trunk Pacific, wages: EE, Feb.
27, 1909, p.1; March 20, 1909, p.6.

Led by the IWW: Leonard, Thousand Blunders, pp.118–24.

p.18

"With backs humped, " "The snows lay deep," "Four days later": Wicks, *Memories of the Skeena*, p.145.

From Frank Leonard I learned: Leonard, *Thousand Blunders*, pp.79–81.

p.19

The Tête Jaune Cache of GTP construction days: Leonard, *Thousand Blunders*, pp.48, 72, 79–81; Marilyn Wheeler, *The Robson Valley Story*, McBride Robson Valley Story Group, 1979, pp.6–14; Richard Bocking, *Mighty River: A Portrait of the Fraser* (Vancouver: Douglas & McIntyre, 1997), pp.18–21; *FGH*, Sept. 28, 1912; May 24, 1913.

p.20

"an end-of-steel village": W. Lacey May, *FGH*, Sept. 20, 1913, p.3.

"We have had Swedes, Italians, Slavs and Greeks": *Port Essington Loyalist*, Jan. 30, 1909, microfilm, Prince Rupert Library.

p.21

"the most drunken and disorderly place": *EE*, July 4, 1908, p.1.

2. SARA ERIKA HANSDOTTER

GENERAL

For the genealogy and family history of Nils Alfred Nilsson, I received information from the personal data bank of Thord Bylund, Senior Archivist, at the Regional Archives in Härnösand, Sweden. For the character and personality of Sara Erika Hansdotter, the *Household Examination Rolls* (the *Husförhörslängd*) of the parish of Resele in Ångermanland, Sweden, provided specific information. These microfilmed documents were made available by the Family History Centre, Burnaby branch of the Church of Jesus Christ of Latter-Day Saints.

Arvid Enquist's *Folkminnen Från Ångermanland*, reprinted in 1986 in no. 2 of the journal *Resele-Historia*, was a rich source of stories of the customs and folk beliefs of the parish, gathered by Enquist in 1912 and originally printed in 1917. I am grateful to Ingegerd Troedsson for sending me a copy of this material and also a photocopy of an essay about the famine of 1867: Vilhelm Scherdin, "Nödåret 1867 i Resele-Socken," *Resele-Historia*, 1992:8.

Also from *Resele-Historia*: Abraham Nyberg, "Sollefteå och Ådalarne, Saga och Sanning," 1988: 4; Vilhelm Scherdin, "Folkskolan i Resele Socken," 1992: 8; Ingegerd Troedsson, "Historien av Anna i Sel i Resele Socken," 1993: 9, all made available by Länsbiblioteket, the regional archives, Härnösand, Sweden.

Gustav Selin, *Resele: bygden med älven, niporna och skogen*, was a valuable resource for the history and daily life of the community.

OTHER SOURCES

"Ångermanland," *Bra Böckers Lexikon*, 1990.

"Catechisms," *Encyclopædia of Religion and Ethics*, 1913.

Richard Dawkins, *River out of Eden: A Darwinian View of Life* (New York: Basic Books, 1995).

Susan Karant-Nunn and Merry Wiesner-Hanks, eds. and trans., *Luther on Women: A Sourcebook* (Cambridge: Cambridge University Press, 2003).

Selma Lagerlöf, *The Girl from the Marshcroft*, trans. Velma Swanston (Howard, N.Y.: Doubleday, Page and Co., 1916).

Doktor Martin Luther's *Lilla Katekes* (Luther's Smaller Catechism of 1529), n.d.

"Luther," *Encyclopædia of Religion* (London: Macmillan, 1987).

3. TO AMERIKA AND THE HOUSE ON ENGLISH HILL

GENERAL

Births, marriages, and deaths of the Aarvik family: genealogical research made available to me by Ingrid Aarvik Solberg and Dorothy Edwards.

The marriage of Kristian Andreassen Viggen and Ingeborg-Oline Aarvik and the death of Kristian: Børsa Parish Record, 1867–1915, research conducted by genealogist Kåre Hasselberg.

Vår Frue Kirke: Ingrid Aukrust to Irene Howard, e-mail, Oct. 24, 2004.

Emigration of members of the Aarvik family from Norway: the emigrant lists of the Trondheim Police Office in Trondheim Statsarkivet, made available to me in correspondence with the archives and by the research of Robert Lundy, an American grandson of Elisabeth Aarvig Lundene.

The story of Sigurd Ullstreng at Vigg: Ann-Carin Bøyesen, *Viggja i Høymiddelalderen: En studie av Sigurd Ullstreng på Vig gods og livet på bygda i høymiddelalderen* (Viggja, Norway, 1991). Johan Bach read the sagas for significant events at Vigg.

"Magnus Berrføtts Saga," and other saga events at Vigg (later Viggen, now Viggja), *Snorre Sturlasson Kongesagaer*, trans. from Snorre by Anne Holtsmark and Didrik Arup Seip (Stavanger: Gyldendal Norsk Forlag, 1970), pp.593–94, 162–64; also the saga of Magnus the Good, p.493, and Olav Trygvesson, pp.162–64.

p.39

A member of the local young people's club: "Fra Viggen," *Søndre Trondhjems Amtstidende (STA)*, Jan. 11, Jan. 18, 1910; also mentioned by Egil Aarvik, *Smil i Alvor: Fragmenter av en liv* (Oslo: Gyldendal Norsk Forlag, 1985), p.22.

p.41

Elling and Ingeborg Anna Aarvik and boatbuilding: Aarvik, *Smil i Alvor*, pp.12–17. Unless otherwise noted, all the translations from Scandinavian languages, including interviews, are mine.

p.44

During the Nazi occupation of Norway: Per Hanson, "Redaktøren ogmennesket-Erik Aarvik," *Sør-Trøndelag*, pp. 3, 4, 22.

p.45

Tuberculosis, a poor people's sickness, taboo: Jan Karlsen and Dag Skogheim, *Tæring: Historia om ein folkesjukdom* (Oslo: Det Norske Samlaget, 1990), p.65.

With Ireland, it had one of the highest rates in Europe: Thomas Dormandy, *The White Death: A History of Tuberculosis* (New York: New York University Press, 2000), pp.82, 242–43.

Spitting, for example, was almost universally quite respectable: Ida Blom, "Don't Spit on the Floor: Changing a Social Norm in Early Twentieth Century Norway," *Pathways of the Past: Time and Thought*, no.7 (Oslo: Novus Forlag, 2002), p.231. This essay gives a detailed account of the campaign to combat the disease in Norway. Re spitting, see also Aarvik, *Smil i Alvor*, p.27.

Women could spread the disease: Blom, "Don't Spit on the Floor," p.236.

TB was noticeably prevalent among tailors: Britt Inger Puranen, *Førelsked i livet*, cited by Karlsen and Skogheim, *Tæring*. I am grateful to Thorstein Sæter for sending me this information.

"Tuberculosis Ravages": *STA*, Dec. 16, 1910.

p.46

He was a left-wing radical: thanks to Ingrid Aarvik for her description of her grandfather (e-mail, Oct. 28, 2004) and for the photocopy of the biographical essay in his memory, *"Redaktoren og Mennesket – Erik Aarvik,"* by Per Hansson in the Jubilee number, *Sør-Trøndelag*, 1958.

In an article about the downturn in the economy: "Idag," signed E.A., *STA*, July 15, 1911.

News items: *STA* re health societies: Jan. 11, Feb. 1, March 1, 8, 15, 1910.

In an editorial addressing the health question: "*Sanitetsaken*," *STA*, Jan. 15, 1909; Karlsen and Skogheim, *Tæring*. I am grateful to Thorstein Sæter for summarizing relevant material in this book for me and to Lise Kvande, who referred me to this book and led me along the research trail with further suggestions. She also engaged in research on my behalf.

p.47

There were scarcely any hospitals available for poor people with TB: Erik Ingebritsen, curator of a Trondheim museum exhibit about TB, e-mail to Lise Kvande, Feb. 19, 2004. My thanks to Erik Ingebritsen for his summary about access to sanatoria and for his suggestions as to further reading.

A search of the registers for 1908–09: "*Protokoll for tuberkulose syke med statsbidrag*" (Records of patients with state support), *Me* 2, 1908–19), Statsarkivet i Trondheim: Elin Jacobson to Irene Howard, e-mail Feb. 19, 2004. I am grateful to Elin Jacobson, archives consultant, for searching these records for me and to Lise Kvande for putting me in touch with her.

p.48

"When the patient coughed up blood": Karlsen and Skogheim, *Tæring*, p.65.

p.50

Her brother Erik printed a departing (anonymous) emigrant's story: Erik Aarvik, *STA*, July 5, 1911.

p.51

Thorstein and Berit Aarvik (later Orvig), biographical details: Mattie Aarvik Frank to Robert Lundy, March 21, 1973, May 25, 1973; a letter from Mattie Frank about her father, T. M. Orwig, appears in Charles M. Defieux, *Vancouver Sun*, April 6, 1967.

When the Norwegian government appointed his father: Thorstein Orwig, handout,

"Estimates given for all kinds and sizes of sea going craft. Yards at Seal Cove, Prince Rupert, B.C., the 20th June, 1918," reprinted in Belle Watt, *The Old Aarvik Place*, self-published, p.33. Belle Watt chronicled the history of the Aarvik family in Canada and the United States, beginning with their roots in Norway. She tells the history of the *Fawn*, pp.30–31.

"In the year 1883, I was selected by the Norwegian government": Thorstein Orwig, handout.

p.52

Port Essington: Large, *Skeena*, pp.35–43; Phylis Bowman, *Klondike of the Skeena* (Port Edward, B.C., 1982), esp. pp.26–28. The history of Port Essington in Bowman's book is told through reprints of newspaper articles, passages from memoirs, and a rich collection of archival photographs.

Further material on Port Essington: E.A. Harris, a binder of comprehensive notes, including the diary of Agnes Harris, Prince Rupert City and Regional Archives; *Port Essington Loyalist*, Nov. 7, 1908, Jan. 9, 1909, Jan. 31, 1909, Prince Rupert Public Library; Agnes Harris, "The Ghosts Walk This B.C. Town," *Vancouver Province*, May 3, 1958, p.19, and "Fun Days at Port Essington before the Big Fire of 1961," *Prince Rupert Daily Colonist*, Nov. 5, 1972, p.3; Phylis Bowman, "Cunningham Built Port Essington . . ." *Prince Rupert Daily Colonist*, Sept. 10, 1967, p.6; *EE*, April 11, 1908, June 20, 1908, p.6, July 4, 1908, p.1.

p.55

"with a Prince Rupert archivist as my guide": thanks to Carol Hadland, who was my guide that day and throughout my research at the Prince Rupert City and Regional Archives.

4. THE NORNS, THE GTP, AND HER BEAUTIFUL BLACK HAIR

GENERAL

The story of Rocher de Boule Copper Mine and the influence of the policies of the Grand Trunk Pacific is told in Leonard, *Thousand Blunders*, ch. 8, and I have drawn largely on his fully documented account. See also *The Omineca Herald*, Sept. 6, 1912; Jan. 17, 1913.

The *Omineca Herald* provides a running account of the development of Rocher de Boule, 1912–15. See also the *British Columbia Annual Report of the Minister of Mines (AR)*, 1914–16.

For the corporate history of Federal Mining and Smelting I have relied on John Fahey, *The Ballyhoo Bonanza: Charles Sweeney and the Idaho Mines* (Seattle and London: University Press, 1971), pp.173–91.

For the U.S. activities of the Industrial Workers of the World and for the campaign of repression waged against them, I have relied on Melvyn Dubofsky, *We Shall Be All: A History of the IWW* (Chicago: Quadrangle Books, 1969); *IW*, 1909–13; Bill Haywood, *The Autobiography of William D. Haywood* (New York: International Publishers, 1958 [c.1929]) (cover title: *The Autobiography of Big Bill Haywood*).

The struggle of the miners for union recognition against the opposition of the Mine Owners' Association is told in Fahey, *Ballyhoo Bonanza*, ch. 4, "Dissent and Dynamite."

Also Al Bannerman, "Duthie Mine Freighting Days," and Bill Leach, "Teamsters," in *Bulkley Valley Stories*, a Heritage Club Publication [Smithers], 1973, p. 158, in Bulkley Valley Museum.

The Library/Historical and Genealogical Collection of the Idaho State Historical Society provided information about the mining industry in Idaho, and I acknowledge them with thanks.

p.60

"The men are working in solid ore ": *The Daily News* (Prince Rupert), Jan. 29, 1913; photo, *OH*, Sept. 12, 1913.

p.61

"a huge mass of cold, hard, defiant rock ": *OH*, Oct. 24, 1913.

p.62

Two-storey steam-heated bunkhouses: *AR*, 1915, K77.

Tramville: Leonard, *Thousand Blunders*, pp.241–242; *AR*, 1916, K107.

p.64

"Rockefeller sat in the train": Fahey, *Ballyhoo Bonanza*, p.183.

p.65

"Beware of the IWW": *The Mullan Progress*, July 13, 1917.

Skandinaviska Propaganda Gruppen: IW, 15 Dec. 1910.

p.67

138 workers... walked out: Robert N. Bell (State Mine Inspector), *Twentieth Annual Report of Idaho for the year 1918*, pp.11, 13. In this report also: wages for contract workers, p.15; ventilation, pp.15–16, 20–21; timbering, pp.16–20; the contract system: how it affects the company and the workers, pp.22–23.

"You know what would happen": *Mullan Progress*, Aug. 9, 1918, p.1.

p.69

"three or four hundred men ... bullpen:" Fahey, *Ballyhoo Bonanza*, p.81.

"the entire male populations": Fahey, *Ballyhoo Bonanza*, p.92.

p.71

In a letter to Ingeborg's brother Erik Aarvik: only two family letters from Idaho survive, both from the summer of 1919.

"The train [to the mine portal] starts and stops": Bell, *Twentieth Annual Report of Idaho*, p.21.

The pay for those miners: a later report says that the usual pay for miners and muckers, that is, those not on contract piece work, was $5.25 an hour. State Mine Inspector, *Twenty-First Annual Report of the Mining Industry of Idaho for the Year 1919*, Boise, Idaho, 1920, p.11.

p.72
"a few unpatriotic agitators": Bell, *Twentieth Annual Report of Idaho*, p.22.

An account of Elling Aarvik's boat accident and death: "Forulykket," *STA*, Jan. 30, 1919, p.2, 3; Egil Aarvik, *Smil i Alvor*, p.16.

A general strike of mines in the Coeur d'Alene district: State Mine Inspector, *Twenty-First Annual Report*, p.6.

p.78
This section is mostly based on interviews with my brothers, Arthur and Verner Nelson. Also, Lillian Weedmark, ["The Bulkley Hotel"], typescript, pp.1-3, Bulkley Valley Museum.

5. THE CABIN ON HUDSON BAY MOUNTAIN
GENERAL
This chapter relies largely on interviews with my three brothers, Arthur, Verner, and Edwin Nelson, and my own memories.

For the description of totem poles I draw on Marius Barbeau, *Totem Poles of the Gitksan, Upper Skeena, British Columbia*, facsimile ed. (Ottawa: National Museum of Canada, 1973 [1929]), esp. pp.132–33, "Pole of Waws, at Hagwelget," and pp.158–71, "Gitksan Crests as Illustrated on Totem Poles: Classified List, According to Types." The book is based on four seasons of field research between 1920 and 1926.

p.94
Emily belonged to the Wet'suwet'en people: telephone interview with Amanda Dennis, Oct. 1, 2004.

p.95
Emily is remembered in the local history: Nan Bourgon, *Rubber Boots for Dancing (and Other Memories of Pioneer Life in the Bulkley Valley)* (Smithers, B.C.: T. and H. Hetherington, 1979), p.34.

p.99
I learned from Emily's niece Mabel: telephone interview with Mabel Critch of Topley, B.C., September 2004. Mabel's father was Matthew Sam, Emily's brother.

p.101
Scotty Aitken . . . the Aitken farm: later the Webber ranch.

6. THE SAGA OF INGEBORG-OLINE AARVIK
GENERAL
Interviews with Verner Nelson (May 22, 1994) and Arthur Nelson.

p.107
The Guggenheim family of financiers and industrialists: Edwin P. Hoyt, *The Guggenheims and the American Dream* (New York: Funk and Wagnalls, 1967), esp. pp.149–59.

John F. Duthie . . . sold a 55 per cent interest: British Columbia: *Annual Report of the Minister of Mines (RMM)*, 1923, A108.

p.114
Duthie Mine prospered: a running account of the development of the mine can be found in *RMM* for the years 1921–29.

"Owing to depressed metal-market conditions, operations were suspended": *RMM*, 1924, B94–95.

p.116
The dissemination of information about birth control: Angus McClaren and Arlene Tigar McClaren, *The Bedroom and the State: Changing Practices and Politics of Contraception and Abortion in Canada,*

2nd ed. (Toronto: Oxford University Press, 1997), p.9.

That law forbade, as "an indictable offence": The provisions of Section 207 are set forth in Mary F. Bishop, "The Early Birth Controllers of B.C.," *BC Studies*, 61 (Spring 1984), fn.11, p.67.

"the motives of the seller, publisher or exhibitor": *Statutes of Canada*, Ch. 29, Section 179.

She kept right on reprinting and disseminating: Margaret Sanger, *Family Limitation*, rev. 8th ed., 16 pp., Angus MacInnis Memorial Collection, Rare Books and Special Collections, University of British Columbia.

Was refusing to be the Angel in the House: Coventry Patmore, "The Angel in the House," 1854, in *The Poems of Coventry Patmore*, ed. Frederick Page (London, Oxford University Press, 1949), p.111. The poet wrote this poem for the woman whom he idolized and saw as the perfect wife: "Man must be pleased; but him to please / Is woman's pleasure, down the gulf / Of his combined necessities / She casts her best, she flings herself / How often flings for naught/ And yokes her heart to an icicle or whim." The dutiful, submissive Angel in the House became the prototype for the good wife for the rest of the century and well into the twentieth.

p.117

"ignorance and inertia of those": Bishop, "Early Birth Controllers of B.C.," p.70. Information about the birth control movement in British Columbia is based on this article, which includes an account of Dr. J. Lyle Telford and the Vancouver Birth Control Clinic that he established in 1932.

"We have kept sex in the gutter too long": Bishop, "Early Birth Controllers of B.C.," p.70.

Women resorted to their own folk pharmacy of contraceptive measures: Sanger, *Family Limitation*. Many of these methods were common knowledge.

p.120

She also claims a place in Canadian statistics: Veronica Strong-Boag, "The Confinement of Women: Childbirth and Hospitalization in Vancouver, 1919-1939," in *Delivering Motherhood: Maternal Ideologies and Practices in the 19th and 20th Centuries*, ed. Katherine Arnup, André Lévesque, and Ruth Roach Pearson (London, New York: Routledge, 1990), Table 1, p.77.

The Commission's *Final Report* recommended: the insurance was recommended for "all regularly employed persons." It was not universal. There was an income ceiling, excluding those who could afford to pay their own medical expenses.

p.122

Inga's life history: Ingeborg Lunder to author, Sept. 14, 2007; telephone interview with Rolf Lunder, trans. his son, Otto Reidar Lunder, and with Ingeborg Lunder, who also kindly answered my questions by e-mail, October 2007.

p.123

In Trondheim, Otto Reidar was: On March 6, 1930, after a vote, the spelling of Trondhjem was changed to Trondheim.

7. GOLD DUST, HOMEBREW, AND CLASS STRUGGLE
GENERAL

For the genealogy of Delina Noel's family in Quebec, I have consulted Le Centre d'Archives du Seminaire de St. Hyacinthe Inc., Ste-Hyacinthe, Quebec, and Société généalogique canadienne-française, Montreal: Parish marriage records, Hyacinthe Létoile and Delina

Bérubé; Charles Castonguay and Adéline Levesque; Joseph L'Italien and Marie Clara Castonguay.

For Joseph L'Italien and the Overlanders: M.S. Wade, *The Overlanders*, reprint (Surrey, B.C.: Heritage House Publishing, 1981 [1st ed., Victoria: Provincial Archives of B.C.]); Thomas McMicking, *Overland from Canada to British Columbia*, ed. Joanne Le Duc (Vancouver: UBC Press, 1981).

For Joseph and Clara L'Italien in Lillooet: Lorraine Harris, *Halfway to the Goldfields: A History of Lillooet* (Vancouver: J.J. Douglas Ltd., 1977), p.24; Irene Edwards, *Short Portage to Lillooet*, 2nd ed. (Mission, B.C.: Cold Spring Books, 1985.

The story of Arthur Noel's mining career and of Delina's partnership with him is told in Lewis Green, *The Great Years: Gold Mining in the Bridge River Valley* (Vancouver: Tricouni Press, 2,000), pp.23–34. I have also used Lewis Green's comprehensive research notes from *The Prospector*, esp. July 14, 1898–June 30, 1899.

Delina's later mining career is told in H. Barry Cotton, "Piebiter Creek: A Personal Reminiscence," *British Columbia Historical News*, 27,4 (Fall 1994), pp.2–4.

The best account of the life of Delina Noel is by geological engineer and chemist Franc R. Joubin, "Delina C. Noel, an Appreciation: Bridge River Pioneer," *Western Miner & Oil Review*, August 1958, pp.36–41.

Arthur and Délina, marriage and death certificates: B.C. Archives.

p.128

The Braatens had emigrated from Norway in 1927: Biographical details about Gunnar Braaten, interviews with Alfhild Gronskei, Salmon Arm, B.C.; Gunnar Brothen's grandson, Gunnar Dybhavn, Surrey, B.C.

p.130

Rich veins of high-grade ore: Howard T.

James, "Features of Pioneer Geology," *The Miner*, 1934, p.347.

p.131

Four dynamite boxes of free gold ore: milling practices at Pioneer varied. See Paul Schutz and Russell J. Spry, "The Pioneer Mill," *The Miner*, August 1934, pp.350–52.

Ben Smith: Green, *Great Years*, pp.111–13.

p.151

"Devoted to drastic cost control": Ross Thompson, "Cost Accounting," *The Miner*, August 1934, pp.355–56.

p.152

Years later Eklof told me what happened: interview, March 1997.

8. CHILDREN OF THE EMPIRE

GENERAL

For school days in Pioneer Mine: interviews with Harry Ashby, Dagny Gronskei, Norman Gronskei, Lissie Jensen, Winnifred Holland, and John Schutz.

Also: *Annual Report of the Public Schools of the Province of British Columbia*, Victoria, 1932, 33, 34, 35; *The Gage Canadian Readers*, Book III, 1927, Books IV and V, 1925 (Toronto: W. J. Gage and Co. Ltd. and Thomas Nelson and Sons Ltd.).

The first-hand accounts of the 1940 strike are from taped interviews and telephone conversations with three union men who were down in the mine: Charles "Ace" Haddrell, April 30, 1997, and May, June, and July 1998; Walter Seretny, May 1, May 14, 1998; Frank Hennessey, June 1998, by Danny Hennessey; and telephone conversation, May 24, 1998.

The union's narrative of the strike is contained in *The Bridge River Miner*, Oct. 12, 1939, Nov. 11, 1939, Feb. 14, 1940, Wm. J. Cameron Papers, Special Collections, UBC, Vertical File 262b; and in "A Brief and an Appeal," in the same file. "*A Statement by the Minister of*

Labour on the Strike of the Pioneer Mines, Limited, Employees and on the 'Industrial Conciliation and Arbitration Act'" is also in this file.

The views of Pioneer Gold Mine, as stated by managing director Dr. Howard James, are printed in full in *Vancouver Sun*, Oct. 16, 1939. Both the *Sun* and the Vancouver *Daily Province* gave full coverage to the strike, as did *The Bridge River-Lillooet News*, which also reported the trials in magistrate's court in Gold Bridge of the union officials.

The role of Workmen's Co-operative Committees in labour-management relations is the subject of "Co-operation vs Unionism," *The Miner*, 12 (October 1939). This editorial expresses the hostility of the mining industry in general towards unionism.

John Stanton, the lawyer representing the union, recalls the strike and his part in the settlement of it in "The Herr Doktor of Pioneer Mine," in *Never Say Die: The Life and Times of John Stanton, a Pioneer Labour Lawyer* (Ottawa: Steel Rail Publishing, 1987), pp.41–54. Handwritten notes of John Stanton's telephone conversations with union officials and MLA Harold Winch are in John Stanton Papers, Special Collections, Box 1, Folder 1, case file 180, University of British Columbia.

As a student on an errand in the Vancouver harbour area in June 1935, Stanton happened to be on the scene when police on horseback and on foot attacked a column of marching longshoremen as they approached the railway crossing at Ballantyne Pier. Writing about his life as a labour lawyer in British Columbia, he recalls police brutality that day in 1935: "four-foot, leather-covered clubs weighted with lead," the wooden billies, the "grey tentacles of tear gas" – and at the head of the marching longshoremen, Mickey O'Rourke, wearing his Victoria Cross and carrying the Union Jack. Young John Stanton, an innocent bystander, was chased by a mounted policeman with a club. When, four

years later, he accepted Local 308's brief, he may have been inexperienced as a lawyer, but he had a realistic idea of what the striking miners might be up against.

Geologist and mining historian Lewis Green gives a complete and well-documented account of the strike in *Great Years*, pp.137–45.

OTHER SOURCES

Duncan Cameron, "Supreme Court Rules That Labour Rights Are Charter Rights," *The CCPA Monitor*, July/August 2007, p.10, first published in rabble.ca.

National Industrial Conference, *Official Report of Proceedings and Discussions* (Ottawa: King's Printers, 1919), "Agenda," item 8, Labour Features of the Treaty of Peace, p.xviii.

Revised Statutes of British Columbia,1937 and 1938.

"Wartime Labour Relations Order [PC1003]," *Labour Gazette* (Ottawa: King's Printers, 1944).

p.157

a long narrative poem: Alfred, Lord Tennyson, "Enoch Arden," *The Complete Poetical Works of Tennyson* (Boston: Houghton Mifflin Co., c.1898, [n.d.]).

p.162

Some time after he had barred down the loose rock: interviews with geologist and writer Glenn Woodsworth, former miner Charles "Ace" Haddrell, Arthur Nelson.

p.164

Following the 1926 report of Lord Balfour: Norman Hillman, "Balfour Report," and "Statute of Westminster," *Canadian Encyclopædia*, 1985.

p.167

The mine managers, governed by the Metalliferous Mines Regulation Act: for mine regulations in metalliferous mines, *Revised Statutes of British Columbia*, 1924, ch. 172; 1935, ch. 46, esp. pp. 202–8 for blasting; pp.211–13 for hoist signals.

p.169

For the death of Gunnar Brothen and other deaths in metalliferous mines in British Columbia that year: British Columbia, *Report of the Minister of Mines*, 1934, G 42.

p.177

As the Canada Labour Code says: Quoted in "Labour Law," *Canadian Encyclopedia*, 1985.

9. DIAMOND FLUSH AND THE BLOWTORCH SOLUTION

GENERAL

The story is largely based on interviews with my brother Arthur Nelson, with added material from an interview with Bob Eklof, March 1997, and telephone interviews with Wyn Hagerstone, 2000, and Norman Gronskei, 2000. Also an interview with Art's friend Anthony Arnold, who was also employed at Polaris Taku.

My archaeological fantasies draw on C.H.V. Sutherland, *Gold: Its Power and Allure* (London: Thames and Hudson, 1959), pp.39–40; and "King Tutankhamen's Tomb" <www.crystallinks.com/tuts tomb> (April 7, 2006).

p.182

In the 1940s my older brothers all worked at Polaris Taku: The mine shut down during the war. It reopened again after the war and was in operation until 1954. British Columbia: *Report of the Minister of Mines*, 1936–41.

p.183

Every man who worked there lost weight: In the song "Taku Miner," the men are underground and getting instructions from the shift boss. The song is a complaint: "A son-of-a-gun, this mining for gold." From Philip J. Thomas, *Songs of the Pacific Northwest* (Saanichton,

B.C.: Hancock House, 1979), pp.143–44. The tune of the song is the same as that of "My Darling Clementine."

p.192

The Canada Flag Bill: *Hansard*, Jan. 15, 1973, p.1327; Feb. 5, 1973, p.936; *Ottawa Citizen*, Feb. 8, 1973.

Ed Nelson on fisheries in Question Period: *Hansard*, July 5, 1973, Jan. 8, 1974.

10. SEARCHING FOR MY HOMETOWN

GENERAL

Information on Carpenter and Seton Lakes, Terghazi Dam: Green, *Great Years*, pp.239–41.

Pioneer, Bralorne, and Minto history: Emma de Hullu, in collaboration with Evelyn E. Cunningham, *Bridge River Gold*, 2nd printing (Bralorne: Bralorne Pioneer Community Club and Bridge River Valley Centennial Committee, 1993 [1967]).

Mission Mountain and the 1930s route to the Bridge River: Base Mapping and Geomatic Services Branch, Integrated Land Management Bureau, B.C. Ministry of Agriculture and Lands, with special thanks to Janet Mason, Provincial Toponymist, for providing detailed information and maps.

For the description of how the ore is processed in the mill, I have relied on interviews with Bralorne Mine Manager Wayne Murton (1997) and geologist and mining historian Lewis Green. I take responsibility for any errors, as well as for oversimplification of a highly complex operation.

Interviews with Norman Gronskei, to whom my grateful thanks. Other interviews: Trish White and Gerry Onischak, Linda Skutnik, Nick Skutnik, Kathleen Doyon, and Christian Doyon.

p.205

Were incorporated as Marmot Enterprises Limited: interview with John Whiting.

Received a $100,000 government grant
to establish a mushroom farm: Green,
Great Years, p.238.

p.207

Katimavik was a national youth training
program: *The Canadian Encyclopaedia*,
2000.

p.208

Bralorne Mine did reopen: *Vancouver Sun*,
April 13, 2004, p. E3.

While working underground, Paul Egan:
Vancouver Sun, Sept. 13, 2004, p. B1.

It was still able to pour "a doré bar from
gravity": Infomine Inc., "News," Bralorne Gold Mines Ltd., June 8, 2007
<http://www.infomine.com/
companies-properties/infodbweb/News.
asp?searchid=10591>.

11. THE PRICE OF
FREE GOLD

p.212

"I'm just a broken-down mucker": Thomas,
Songs of the Pacific Northwest, p.146.

They were called "red fumes": Thomas,
Songs of the Pacific Northwest, p.147.

p.216

1935 strike: *Daily Province* (Vancouver), May
7, 1935, p.22 and May 8, 1935, p.4; Green,
Great Years, p.137.

He was told he had silicosis: The progress
of my father's disease is documented
in Claim 90002, Reel 722B, Disclosure
Department, Workers' Compensation
Board. These records have been an
invaluable resource, reviving and clarifying my own memories, and I'm grateful
to Stephen Chan for making them available to me.

p.218

Years later in my archival research ... I came
across an inquest report: Ted Ward, Issue
No. 8, Daily Report: Compensation Investigation, Marine Workers and Boiler-

makers Industrial Union, Local No. 1 and
Mine, Mill and Smelter Workers Union,
in Wm. J. Cameron Papers, VF262a,
Special Collections, University of British
Columbia Library. I withhold the name
of the deceased out of deference to the
memory of this miner, unknown to me.
The date of the report is July 20, 1937.

That was the case with Jack Zucco: My
account of the Zucco case is taken from
Stanton, *Never Say Die*, pp.170–77. Stanton was the Zuccos' lawyer. The daily
press followed the Zucco story closely
and with sympathy.

p.219

They slept in a room in the Parliament Buildings ... Lyle Wicks: *Vancouver Sun*, Feb.
28, 1956, p.3; the fourth child appears
not to have been with them.

"You are butting your head against a stone
wall": Phil Gaglardi, Minister of Highways to Beatrice Zucco, Dec. 20, 1956,
quoted by Stanton, *Never Say Die*, p.174.

p.220

Beatrice Zucco, however, received a settlement: "Silicosis Victim's Widow Sues
Compensation Board," *Vancouver Sun*,
April 23, 1958, p.2. For the two autopsy reports: "Belated Victory for Mrs.
Zucco," *Vancouver Sun*, April 24, 1958,
p.10.

The *Vancouver Sun* published a stern editorial: "Make Amends to Mrs. Zucco," April
24, 1958, p.4.

Meanwhile he was writing letters: Alfred
Nelson to the editor, *CCF News*,
Aug. 1, 1939.

EPILOGUE

p.225

"More than once it has been declared":
Eaton's Golden Jubilee, 1869–1919
(Toronto and Winnipeg: The T. Eaton
Co. Ltd.), p.152. Eaton's catalogue,

1915, listed the china cabinet at $18.50 ($349.58 in today's money). Special thanks to the librarians at Vancouver Public Library, so faithful and resourceful in answering my questions for so many years.

LIST OF INTERVIEWS

Ingrid Aarvik/Solberg, Oslo, Norway, 1975
Anthony Arnold, Vancouver, 1996
Harry Ashby, Vancouver, 2000
Harry Brown, Salmon Arm, B.C., Sept. 28, 1999
Mabel Critch, Topley, B.C., September 2004
Amanda Dennis, Moricetown, B.C., by phone, Oct. 1, 2004
Christian Doyon, Bralorne, B.C., September 1997
Kathleen Doyon, Bralorne, B.C., September 1997
Violet Dragvik, Maple Ridge, B.C., Sept. 23, 1999
Bob Eklof, Abbotsford, B.C., March 1997
Alfhild Gronskei, Salmon Arm, B.C., Sept. 28, 1999
Dagny Gronskei Smith, Salmon Arm, B.C., Sept. 29, 1999
Norman Gronskei, Bralorne, B.C., by phone, September 1997
Charles "Ace" Haddrell, Vancouver, April 30, 1997, by phone, May-August 1997
Rolf Halvorsen, Salmon Arm, B.C., Sept. 28, 1999
Danny Hennessey, Quesnel, B.C., by phone, May 24, 2008
Frank Hennessey, Quesnel, B.C., by phone, June 1998
Wyn Holland/Hagerstone, Revelstoke, B.C., by phone, 2000
Lissie Jensen, Victoria, B.C., 1999

Kristine Kongsvik, Orkanger, Norway, 1975
Ozzie and Rita Lorenskeit, Langley, B.C., by phone, May 20, 2008
Rolf and Ingeborg Lunder, Ålen, Norway, by phone, 2007, 2008
Wayne Murton, Bralorne, B.C., September 1997
Arthur Nelson, Vancouver, Jan. 16, 1973/74, July 11, 1993, Feb. 4, 13, 1994, March 6, 1994
Verner Nelson, Langley, B.C., Jan 16, 1973, May 22, 1994
Gerry Onischak, Bralorne, B.C., September 1997
John Schutz, New Westminster, B.C., Nov. 3, 1999
Walter Seretny, Vancouver, May 1, 14, 1998
Linda Skutnik, Bralorne, B.C., September 1997
Nick Skutnik, Bralorne, B.C., September 1997
Belle Watt, White Rock, B.C., Aug. 12, 1993
Trish White, Bralorne, B.C., September 1997
John Whiting, Bralorne, B.C., September 1997
Glen Woodsworth, Vancouver, by phone, July 22, 1999

INDEX